QABALAH FOR THE 21ST CENTURY:
LIVING THE TREE OF LIFE
Book One

"The Teacher who is indeed wise does not bid you to enter the house of their wisdom but rather leads you to the threshold of your mind."

-KAHLIL GIBRAN

"When I met Amber in 1969 she was an enthusiastic and dedicated Qabalistic Tree of Life and Tarot student and beginning level teacher. Her knowledge and ability to communicate these subjects has blossomed over the years, making her new series an essential contribution to these fields and to the lives of her readers."

-STEVEN HALPERN
Grammy® nominated sound healer and author, StevenHalpernMusic.com

"We are all students of life, and some among us are perfecting their knowledge of life through teaching. A real teacher in any subject is one who brings enthusiasm, joy, and humor to their instruction, besides a thorough knowledge of the field they teacher. Amber Jayanti is such a teacher. The common danger in teaching a subject like the Tree of Life is becoming a 'guru', especially in one's own mind. Amber presents this subject with such vulnerability that she completely avoids this sticky, ego-elevating trap."

-REVEREND JOSEPH NOLEN
President Emeritus, Builders of the Adytum

"Firmly based upon the traditional teachings from the mainline of schools of the Western Esoteric Tradition, Amber Jayanti ably translates them into practical advise for seekers of guidance and wisdom in the modern world. An invaluable opening of the doors of the arcane wisdom to let the light shine forth into the practicalities of contemporary life."

-GARETH KNIGHT
Author, A Practical Guide to Qabalistic Symbolism

Book One

QABALAH FOR THE 21ST CENTURY: *LIVING* THE TREE OF LIFE

Amber Jayanti

ISBN: 979-8-9899264-0-4

DEDICATION

In loving memory of Paul Foster Case, Anne Davies, Joseph Nolen, Paramahansa Yogananda, Baba Muktananda, Sathya Sai Baba, and other Great Souls who have nurtured and inspired me on my journey through the Tree of Life. To the Builders of the Adytum for their years of selfless service. With gratitude to my remarkable students, without whom this book would not have been possible. Last yet not least, special thanks to Andi, Shanin, Jah, Maria, Shari, Marc, Tracy, Bonni, editor, Emily Shurr, and last yet not least, Brent Spears, artistic director and hand-holder extraordinaire.

With Respect and Love in Darkness, Light, and In-Between,
Amber Jayanti

Book One

QABALAH FOR THE 21ST CENTURY: LIVING THE TREE OF LIFE

FOREWORD

Dear Reader:

Several years before my remarkable mentor, Joseph Nolen President Emeritus of Builders of the Adytum passed away in 2003 we thoroughly discussed this project. At the time it was a detailed outline and innumerable Word files. After patiently reviewing these, Joseph enthusiastically endorsed the project, thoughtfully adding, "Just in case I pass on feel free to adapt the Forward from LIVING THE QABALISTIC TAROT, to your QABALAH FOR THE 21st CENTURY: *LIVING* THE TREE OF LIFE." Now more than twenty years later, I am taking Joseph up on his uplifting offer.

This Book is Important for Two Reasons

First, the subject is important: the Qabalistic Tree of Life. Second, the motivation of the author is important. Either one can obscure or elevate the importance of the material.

In a world filled with the delusion of appearances, the Qabalistic Tree of Life and the Tarot are clear windows into reality—a reality larger and more unitive than our local, individual stories. These are marvelous beyond any written doctrine because they are expressed in the universal language of symbols that we all have the potential to understand. Due to the influence of movies, TV, the computer, the Internet, and the like, the world and we ourselves have become increasingly responsive to imagery. Because these media help us to communicate across different languages, they are in many ways, facilitating a "one-world culture."

This universal symbol-language is continually communicating to our subconscious minds and seeding ideas in the collective unconscious. Essentially, we humans are creatures of symbol! Symbols create us, and our world, in that they set non-verbal, subliminal standards for living that we are being subtly, and not so subtly, compelled to live up to. Such are a combination of our present norms and those that are in the midst of change. A potent example of this type of shift would be mainstream advertising finally showing multi-racial individuals, racially mixed and same-sex couples, rather than only white heterosexuals. (We must assume that market research showed the financial benefits of making this change!) Essentially, when we change our symbols, we change ourselves, and in time, the world.

We are all students of life, and some of the more advanced among us are perfecting their knowledge of life through teaching. A real teacher in any subject is one who brings enthusiasm, joy and humor to their instruction, besides a thorough knowledge of the field they teach. Amber Jayanti is such a teacher. The common danger in teaching a subject like the Qabalistic Tree of Life and the Tarot is that of becoming a "guru," especially in one's own mind. Amber presents her subject with such vulnerability that she completely avoids this sticky and illusive, ego- elevating trap.

In addition, if a subject like the Tree of Life is presented as either very occult or "super-holy," the learning process is debilitated. Amber has a very wholesome, natural approach to the Qabalistic Tree of Life and the Tarot that dispels the phony mystery and superstition surrounding these subjects, making them as workable as a cooking recipe.

Spiritual Security

In times of personal, national and world crises, which we are certainly experiencing at present, individuals look to spiritual security with intensity commensurate with the predicament they feel is upon them. Some return to the fundamentalism of their childhood where they only had to believe, to be saved; understanding was unnecessary. Consequently, we have been seeing a tremendous resurgence of religious fundamentalism in the world—a trend that is presenting social, political, and environmental problems in many countries. Paradoxically, because of the same pressures, other individuals are seeking a deeper understanding of themselves and the mysteries of life in order to find peace with the reality of *what is*. These conditions are producing a great wave of searchers for reality, or spiritual aspirants. "When Life desires, Life also answers." QABALAH FOR THE 21st CENTURY: *LIVING* THE TREE OF LIFE is one of the answers.

—REVEREND JOSEPH NOLEN
President Emeritus, Builders of the Adytum

"Qabalah conveys the sweetness that is the essence of life's harshness and the hunger of what is Above to consciously be inhabited by all that is Below." *Unknown*

PREFACE

Receiving and Extending the Light

ABOUT THIRTY YEARS AGO, Dion Fortune's book *The Mystical Qabalah* came to my attention and I was entranced. Although published in 1935, it was the first book on Qabalah that actually made sense. In fact, it seemed as if Ms. Fortune herself were whispering into my ears.

The foremost assignment of any student or aspirant of a mystery school is that of continuously applying, or in mystery school speak, "cleaving to its teachings always," to make themselves better people and the world a better place. The role of practitioners is to keep these teachings alive. This role includes, when fitting, sharing personal examples of the workings of Ageless Wisdom through their desire to demonstrate the effectiveness of the material. In doing so, they inspire others to do likewise. This practice is known as, "Receiving and Extending the Light." Dion Fortune speaks of doing this in her Foreword, stating: "It is not my aim to write a historical study of the sources of the Qabalah, but rather to show the uses that are made of it by modern students of the Mysteries." I came to understand and experience living in this way as being a practical mystic. Over time, so have many of my students.

Although Ms. Fortune does not refer to her students specifically, she does mention "the influence of MacGregor Mathers, in matters of Qabalistic mysticism." Much as Dion Fortune extended, continued and elaborated upon, the teachings of her teachers, QABALAH FOR THE 21st CENTURY: *LIVING* THE TREE OF LIFE aims at doing likewise. I must humbly acknowledge the extension of the Light from the Builders of the Adytum (BOTA) teachers Paul Foster Case, Ann Davies, and Joseph Nolen. I have also been blessed to study and interact with uplifting teachers from the Hindu, Buddhist and Sufi traditions. As if this were not enough I am continually inspired by my Tree of Life and Tarot and students who are practitioners of these and other traditions such the Native American Way, Islam, Wicca, and Gnosticism.

Eventually, I began regarding Qabalah to be a Henotheistic tradition. Henotheism is a system in which devotion is to a single deity such as the Most High or One Great Spirit of Life, Kether, Crown of the Tree of Life, while not denying the existence of other deities, leaving room for them too. These expanded Qabalah beyond its traditional Greek, Islamic and Judeo-Christian roots, metamorphosing it into Universal Qabalah—a perfect fit for the 21st century! Before proceeding, with the Universal Qabalah, I am being prompted to briefly explain the various forms of this often-perplexing tradition.

KABBALAH, CABALA, QABALAH

Kabbalah

When spelled with a "K" as in Kabbalah, Kabalah, or Kabala, thought to be of Jewish origin alone, is only one of many terms used during a 2,000-year period to designate Jewish mysticism, its teachings and practitioners. Simply put, Kabbalah is not "strictly kosher" as it has many influences. Among these is that of the *Kalam* schools of Persia.

Kalam meaning "science of debate," is the branch of Islamic philosophy; influenced by the rational thought and inquiry of the Greek philosophers; Plato, Socrates and Aristotle, as well as by the Gnostic Heresies. Here the focus is on questioning and reasoning out the appropriateness of religious commands, obligations and theological principles through logical discussion. The *Mu'tazila* Kalam School of the eighth and tenth centuries greatly influenced Kabbalah.

Cabala

When spelled with a "C", most commonly as Cabala, also with its alternative spellings, refers to the spread of Kabbalah into Christianity. This movement originated in Spain and southern France in the 12th century and continued into the Italian Renaissance. Cabala's mid-Renaissance roots were tied with the Neo-Platonic leanings of the Platonic Academy, founded by the brilliant Lorenzo de' Medici and headed by the brilliant Pico Della Mirandola.

The Renaissance marked the end of the Age of Faith and ushered in the Age of Reason. This change resulted in a decline in churchgoers. Because Jesus was born Jewish, cutting-edge thinkers under the tutelage of Mirandola imagined a way of reviving interest in Catholicism was to combine Christianity with Judaism. Although this idea drew support from prominent religious leaders and scholars, however a powerful combination of the Pope, in response to beginnings of the Protestant Reformation, quashed the plan.

Analogous to the early Kabbalah, Cabala was but one of the many names its founders and teachers gave to their work.

Universal Qabalah

Nonsexist, Nonracist, Non-Homophobic and Pan-Denominational

When spelled with a "Q," Qabalah, at times spelled Qabala and Qabbalah, is the mid-nineteenth spelling assigned by those who knowingly combine teachings from the Kabbalah and Cabala with the Hermetic Arts and Sciences—alchemy, tarot, astrology, numerology, and sacred geometry. This spelling is further meant to include key material from the ancient orders noted above addition to such from the more recent Rosicrucian, Masonic, Theosophical and Golden Dawn orders.

Working with students from a wide array of background and having familiarity with Hindu, Buddhist, Sufi, and Pagan traditions, prompted me to adopt this spelling and expand its meaning. Qabalah spelled with the letter "Q" evolved into "Universal Qabalah."

As I grew to know, live, love, and teach it, Universal Qabalah flowered into a remarkable 21st century nonsexist, nonracist, non-homophobic, pan-denominational mystery school tradition of universal and natural laws, truths, and principles that bridges the world's foremost esoteric or inner religio-spiritual traditions of East and West, aligning it with the Eternal Verities and Perennial Philosophy of antiquity. These view such traditions as sharing a single, metaphysical truth or origin from which the entire body of esoteric and religious knowledge and doctrine evolved. Yes, the philosophical practice of recognizing and accepting differences and commonalities is nothing new—accomplishing this is basic to the evolution of human consciousness. However, the study and practical application of the wisdom of the Universal Qabalah and its symbolic representations, the Tree of Life and the Tarot, visually enhance and add new dimensions to these, helping support and build the critical mass toward this goal. On that note, I am now being prompted to introduce the Qabalistic Tree of Life.

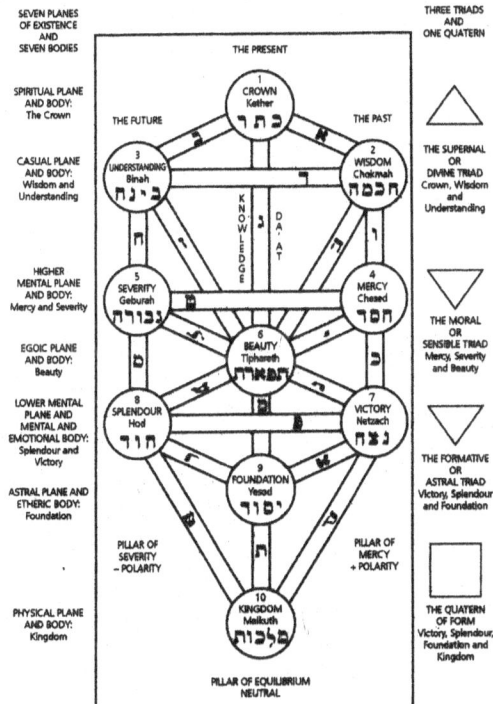

The Qabalistic Tree of Life. The central image shows how the Tree's three pillars relate to time and nature's polarities. The right side of the diagram divides the Tree into the building blocks of creation—three triads and one quantern of form. The left side of the figure charts the Tree's seven planes or levels of existence and their corresponding energy bodies.

INTRODUCING THE QABALISTIC TREE OF LIFE

Shorthand for Qabalah

Before detailing the Tree of Life's ten spheres or sephiroth, it is essential to have an overall picture of this potent symbol. Because the Universal Qabalah encompasses the esoteric or inner traditions of both West and East and we humans tend to be visually oriented, it is essential to understand its symbolic representation, the Qabalistic Tree of Life that presents its fundamental principles in picture form. Symbols are physical representations of nonphysical, abstract laws, truths, principles and theories the Tree of Life is a type of shorthand for the mystical system of Qabalah.

To help you more fully understand the Qabalistic Tree of Life, I begin by explaining some of the many ways trees serve humankind as maps of divine and human activities in such forms as oracles, healers, bearers of fertility, wisdom, and immortality symbols, sacred markers, and the homes for ancestral spirits, gods and goddesses. Trees have also been used since time immemorial to signify the change of seasons as well as the ebbing and flowing of the life cycle.

Trees Across Time and Cultures

Some trees remain forever green while others bud, blossom, bear fruit, shed their leaves, and appear dead, yet come to life again in another season. Because trees are regarded to signify eternal life as well as the cycles of nature and human life, many groups have held them in high esteem, since the beginning of human history.

From the most ancient times, trees have been considered holy and dedicated to sacred use. The European Maypole, originally a symbol of fertility, was a tree brought into the village in springtime to represent the spirit of the fruitful harvest to come. At the opening ceremonies for the 1998 Winter Olympics in Nagano, Japan, a group of men sang as they raised trees. When interviewed about the presentation, one elder Japanese said he was shocked to see this secret fertility rite performed in front of the entire world. Another symbol of Western origin was the Green Tree or Green Man. The Green Tree embodies the potent male energy, which impregnates Mother Earth with life.

Chinese Taoist tradition links the peach tree with eternal life. Although Buddha disapproved of tree worship, the bodhi or pipal tree under which he meditated and achieved enlightenment is revered by Buddhists in India. In Hindu India, the pipal tree is looked upon as a physical manifestation of the god, Vishnu, and it is forbidden to cut its leaves or branches except for use in acts of worship.

For thousands of years, the Jews have celebrated the Feast of Tabernacles or *Sukkoth*, marking the end of the harvest season. The *lulog* or palm branch and *ethrog*, fruit of the citron tree, play key roles in the festivities. Palm branches used in the acknowledgment and celebration of royalty and victory, were spread before Jesus as he entered Jerusalem on what became known as Palm Sunday. The United States military awards soldiers palm emblems to recognize outstanding service.

Besides, the many oracular trees mentioned in the Old Testament, trees such as the laurel at Delphi are believed to have psychic powers. Connected by its roots with the underworld, the laurel provided access to the foreknowledge of the dead. Most likely a tree, the early Greek oracle of Dodona in Northwestern Greece was first devoted to a Great Mother Goddess and later to the Greek god Zeus. The Oracle of Jupiter in Epirus was situated in a grove of oak trees; answers were interpreted from the rustling of the leaves. There is an old Yaqui Indian tale about a young girl who listened to a talking tree and carried its prophecies to her people. Giving it some thought, it is not surprising that a Disney animation shows the North American Indian woman, Pocohantas, consulting "Grandmother Willow" for guidance.

The ancient Scythians practiced divination with the aid of willow rods—a forerunner of dowsing rods. The Druid priests of the Celts celebrated their rites in sacred woodlets—small especially cultivated woods without undergrowth to help facilitate sacred gatherings. The Saxons or early Germans held their ceremonies in the forest as well. In the old Russian province of Moldavia, tree worship was practiced for countless generations.

In Greek mythology, the garden of Hesperides is supported by Mount Atlas. It was there, that Hercules overcame the multi-headed dragon that guarded the sacred tree and snatched its golden apples, the fruits of knowledge. In this tradition, the olive tree is holy to the goddess of wisdom, Athena, and the cypress to Artemis, the virginal Goddess of the hunt. The fir tree, into which Cybele turned her priest Attis (also known as Adonis) as punishment for breaking his vow of chastity, is central to the cult of Cybele. On the first day of the annual spring festival, the sacred fir wound with woolen bands was carried through the streets of Pessinus.

Trees as the Universe, Givers of Life, Nourishment, Wisdom, and, Immortality.

Trees span three worlds—their branches stretch up to heaven, their roots reach into the underworld, and their trunks and foliage live on earth. Resultantly trees came to signify both the eternal universe and sacred sustenance.

In ancient India, the Tree of Life was the fig or *Ashwattha*. The Hindu avatar Krishna instructs his pupil Arjuna through the symbolism of this tree in the *Bagavad Gita*. The idea of the tree as the universe was known to the Scandinavians of old in the form of an ash tree called the *Yggdrasil*, or World Tree.

Cosmic trees usually bore fruit, which the gods and goddesses ate to ensure their immortality, and so in this way became known as Trees of Life. The Koran tells of an enormous *tooba* tree covered with different kinds of food growing in the seventh or highest level of heaven. When the nomadic peoples and wild animals of Africa and Australia are unable to find enough water from their usual sources during a drought, they would be in danger **of** dying from dehydration were it not for the *Baobab* Tree. People cut the **tree**'s branches or trunk to access its life-giving waters while animals chew on the tree branches and then use them like straws to drink. Large Baobab trees may contain more than 30,000 gallons of water at once. It is no wonder that the Baobab is called the Miraculous Tree of Life. The juices of the psychedelic Persian *haoma* and Indian *soma*, known as "the pillar of the World," were taken to ward off disease, lengthen life, and bestow transcendental experiences.

Because the Tree of Life was believed to bear life everlasting, tribal people were buried wearing them as talismans. A few years ago, the body of a 2,400-year-old Siberian "Ice Maiden," was discovered during a thaw wearing a funerary headdress in this design. On the other hand, the newly Christianized King, Charlemagne ordered that the Saxon people's *Irminsul* meaning "a mighty rising pillar," be destroyed when he took power. Germanic pagans believed the Irminsul, likely a mammoth tree trunk, was an embodiment of their great god Odin.

There were also the mystical trees of the Garden of Eden. Tradition states that the Tree of Knowledge of Good and Evil was an apple tree. Although the exact species of the Tree of Life is not disclosed, this representation of perfect harmony and spiritual immortality was probably an evergreen. The ten "fruits" spheres, *sephiroth*, or palaces in the branches of the Tree of Life symbolize the byproducts of spiritual growth. These are believed to be manifestations of the Great Spirit of Life signified by the Crown at the tree's top. It is thought that those who eat the fruits of the Tree of Life or drink an essence extracted from this holy tree receive eternal life. On the Eastern side of California's Sierra Mountains, in a climate zone similar to that of the Middle East, is a Bristle Cone Pine forest. Bristlecone pines are regarded to be the oldest genus of trees in existence—the forest's Methuselah tree is more than 5,000 years old.

The Jewish Talmud speaks of two paradises connected by a pillar or ladder, sometimes called "Jacob's Ladder," in which the souls of the righteous ascend on the Sabbath to enjoy the splendor of divine grace. Similar to this is the Jews' speak of an Inverted Tree, which has its roots in heaven and grows down toward the Earth. Illustrates the belief that all of life is the descent of spirit into bodily form. Chinese, Native American, and South American Indian legends mention the living and dead climbing to and from heaven up and down the trunk of a tree.

Black Elk, a modern Oglala Sioux visionary, speaks of the Tree of Life within his "Great Vision for men." He taught that the roots of the great Tree of Life are still alive in the hearts of each one of us. The Big Tree of Tule, a majestic Montezuma bald cypress, measured at over 121 feet around, presently grows in the churchyard at Santa Maria del Tule, in the southern part of Oaxaca, Mexico. This giant symbol of eternal life was supposedly planted by the Aztec prophet Pecocha in the sixth century B.C.

Representations of sacred palm, pomegranate, and cypress trees are found on Chaldean, Babylonian, and Assyrian engravings and temples. In Assyro-Babylonian mythology, the hero Gilgamesh reached the holy Mount Mashu "whereon arose the tree of the gods." Sacred trees of life were also associated with the worship of the deities of the earth and air, Bel and Enlil.

In ancient Egypt, the tamarisk was sacred to the god Osiris. Egyptian lore also tells of the sycomore tree that grew on the border of this world and the next. On reaching these trees, the souls of the departed would receive supplies of food and water from the spirits dwelling within its foliage. On another side of the globe, both the European May Pole and Celtic Green Tree or Green Man signify divine male energy descending to impregnate Mother Earth with life.

The North American Indian tribes such as the Sioux and Dakotas among others, suspended dead bodies on burial platforms or tree branches helping their ascent. Certain tribes of India and central Australia continue using these methods. This is further aligned with the practice of "the return to the Mother tree," existing in the beliefs of the Mongol Selkups. There is also a small Balinese sect living in Truyan Northeast Bali who continue their pre-Hindu practices. The Truyans lay the bodies of the dead in bamboo enclosures under their ancient "mother tree' to decompose. These people hold the belief that this custom stops the corpses from smelling fetid.

In 1998, a massive 4,000-year-old oak tree (Early Bronze Age 2,000-1,000 BC) emerged upside down from the shifting sands of tidal erosion at the seashore of Norfolk, England. The tree is called Seahenge, "A wooden relative to Stonehenge." The leading archeologist, Mark Brennand suggests that the tree-temple was built on swampy ground some way inland, which the sea later covered. Brennand believes the purpose of the site was likely excarnation—the practice of exposing the bodies of the dead to the elements so that their flesh rotted more quickly, hastening the spirit on its way to the afterlife.

On a somewhat different note, the practice of planting trees as a memorial to one's loved ones in Israel, is yet another way of keeping their spirit alive, as is the burying of a child's placenta and then planting a tree over it. There is also the tradition of making the poles of a couple's wedding canopy from these trees after both the child and tree have reached maturity. It best be noted that the tradition of burying a placenta and planting a tree is also practiced by Navajos, Indonesians, Maoris, Cambodians Costa Ricans, and Bolivians among many others.

Finally, one of the chief man-made amazements at Disney's Animal Kingdom is a 14-story (145 ft tall), 50 foot-wide, Tree of Life. This sculpture of a Baobab tree—detailed above, lights up the park at night. Due to its immense popularity, the Tree of Life is marketed in story, seed, powder, bonsai, various toys, and desk lamp forms.

Trees as Sacred Ladders

As a child, I remember how, when I climbed a tree, feeling safer from the real and imaginary dangers on the earth below because I was closer to heaven. Trees or ladders have performed similar functions in numerous traditions. One of the best known is Jacob's Ladder, spoken of in *Genesis 28:12*. "And Jacob lay down...and he dreamed, and beheld a ladder set up on the earth, and the top of it reached to heaven, and he beheld the angels of God ascending and descending on it."

Part of the initiation ceremony of the Buriat sect of Siberian shamans one scales a live birch tree, the *udeshi burkhur* meaning "the guardian of the door." The tree which is rooted in the earth and projects through the smoke home of the yurt, is believed to bridge the way to the spirit world for those who reach its top.

In the ancient Persian cult of Mithra, initiates had to climb the *Klimax*, a perilous seven-rung ladder made of the seven planetary metals to enter the heavenly realms. The Prophet Mohammed's famed *mir'aj*, ascent to heaven on horseback, is considered to be another type of ladder.

The Native American and South American shamans are said to ascend a sacred rainbow serpent whose seven colors represent the seven levels of heaven. Seven-storied, many-colored ziggurats or pyramids were prominent in the Babylonian, Egyptian, Mayan, and Aztec civilizations. Reaching the seventh level was equated with reaching the summit of the cosmos.

As part of their rites, Taoists in Taiwan and Yamabushi monks in Japan still perform the miraculous feat of climbing a ladder built of razor-sharp swords in their bare feet. The ascent of a living birch tree plays an important role in the initiation ceremony of Siberian shamans. The tree, which is rooted in the earth and projects through the smoke hole of the *yurt* or dwelling, is believed to bridge the way to the spirit world for those who get to its top. While all discover that to ascend means one must descend again, both paths do bring universal consciousness.

What is the Qabalistic Tree of Life?

Essentially: The Tree of Life is a map of the involution—from the top to the bottom, and evolution from the bottom to the top—of human consciousness while living IN the physical world and body, and as such, depicts the building blocks for all of creation. In other words, it is a mathematical and diagrammatic account of the development of life and awareness.

From the perspective of those who study Universal Qabalah, the Tree of Life is a global, nonsectarian, or pan-denomination symbol that shows us what we and the universe are, manifestations of the One Self, Most High, God/dess, Spirit Divine, and so on and how we and the universe function and interact.

The Tree of Life depicts the ten basic facets of the One and how these are interrelated. In this sense, the Tree of Life is, as mentioned, a pictorial representation of the ancient Hebrew Kabbalah, Christian Cabala, and Universal Qabalah. This potent glyph shows humankind's role as co-creators with the Universal Life Force. The Tree is simultaneously a diagram of our progressive mastery of the universal forces that surround and play through our lives coupled with our gradual recognition that these forces have the ultimate say over the physical world.

The Qabalah's main tenet, whether Hebrew, Christian, or Universal, addresses the unfolding of the hidden and unknowable Godhead into the "fullness" of the manifest, visible Godhead. This arises by way of the appearance of the physical universe and its myriad forms and humans growing to know, hear, see, feel, taste, touch, or perceive the Spirit of the Most High, God/dess in all people, creatures, things, places and situations at all times. The process of manifestation is, in actuality, the transformation of the super-physical into the physical. It is the Great Spirit of the Universe "coming into being."

Prior to creation, it is believed that the Most High existed in an original undifferentiated state called *Ain Soph* the Infinite. The foundation of existence or four elements, fire, water, air, and earth, were birthed from Divinity's first utterance, the "The Word," or *Logos*. Consequently, the Most High's Hebrew name known as the *Tetragrammaton* (a word of four letters and transliterated as either YHWH, IHVH, or JHVH), *Yod, Heh, Vav, Heh,* is assigned to this pronouncement. The Holy Tetragrammaton means, "That which was, That which is, and That which shall always be." Each of its letters represents one of the four elements: Yod, fire, Heh, water, Vav, air, and Heh, earth. Nature's elements are further analogous with the Most High's fourfold nature—ideation, creative imagination, mental formulation, and physical manifestation, which humankind mirrors. Although this concept divides the One into the many, it is essential to remember that all comes from one Source. These only appear to be separate entities in the same way that steam, water, and ice are different forms of the same element. The next tangible results of this Divine emanation--from the undifferentiated state into differentiated form—are the solar system, the Earth, and all upon it. The Tree of Life is the Qabalistic way of illustrating both the genesis of life and the creative processes of the human mind.

As stated, when the word "Qabalah" is spelled with the letter Q it represents an inclusive tradition that is not limited to or associated with a specific religious denomination. Therefore, the Qabalistic Tree of Life presents a harmonious blending of the wisdom traditions of the East and West. When pondered this remarkable glyph depicts the principle that there are as many ways to know God/dess as there are people on the face of the Earth and that each person will achieve this knowledge in their particular way and time, a concept depicted by the numerous paths leading to the tree's top. It is helpful to refer to an image of the Tree of Life while reading the following section.

A Computer, Map, and Chart

The Qabalistic Tree of Life is a cosmic computer. Akin to the computer, the Tree of Life is accessible to beginners and experts alike. Both the computer and Tree of Life are filing systems for storing enormous amounts of information. The Tree of Life and computer also mirror the mind and imagination of those who interact with it. Although this is shifting somewhat with the use of Artificial Intelligence, AI might function to expand our understanding of this universal symbol.

Qabalists believe that the Tree of Life is Divinity's design for humankind, as well as our design for ourselves—the principles inherent within this design may help us to fulfill the divine plan—each of our "contracts" for this incarnation.

The Tree of Life is a map of divine and human consciousness: It depicts the unending journey between spirit and matter. Spirit changes into matter by invo-lution—movement from the Crown at the top of the Tree to the Kingdom at the bottom. Matter changes into spirit by evolution--movement from the Kingdom at the bottom of the Tree to the Crown at its top. Because it represents both the cosmic and personal experience of life, the Tree of Life is thought of as both constantly transforming and stable realities. This remarkable symbol offers us a systematic approach to life as it diagrams the development of human awareness while we live in the physical world and body.

The Qabalistic Tree of Life is a graphic representation of the interactions contin-ually occurring between universal and personal consciousness. The very structure of the Tree of Life illustrates how, through the alchemy of our life journey, we are brought into a conscious relationship with the greater impersonal Self. While there are innumerable ways to expand awareness, the Tree functions to chart our step-by-step mastery of the universal forces that surround us and play through our lives—and that forces' mastery of us. The Tree of Life is a symbolic cross-cultural and pan-denominational attempt to bring our personal self together with our bigger impersonal Self.

Because the Tree of Life also depicts the various stages or steps through which humankind matures to achieve higher consciousness, it verily makes the powers and abilities that result from spiritual evolution perceptible. Along with this, it's important to remember that what we understand is always a reflection of our understanding at that moment in time. Therefore, we may contemplate the Tree of Life today and see it one way, while at another time might see it quite differently.

Finally, although seemingly contradictory to the idea of Oneness, the Tree of Life identifies the ten facets are one-and-the-same.

A Model of Creation

Whether Hebrew, Christian, Hermetic, Pagan, or Universal in origin, the Tree of Life is a paradigm of creation. It lays out the ten steps that characterize the process of creation—the unfolding of the hidden and unknowable godhead into the "fullness" of the manifest godhead by way of the physical world and its myriad forms. In this sense, the Tree of Life is a mandala—a geometric figure representing life in the universe.

The Qabalistic Tree of Life is like a cosmic Christmas tree: Its ornaments are the joys and sorrows of daily life, and its gifts are the love, wisdom, and understanding that come to us through these experiences. The Tree of Life is truly unique in that it is a physical form, whereon every human feeling, thought, and experience may be placed, contemplated, identified, and understood.

A Divine Plan

A plan is a detailed scheme that shows us how to go about achieving a particular goal. Although each person's goals differ, our goal as a race is to discover and live out our soul's purpose with as much wisdom, understanding, and love as we are capable of achieving and expressing.

Qabalistic lore tells us that its teachings are gifts from the Most High to humankind. The word Qabalah is translated as "from mouth to ear," making it both an oral and aural tradition—the teachings of which have been transmitted to humankind through the likes of angels and wise ones and people like us through our words and actions for thousands of years. The Qabalah, by way of the Tree of Life and the principles encoded with it, offers guidelines that are designed to help us live in harmony with divinity, our human sisters and brothers, the planet, and the totality of creation—and of course, our selves. This symbol also charts ways to better play our roles in the world and by doing so, to attain more expansive levels of awareness and, in time, enlightenment. For these reasons, the Qabalah and Tree of Life are considered a divine plan.

Although many books, including the one before you, attempt to explain this plan, for me and many I have had the privilege of facilitating, none is quite so revealing as the insights and information that arise from one's personal contemplation of the Tree of Life. While we do live in a fast-track world, taking the time to do this is enormously rewarding, since it unveils the mysteries encoded in its structure. Most importantly, I have found that teachings revealed in this way are always relevant to what I and others need to be cognizant of at that moment.

Discovering and living out the principles of the Qabalistic Tree of Life through the pages ahead is intended to bring readers into an increasingly intimate relationship with the God/dess within us, and all of existence. Through this closeness, we begin to genuinely understand the divine plan—in terms of who and what we genuinely are and our place in the world. Furthermore, while contemplating each of the ten sephiroth ahead we recognize the truth that the Tree of Life is a living breathing being and that each of us is a Tree of Life. This may be seen in the figure of Adam Kadmon.

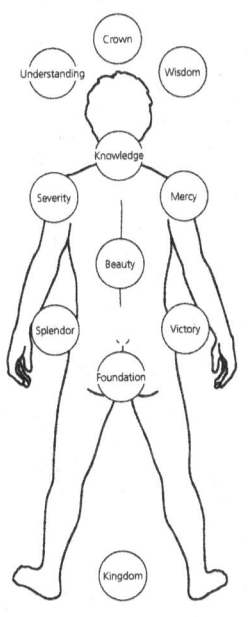

Adam Kadmon

The name Adam is a generic or general term from the Old Testament referring to the entire human species. Qabalists have superimposed the body of Adam Kadmon, a symbol of "Every Human," on the Tree of Life for countless generations. Traditionally, the body is shown backward thereby gender-neutral or non-binary to indicate that it is, in fact, Every Human. Because the Tree of Life also represents the cosmos, the Tree of Life in human form is a simple way of reminding us that we are made in the likeness of our cosmic parents.

Like other great systems, the Qabalah asserts the infinite nature dwelling within the heart of humankind. Adam Kadmon is an actual picture of the relationship between the human race and the godhead. This figure was created to depict two basic Qabalistic principles: 1) We are children of the Most High and are divine in essence and origin, and 2) The one divine Self continuously lives in and through us. Adam Kadmon is such a potent concept that it has been used as a teaching and meditation guide for centuries.

Qabalists teach that as practitioners' thoughts, words, and actions become more consistently aligned with God/dess consciousness, the structure of Adam Kadmon transforms from "Every Man" or the ordinary human into the extraordinary human. This "Superperson" is the fully aware, enlightened individual through whose everyday life the one divine Self is actually perceived.

A Qabalistic Feast

Living, studying, consulting with, and teaching Universal Qabalah for nearly fifty years has been helping me to keep these potent tools front and center. It also allows me to witness and experience the innumerable ways students apply what they learn in class to solve the mysteries of modern life. In doing so, they improve and upgrade their lives, and, at times the lives of those around them. Through these combined personal and professional experiences the first of three parts of QABALAH FOR THE 21st CENTURY: *LIVING* THE TREE OF LIFE is before you.

When the original length of this book came to nearly a thousand pages the fruit of more than twenty years of collecting material and writing, I needed to make an important decision. After much angst, prayer and meditation, Spirit moved me to divide this veritable Qabalistic feast into three books with each chapter offering four scrumptious courses: an appetizer, an entree or main course, a palate cleanser, and a dessert. In addition to Book One, now in your hands, Books Two and Three, now well underway, will soon follow. The sequence is served up like this:

BOOK ONE: The Crown, *Kether*; Wisdom, *Chokmah;* and Understanding, *Binah.* The Supernal Triad on the Spiritual and Causal Planes.

BOOK TWO: Mercy, *Chesed*; Severity, *Geburah*; and Beauty, *Tiphareth.* The Triad of Integrity on the Higher Mental, and Egoic Planes.

BOOK THREE: Victory, *Netzach*; Splendor, *Hod*, Foundation; *Yesod*, and Kingdom, *Malkuth.* The Quaternary of Form on the Lower Mental, Astral, and Physical Planes.

With Respect and Love in Darkness, Light, and In-Between,
Amber Jayanti

INTRODUCTION:

YOU ARE CORDIALLY INVITED
TO A QABALISTIC FEAST!

Ta ta ta taaaaa...! You are cordially invited to a Qabalistic Feast! The following menu describes how the teachings and practical application of the nonsexist, nonracist, nonhomophobic, pan-denominational Universal Qabalah's Ageless Wisdom for 21st century life will be served.

Each of the three chapters of this gourmet meal is divided into four delectable and nourishing courses. These are:

- *The Appetizer: Personally Speaking*
- *The Entree or Main Course: General Information and Symbolism*
- *The Palate Refresher: Homeplay Suggestions for Practical Application & Integration of each Sephirah*
- *The Dessert: Affirming, Confirming, and Inspiring Student Experiences*

Teasing the Appetite, the Appetizer

Like all fine dining experiences, this begins with an appetizer—or as I prefer, the "appe-teaser," to stimulate hunger for the upcoming meal. After many hours experimenting in the "kitchen," I opted to begin our banquet and each chapter by presenting "The Appetizer: Personally Speaking," an example of my perfectly-imperfect experiences in living out the teachings of the Qabalistic Tree of Life. My aim is for this dish to create a craving for the Entree, plus inspire diners to also apply and integrate, what has been for me, these inspirational teachings.

Enter the Entree

Our Feast's sumptuous entree or main course, "General Information and Symbolism," serves up the banquet of the Tree of Life philosophy and symbolism coupled with each of the Tree's ten *sephiroth* or spheres. These have been enticingly seasoned to appeal to almost any palate. All detail the English and Hebrew names, letters, and images in the form of their corresponding Qabalistic Tarot cards, Spiritual Experiences, and Intelligences. Each are specially spiced with matching colors, scents, gems, plants, animals, medicine and drugs, corresponding Sacraments, Divine and

Archangelic Presences, and Alternative Titles. The exotic flavors of Mythology, Corresponding Tools, Talismans, Amulets and Sigils, Grades on the Tree of Life, Astrological counterparts, and more are also set out.

The Pause That Refreshes, the Palate Refresher

"The Palate Refresher: Homeplay Suggestions for the Practical Application and Integration" for each sphere or *sephirah*, presents a refreshing menu of experiential "try and see" possibilities. Homeplay is homework, without the pressure! This course proposes numerous ideas on the "how to's" of integrating each entree's "General Information and Symbolism" into daily living, facilitating digestion of the Qabalistic feast. Certainly, this intermediary dish is also aimed at stimulating participants to cook-up their own "Suggestions," and they surely have come up with some astonishing ones.

Homeplay, with its tried and true recipes, serves as a gentle reminder that knowledge without its application is only half the story. As the Zen proverb reminds us, "A donkey carrying a pile of holy books, is still a donkey!" Lastly, Homeplay sets the table for the rewarding and flavorful Dessert of *living* the teachings of the Qabalistic Tree of Life, which contain the potential to stimulate new neural pathways and in doing so enhances and expands consciousness—opening the Doors of Perception to one's Self, and life.

Just Desserts, the Dessert

As the old saying goes, "The proof of the pudding is in the eating." It means that something is a success only after it has been put to the test of use. The proof of this Qabalistic Feast comes with its taste and digestion or practical application served up as the final course, "The Dessert: Affirming, Confirming and Inspiring Student Experiences."

This book is entitled QABALAH FOR THE 21st CENTURY: *LIVING* THE TREE OF LIFE. Essential to a class completing the study of a sephirah, students share their Homeplay experiences. Just desserts prove that feasting on the teachings of the Qabalistic Tree of Life and its Homeplay recipes is nourishing. Taken directly from transcriptions, these segments reveal participants putting the "Suggestions for the Practical Application and Integration," into practice in their own unique ways.

Stories detail class members applying the teachings of the ancient Qabalistic mystery school tradition coupled with a sephirah to upgrade awareness and solve the mysteries of 21st century living. The act of affirming or testifying to the presence of the mystical existing in the mundane and the mundane existing in the mystical validates how with practice, the distinction between spiritual and worldly activities not only blurs—spiritual and worldly becomes one-and-the-same. By doing this, we not only grow wiser, we subtly contribute to the evolution of our human family and planet Earth.

KETHER, THE CROWN

AUTHOR OF LIFE, THE ONE IN ALL, AND THE ALL IN ONE

THE APPETIZER: PERSONALLY SPEAKING

As I started to study *Kether,* pronounced Ket-er as in sweater, the Tree of Life's Crown sphere or *sephirah,* the Supreme Spirit of the universe, while reading books about the mystics and saints from various mystical and spiritual traditions, I began longing for Kether's spiritual experience of, Unified Existence. It was breathtakingly described as stepping away from one's personality and physical body to merge with the Oneness of all creation! In this ecstatic state of "at-one-ment," we take the quantum leap from being a distinct part of the universe and separate from Divinity to being part of the whole of the universe and at one with Divinity-no small change. Like other traditions, Qabalah teaches that transforming from "something-ness" to "nothingness" happens *only* when we are ready. Despite having a certain amount of fear regarding the extinction of my individuality, my longing kept building.

Up until that time, what I had received from my mystically adept Qabalah and yoga teachers had been passed on without meeting in person. Despite connecting with them in dreams and other non-physical ways, I yearned to be in the flesh and blood presence of a genuinely Enlightened One. As a result, I began "interviewing" teachers.

For several years of disappointing meetings such as: Following six hours of prepping and mere moments before bestowing us with enlightenment, one "master" demanded students "surrender, all money and possessions," to his organization. (By that time I was enlightened enough to head for the nearest exit!) Another "enlightened one" downed nearly two six-packs of beer while heatedly lecturing on detachment, a teaching I was not ready to fully get. (I read that he eventually died from a combination of alcoholism and drug addiction.) There was also the well-known self-proclaimed celibate "holy man," having a clandestine affair with his physician that he was forced to relinquish due to the cultural prohibition against homosexuality.

I'd just about given up when a friend gave me a biography by an increasingly popular yogi Swami Muktananda, called "Baba," an honorific name meaning "Spiritual Father." Seeming less likely that a genuine teacher would be a full-on public figure, I reluctantly began reading his story. Yet, quite unexpectedly, my meditations began growing deeper and more intense. I also began experiencing some extraordinary insights. It wasn't long before I found myself thinking I'd found a true teacher, or in 1970s terms, "the real deal." Shortly after finishing his book, I learned that "Baba," was offering a weekend retreat within driving distance and eagerly signed up.

By the time the retreat rolled around, some two months later, I was in a somewhat elevated state most of the time. My sensory perceptions—what I was seeing, hearing, tasting, and so on—became clearer and more vivid than I ever could have imagined. I was also sleeping less, dreaming vividly, and at times knowing what others were going to say before speaking. While packing to depart, I felt that a new door was opening.

When at the retreat's onset, Baba came gliding into the incense-scented, flower-bedecked hall; I felt the air flooding with electricity. I experienced a mixture of joy, fear, and excited anticipation as he led the group in chanting and then into meditation. Both of these practices aimed at amplifying and elevating participants' spiritual energies or *Shakti*, the divine power of creation, flowing through us.

Closing my eyes and praying to experience Kether's sacred Unified Existence, I began sensing Baba moving about the semi-darkened room. The closer he got to where I was sitting, the warmer I began to feel. It was like getting closer and closer to a great furnace. Although it seemed like forever until he reached my place on the crowded floor, he finally did. Inhaling his exquisite scent, my heart began racing as if I were in the midst of doing Jazzercise. Reaching down he began my *Shaktipat* initiation by dusting the top of my head with his peacock feather fan and then vigorously rubbing both the crown of my head and place between my eyebrows. With this, suddenly, unexpectedly, and amazingly, "I" was gone. Difficult, as it is to explain the unexplainable, the personal "me" melted into an enormous ocean of supremely blissful diamond-like radiance. Awareness of my physical body and personality vanished when for what seemed like forever and in a split second; Kether's crowing experience of Unified Existence enveloped me. Psychologically speaking, the rug of the physical world had suddenly been pulled out from beneath me!

Mulling over the event for hours afterward, I began laughing aloud as the words, "You got what you paid for," came to mind. Muktananda's elevated consciousness temporarily raised my own to that of cosmic consciousness, aka the transcendent state of Unified Existence or Oneness, Kether's spiritual experience. This was further confirmed when speaking with an attending swami monitor on the last evening of the retreat. She calmly explained that I'd experienced a transcendent state, which when permanent brings *moksha*, the complete freeing of oneself from karma and its ongoing cycles of life and death.

Although I continued spending time with Baba, meditating and chanting according to his instructions, the experience did not reoccur. Despite this, my desire to know the Unified Existence of Kether was fully satisfied. Feeling blessed, to have "visited" this transcendental state and understood that I would eventually, in Divine time, grow into the state of Ketherian Oneness. Presently, the best way for me to arrive there is by concentrating on integrating Qabalah's Ageless Wisdom of universal and natural laws, truths, and principles—aka Eternal Verities or Perennial Philosophy-into my life with as much awareness as I'm able.

This state of being is summed up by a student sharing a modification of an ancient Zen Buddhist proverb: "Before enlightenment, I chopped wood and carried water; after enlightenment, wood was chopped and water was carried, ending the illusion that I did it, or anything!"

Okay! Now that you've had an appe-teaser, perhaps you're ready for the main course. Many more examples of *living* the Qabalistic Tree of Life, from students and I are coming up.

THE ENTREE:
GENERAL INFORMATION AND SYMBOLISM

KETHER IS THE HEBREW WORD FOR CROWN

Kether, again pronounced Ket-er, as in sweater, means Crown in Hebrew. The English word Crown is derived from the Greek, *korone,* meaning "curved horn," and Latin, *corona*, meaning "wreath of light."

The Crown of the Tree of Life is the eternal source and superconscious intermediary, the author of life from which all life originates and emerges. It is fittingly defined as a blessing and filling to overflowing—deeming it a horn of plenty. A wreath of light describes the aura or halo of otherworldly light surrounding the head of a holy one or sacred relic. Yet, for those who do not or tentatively subscribe (i.e. atheists or agnostics) to the notion of the Most High, or a Supreme Spirit, God/ dess, or other Deity, scientific photos showing the creation of the universe depict it enveloped by radiant light. From almost any perspective, Kether is the One Great Reality. Although it is often referred to in terms of Divinity or Spirit, Kether is the ultimate Source that emanates nature's positive and negative polarities.

A crown is the highest point, summit, or pinnacle of anything. From this perspective, such is also the ideal state or type, the acme or crowning glory. Fittingly, the flawless, mysterious, mystical, omnipresent, omniscient and omnipotent Kether crowns, and is the crowning glory of, the Tree of Life.

Wes, a Tree of Life student, and physics major likened Kether to the "God particle," or Higgs boson. Physicists propose that this particle, present in all of creation, is responsible for giving all other particles their mass.

Kether may be viewed as eternity, or the Oneness existing before time came into being, and from which all beingness has been emerging. This sephirah is the seemingly contradictory Non-existent All-Being. It is the Tao of Chinese philosophy, the absolute principle underlying the universe, combining the principles of *yin* and *yang*. Gnostics refer to this Oneness as the great androgynous masculo-feminine power. This harmonious relationship of opposites was influenced by Plato's myth of androgyny. This tale was elaborated upon by Rabbi Samuel bar Nachman, who in doing so refers to this passage in *Genesis 1:26-27*: "Then God said, Let us make man (Adam) in our image, after our likeness, in the image of God was created them." He goes on to state:

"When the Holy One first created Adam (humankind), he created humans with two faces, two sets of genitals (male and female), four arms and legs, back to back. Then he split Adam in two, and made two backs, one on each side."

Traditionally Hebrew Qabalists, view the *sephiroth* below Kether the Crown—*Chokmah*, Wisdom and *Binah*—Understanding, to be holy sparks that have descended to be confined in shells, or according to others, imprisoned in flesh. Certainly, physical captivity may also be seen as an opportunity to earn one's freedom.

A crown is also an ornamental garland or wreath worn on the crown of one's head symbolizing victory, honor, and distinction, endowing the wearer with authority and dominion. When I was a little girl my grandmother would braid my hair into a crown would sing "My Little Shabbat Princess," as we danced around the Shabbat candles.

Crowing further signifies Rulership by Divine Right, the ancient principle granting monarchs the "right" of governance by being born into a particular place in a particular family. The concept of Rulership by Divine Right is practiced by governments agreeing that monarchs receive their authority to rule directly from Spirit rather than from people. From the Qabalistic view, Rulership by Divine Right signifies that each-and-every one of us is descended from a divine lineage, making all of creation spiritual royalty. Going forward to living in this way requires basing our thinking and doing on the likes of the Qabalistic Tree of Life's universal and natural laws, truths, and principles, rather than on bloodlines, personal biases, and power grabs. Kether, the Crown symbolizes the sacred authority handed down from on high to one, and all.

Surely, part of our evolutionary journey is growing into desiring and then learning to respect and willingly yield to the revered Source from which we originate!

Crowning

Anatomically, a crown also signifies the top of the head. Immediately before birth, a baby's head is said to be "crowning," much as Kether symbolizes the state of the universe immediately before its birth. In this sense, crowning may be understood as a border between Beingness and Nothingness—the prerequisite to creation that we'll explore under the Three Veils of the Absolute,

Crowning also indicates a successful conclusion, intimating that this first sephirah is both an ending and a beginning. Much as homing pigeons are drawn to returning to their place of origin, this crowning glory of the Tree of Life is continuously sending and drawing all life forms out from and back into itself. In this sense, Kether signifies both the soul's departing from, and returning to, the world of pure spirit.

Anecdotally, while learning to ice skate on a sunny wintery afternoon at about age seven, I slipped and fell receiving an unforgettable "crowning." This truly memorable blow to the back of my head filled the afternoon sky with stars. Oops, I almost forgot! When playing the game of checkers there's the act of "crowning," giving "crowned" players the supremacy of moving in any direction on the board--definitely a Kethe-rian quality.

Lastly, whether the Crown symbolizes the Godhead or the "Nothingness" at the center of the cosmos is a matter of personal belief and experience. However, in either instance, according to the Sephirotic Doctrine, explored next Kether encompasses and presides over the entire universe.

A SHORT HISTORY LESSON: HEBREW LETTERS AND TAROT CARDS

The ancient *Sepher Yetzirah,* or *Book of Formation*, was most likely written or "received," by Rabbi Akiba, an enlightened leader of the Palestinian Jews in about 100 CE This work was aimed at teaching children the Hebrew alphabet. It also explained that the universe was created by a mysterious combination of Hebrew letters, which form the basis of the Tree of Life's ten sephiroth, known as Sephirotic Doctrine. Taking this a step further, the Hebrew word for Qabalah means both, "from mouth to ear" and "to receive."

The passion to share this guide to uplifting the earth and all upon it birthed the elaboration of the Hebrew alphabet in the form of the Qabalistic Tarot's twenty-two Major Arcana cards. Each tarot image was "received" through deep meditation and contemplation on each of the letters of the Hebrew alphabet. The purpose of doing this was to provide another way of communicating the universal and natural laws, truths, and principles aligned with the Sephirotic Doctrine, and bringing heaven to earth and earth to heaven.

Now, we move on to a segment that appears in each chapter of this book. I encourage one-and-all to surprise and perhaps delight yourself by "playing" with it.

KETHER IN PICTURES

The Hebrew word Crown, Kether, is composed of the letters *Kaph, Tav* and *Resh*. Again, some of the most profound understandings of the Crown sephirah, and all of the sephiroth, may be received by contemplating the individual Tarot cards corresponding to the Hebrew letters making up each sphere's name.

Breaking down the word Kether: Kaph means a human hand in the act of grasping—the Wheel of Fortune card. Tav denotes a signature or mark of completion and measurement of depth—the World card. The letter Resh signifies the human face and head—the Sun card. Before moving on to read my ideas, remember there are no completely right or wrong interpretations. That said, be adventurous and try it yourself!

My contemplation revealed the following:

The Wheel of Fortune Card and Hebrew letter Kaph

The Wheel of Fortune emanates from the Hebrew letter Kaph: the grasping hand indicates circular movement. This reminds me of the old saying, "Spirit is a circle whose center is everywhere and the circumference nowhere." Looking at my own hand poised to grasp, it becomes a spiral, adding Kether's spiraling dimension to what initially appears circular. Kether is also known as the "Beginning of the Whirlings and Swirlings." This refers to the true geometrical movement of both the Wheel of Fortune and Kether—a curving, cork-screw-like motion generated by a point, the universe, which humans are continually approaching or moving away from.

The Wheel of Fortune is also coupled with memory—a reminder that life originates from the spiraling center of the cosmos. The wonder of movement is found at every level of existence—from subatomic and atomic particles to the cells of inanimate and animate beings. Motion is continually occurring from planets rotating in their orbits to our own DNA and back again. Observing a Sufi Dervishes' spinning meditation *Zikir*, meaning "Remembrance,"—another stirring and memorable example of this principle in action.

The World or Universe Card and Hebrew Letter, Tav

The World or Universe card evolved from the Hebrew letter Tav a signature or "mark," denoting personal identification, ownership, and responsibility. I am a soul, spirit being who "signed on" to take a physical body and a worldly journey and will "sign off" when my work is done and it is time to return to the universe. The Tav cross is an ancient Egyptian tool marking the depth of water to facilitate safe passage. (I have nearly drowned by not being prudent and getting into situations over my head.)

The card's link with the planet Saturn, called both "the Teacher and Taskmaster," is a reminder of limits, restrictions, time, and learning and the Qabalistic opposites of dominion and slavery that result from our attitudes towards encountering, handling, and overcoming these constraints. Accepting and learning from these helps to deepen my understanding of the sacred nature of the physical world and myself. From the overview, my worldly adventures aim at reuniting me with the Oneness at the heart of the universe.

The Sun Card and Hebrew Letter, Resh

The Sun card radiates out from the Hebrew letter Resh, meaning "face" and "head" as well as the Vast Countenance or Face of Spirit Supreme. Qabalists call Kether "the Sun behind the sun," as is the source of the sun's light and the real light of the world. The Sun card is also coupled with the human heart and Heart Star or chakra. This glowing image inspires me to face the fact that wherever I turn my head the Great Spirit of Life, Kether, is reflected in the faces and features of every creature and thing in our solar system.

LOCATION, LOCATION, LOCATION:

KETHER'S PLACEMENT ON THE TREE OF LIFE

Kether, the first sphere or sephirah—a Hebrew word meaning, "a shining jewel or emanation from on High,"—tops the Qabalistic Tree of Life. This sephirah presides over the Tree's middle, neutral, non-binary Pillar of Mildness, which contains the potential to manifest the entire spectrum of sexual characteristics—physical, emotional, mental, and so on. Kether is the Source and primal activating principle hovering above and containing the positive and negative polarities, plus their variations, of Chokmah and Binah, Creator/Creatrix. Kether is situated in the time zone interchangeably termed: the present, now and eternal moment. Tibetan Buddhist teachings propose that the current moment is a continual *bardo*, the transitional period, or void eternally suspended between the past and future. It may also be understood as an ever-existing state between life and death.

When giving my complete attention to whatever is before me, I feel completely alive and energized. Of course, this attitude is easy in the midst of what I am interested in and enjoying. Yet if I am feeling bored, wanting to elsewhere, or doing something other than what is in front of me and *must* now be done, is a different story. At such junctures, I have learned that (when possible) flavoring unpleasant tasks with something uplifting, such as music, makes being in the here-and-now more palatable.

A Qabalah student and Buddhist practitioner referred to this state as the "One Taste," wherein all things are perceived equally when viewed from a non-dualistic state of mind. Coaching myself to chant and sing while doing laundry and other boring chores makes doing these less tedious and helps me to progress in this direction. With the advent of COVID-19, I began singing along with Ella Fitzgerald while riding my stationary bike provided me with a greatly needed lift.

Backing up this practice germinated while living in an ashram in India when I was assigned the mind-numbing task of Accident Prevention. Such involved carefully removing stones, twigs, bits of glass, and metal from huge vats of rice, split peas chick, peas, and lentils before these were sent to the kitchen to become our meals. Initially, I thought I'd go bonkers with boredom, yet when I heard other ashram residents chanting while laboring, I became inspired to do likewise. Accomplishing this, I have grown increasingly able to call up this selfsame," being in the here and now," centering attitude and behavior. Certainly, the more I am able to surrender to the present moment, the better I am at whatever I am doing. And as a bonus I get to improve the quality of my life. I am slowly integrating the fact that everything we do in life can be viewed as a spiritual practice. This is what Ram Dass creatively centered on in his landmark book, *Be Here Now!*

A Peak Experience

The Tree of Life maps-out the seven planes or levels of existence and four stages in the transformation of spirit into matter—three triads and one quantern of form.

Kether, the peak or pinnacle of the Tree of Life, is enthroned at the head of the Supernal Triad, composed of Kether, Chokmah, and Binah, from which creation originates and flows, encompassing the spiritual and causal planes. This Crown of the Supernal, Cosmic, or Divine Triad, is the sole sephirah on the Tree's spiritual plane. Representing the all-pervasive, most elementary component of life, Kether is the unchanging substrate of existence; it is the One Vital Principle encoded within every physical form-animate and inanimate alike. It is the realm wherein very simply, "All are one, and the One is in all."

Sitting in the world of pure or abstract spirit, Kether precedes every form of existence. Yet, Kether's solo placement on the plane of spirit is the first phase of manifestation, the totality of the visible world in its potential. This first sephirah is equated with the pre-material material for life *before* it differentiates the process during physical growth wherein cells or tissues change from a relatively general to a specific kind. Mindboggling as conceptualizing this might be, Kether's undifferentiated state simultaneously represents a whole, absolute unit and the beginning of evolution. The animals, vegetables, and minerals that will be manifesting in their season as Kether's energy streams out and down throughout the Tree of Life.

It is essential to be aware that the spiritual plane and sphere of Kether draws its energetic sustenance directly from the Great Unmanifest, the three-stage reservoir of *Ayin, Ayin Soph,* and *Ayin Soph Aur,* directly above and behind this plane. A description of the infinite's Three Stages of Cosmic Development from No-Thingness into the pre-material for Some-Thingness, or the illusion of such, follows

Unveiling

When something is unveiled, it lays whatever is beneath it bare. Consider this while pondering this description of the three sacred Veils of the Absolute, *Ayin, Ayin Soph* and *Ayin Soph Aur,* and their inseparable relationship with Kether.

Ayin: Imagine an Ocean of Infinite Light or Spirit existing in a static universe. Although this ocean has no polarity or movement, it contains, like Kether, pure potential.

Ayin Soph: Next, Spirit begins using its only "tool," thinking. The force of Spirit's thought process initiates a rhythmical oscillation of Father Chokmah and Mother Binah, centripetal and centrifugal forces, respectively. Briefly, centripetal force acts on a body moving in a circular path and is directed toward the center around which the body is moving. Centrifugal force causes a body moving in a circular path to move out and away from the center of its path.

Ayin Soph Aur: The One becomes Two, which then becomes the All.

As described the intimate relationship between the centripetal force of Chokmah's positive polarity and the centrifugal force of Binah's negative polarity results in a cyclical wave of movement. This undulating motion of polarities is the dance of creation from which all life emanates.

The cycle of waves gives us intervals and each interval vibrations, which presents us with the impression, or better yet illusion, of the different physical elements or mass. The subtle motion of the waves tricks our senses into thinking there is mass or physical things. This line of thinking obscures except from the most perceptive individuals, the one and only Reality that of Kether's still Ocean of Infinite Light, Ayin.

Kether is often called the No-thing, underscoring the fact that No-Thing really exists except Spirit. This three-fold progression lays out what Spirit, Ayin does with its only "tool"—its power to think—and how everything is made of the same primal substance. It renders this potent combination to be the channel for life, as we know it, to flow through.

Lastly, as a photographer who has loved working in the darkroom, I liken the Three Veils of the Absolute to a photographic negative, resulting in Kether's photographic positive or picture of life.

Connecting the Dots

Kether the Crown tops the Tree of Life. As the causative force or One Will or "God beyond God" behind all of the creation, Kether is seen to represent the "ground of being," which contains what an architectural student termed, "the general plan for the universe." This explains why Qabalists teach that the bible begins with the second letter of the Hebrew alphabet, *Beth,* which is equivalent to the number two. It is a reminder that Spirit created everything on two levels: all in the heavenly world has its analog or *exact,* perfectly-imperfect double in the physical world or Garden of Eden. This *hints* at the often unknown and unrecognized, yet essential Qabalistic reference to the part creation plays in fulfilling Divinity.

THE SEVEN PLANES OF EXISTENCE

SPIRITUAL PLANE:
KETHER/THE CROWN/SUPERNAL TRIAD
THE COSMIC SELF. SOURCE OF THE UNIVERSE. POTENTIALITY

CAUSAL PLANE:
CHOKMAH/WISDOM/SUPERNAL TRIAD
THE VIBRANT FIRE OF LIFE AND CREATION, *CHAIAH*, THE WORD.
DIVINE MIND

CAUSAL PLANE:
BINAH/UNDERSTANDING/SUPERNAL TRIAD
SACRED ENSOULMENT, *NESHAMA*. WOMB OF THE WORLD. DOORWAY TO
EARTH AND GATEWAY TO HEAVEN, THE PEARLY GATES

HIGHER MENTAL PLANE:
CHESED/MERCY/ETHICAL TRIAD
LOVING-KINDNESS. PERMISSION. MEMORY. RETROSPECTIVE-PAST

HIGHER MENTAL PLANE:
GEBURAH/SEVERITY/ETHICAL TRIAD
WILL. VOLITION. RESTRICTION. PROSPECTIVE-FUTURE

EGOIC PLANE:
TIPHARETH/BEAUTY/ETHICAL TRIAD
CENTER OF PERSONALITY. SPIRIT EMBODIED IN FLESH, *RUACH*
UNCONDITIONAL LOVE, *AGAPE*. SELF-REALIZATION

LOWER MENTAL PLANE:
NETZACH/VICTORY/ASTRAL TRIAD AND QUANTERN OF FORM
EMOTIONS. FEELINGS. CONDITIONAL LOVE, EROS. WISHES, CREATIVE
IMAGININGS AND PROMPTINGS

LOWER MENTAL PLANE:
HOD/SPLENDOR/ASTRAL TRIAD AND QUANTERN OF FORM
INTELLECT. CRITICAL THINKING, LOGIC AND REASONING

ASTRAL PLANE:
YESOD/FOUNDATION/ASTRAL TRIAD AND QUANTERN OF FORM
THE VITAL SOUL-ANIMATING PRINCIPLE *NEFESH*, WITHIN ALL OF CREATION

PHYSICAL PLANE:
MALKUTH/KINGDOM/ASTRAL TRIAD AND QUANTERN OF FORM
SPIRIT EMBODIED IN PHYSICAL FORM

Present Time

Kether is situated in the present time or now, which may be influenced by the past and influence the future. Signing on to being born into a physical body means, depending upon our evolution and belief system, knowingly or unknowingly entering into a maturation process that involves engaging with ourselves, others, and life events with as much awareness as we now have, and in proceeding, maturing further. Doing this offers us the opportunity of updating our thinking and doing, something that is, at times, contrary to what our personality prefers. At such junctures, I find it helpful to remember the words of one of my teachers, "Life is a course in self-improvement." Put differently, all actions have results that potentially contribute to our evolution.

An Inconvenient Truth

The path leading from the Kingdom to the Crown or *Malkuth* to Kether, on the Tree of Life, is the straightest, fastest, and therefore, most grueling journey to cosmic union. Taking this route moves travelers to develop and diligently maintain a sense of mental and emotional balance, what is interchangeably termed Equanimity, Witness Consciousness, and Mindfulness among other labels. In this state, Kether's time frame of the eternal present is front and center.

Developing our powers of observation—the ability to perceive—see, hear, feel, and so on, what is now occurring in life without getting overly enmeshed, offers a great sense of inner peace and accomplishment. Such proffers the growing ability to stand back, observe, and then reconcile life's seeming incompatibilities. From this neutral position to proceed to say, think, and do what we honestly think and feel is for the benefit of ourselves and all concerned. It is a practice that I, at moments, find myself regarding as an inconvenient truth! Simply, there are times, when taking the high road goes against my personal preferences. Living in a naturally dualistic world wherein having personal likes and dislikes is necessary and normal can make letting go and shifting into neutral, although potentially beneficial, feel unnatural and disorienting. Yet with practice, cultivating Kether's neutralized view can provide an invaluable and ultimately uplifting way of perceiving ourselves, others, and life in general.

All Roads Leading

The inspirational Chasidic Master, Rabbi Israel Baal Shem Tov termed present time Equanimity. He taught that Equanimity is achieved when we receive criticism with the same response with which we receive applause. When seeking applause, we wind up being controlled by those from whom we desire praise. When looking to avoid criticism, we adjust our behavior to continually please others. In either instance, we are caught in the demands of the separate self. Herein we are not only far from the state of Equanimity, we become closed to the wholeness and inclusivity Divinity compassionately offers. The Baal Shem Tov prescribed the exercise of taking the phrase: "I set the Eternal before me always," as a focus for meditation.

Paralleling Equanimity is the yogic technique of Witness Consciousness, Buddhist Mindfulness, and the Qabalistic practice of Solution, which add the mind-body component of calmly acknowledging and accepting each thought, feeling, and bodily sensation while practicing. The Buddha described Mindfulness as a mind and heart filled with serenity as "abundant, exalted, immeasurable, without hostility, or ill-will." When we refrain from taking another's offensive words personally, we become, over time, less likely to react to what was said. Refraining from reacting opens the possibility of responding wisely. Doing this may be compared to being a grandparent. Grandparents love their grandchildren, but thanks to their experience with their own children, are less likely to be caught up in the drama of their grand-children's lives. Fittingly, this practice also became known as "Insight Meditation."

Anthropological research shows that these and like techniques have been practiced cross-culturally from time immemorial. Ethnological studies reveal that psychoactive substances have sometimes been added to unlock the gateways to greater wisdom, understanding, and spirituality—or as Aldous Huxley dubbed it, "The Doors of Perception." This explains the current resurgence of psychedelic therapy by physicians and clinicians to treat psychological conditions that are unre-sponsive to more traditional means.

Cultivating dispassion and our ability to relax and simply *be* may be developed through almost any form of meditation. Developing practices that bring us into Kether's eternal present, offers us the skill and confidence to handle whatever life jettisons our way. When a dear family member was diagnosed with a life-threatening illness, one of the main ways I became able to handle and endure all that required doing, including researching an innovative treatment that ended up saving her life, was by focusing on the here and now.

"It is what it is"

The words "It is what it is," are commonly used to express resignation to, or frustration with, a life situation. This phrase is also exclaimed to answer a question that cannot be adequately answered as well as to justify or acknowledge the perceived reality of our circumstances. Such is further used to denote, akin to Kether, impartially observing what is presently occurring, right now, exactly as it *is*, without any positive or negative judgment. This statement is in strong contrast to rejecting what is now transpiring because we want it to be otherwise. Alternatively, while this expression may be seen as a step on the road to Kether's expansive, cosmic consciousness, I have certainly called it up as an excuse to avoid unpleasant, yet necessary, action. Of course, I have always "paid" for doing this in one form or another.

The Gift of Imbalance

It is essential to remember that we humans are always in the midst of re-equilibrating ourselves. Without imbalances, there would be no movement in life. Simply, our evolutionary journey would not exist. Moving between the Tree of Life's positive and negative polarities is a normal and natural part of daily living. Being completely balanced at all times is stasis or death! Much as the metabolism of our physical bodies builds up and breaks down during the anabolic and catabolic processes, we are always doing likewise. Simply, ongoing physical, mental, and emotional aka spiritual construction and destruction is unavoidable and required. Certainly, deciding how to adjust to these natural processes is key.

Remembering we have the Tree's Middle Pillar of Equilibrium to help us focus, balance, and center in the midst of uncertainty and upheaval, is a gift. Cultivating the ability to slip into neutral is proven to clarify perspective, and in doing so, our prospective actions. Essentially, we decide from this stable place what we best do, or not do, next. Yet no matter what we choose, over time, life is slowly and surely teaching us to pursue what is for the upliftment and benefit of ourselves and all concerned.

Self-Stirred Existence

Kether may be likened to Aristotle's Cause of All Causes and Prime Mover. This uncaused cause, what Plato termed the Unmoved Mover, is the self-stirred existence urging the Universal Life Force into motion. Simply, the Unmoved Mover moves other things, yet is not itself moved by any prior action. Kether's power of actionless existence is fixed or static, rather than a dynamic force that energetically permeates and maintains all existence. Nita, an electrical engineer and Qabalah student likened Kether to the production of stationary or motionless charges.

Kether may be understood as an act of cosmic intention: Spirit, Divinity, Most High, God/dess, Cosmos, and so on, turning inwards to a point within itself, and in doing so, initiating the life process. In physics, the act of compressing energy inward at its center decreases its volume, resulting in rotation. Essentially, what's transpiring in this first sephirah corresponds to compression.

Kether's activity is comparable to what happens when we turn inwards during deep meditation and contemplation—such results in the stirring of the depths of our being. The workings of Kether may also be likened to the process of breathing: Breathing in is the building-up of energy. Breathing out is the outpouring of energy, or creation itself. However, at this early stage of creation, there's nothing except pure potential to generate. While the manifestation process *begins* in Kether, it actually *becomes* in the remaining spheres or sephroth.

Possibility vs. Actuality

The first statement from Paul Foster Case's *Pattern on the Trestleboard* clarifies the aforementioned act, declaring: "All the power that ever was or will be is here now. I am a center of expression for the One Divine Will to express itself, which eternally creates, sustains, and transforms the universe." This potent assertion designates Kether to be the capacity for existence, yet not existing. This first sephirah is the uncreated preceding all creation and beingless potential of Beingness. Kether is the cosmic incongruity of, that which is, and yet is not. Alternatively, Kether symbolizes the *possibility* of existence versus the *actuality* of existence, which is the byproduct of Kether radiating its energy into the next sephirah, Chokmah. Chokmah's dynamic creative activity is aligned with "The Word." Receiving Kether's energies, Chokmah then projects them into Binah, rolling the ball of physical manifestation along.

Comparing Kether to an old-fashioned wind-up clock before it starts unwinding is a fitting example of Kether's workings. Kether is the uncreated, beingless, indefinite, unformed universal potential immediately before the unmanifest world starts winding down and out into manifest form.

The Source

Because Kether is not an actual emanation from the Godhead, Spirit, Cosmos, Universe, and so on—it *is* such—some Qabalists refrain from including it among the sephiroth. Beginning or crowning the Tree of Life with Kether indicates that it is the source, origin, or cause behind the creation and the remaining sephiroth. From this point of view, Kether symbolizes pure spirit, the one invisible, vital principle energizing and supporting the entire visible universe. This may be likened to the Gnostic idea of the "depth of all being," *pleroma* or fullness. The loftiest principle in their theogony is viewing the spiritual universe as the totality of the divine powers and emanations

Similarly, some Jewish Kabbalists regard Kether as the "supernal serpent," the universal world spirit, which is everything and no thing. When wearing the guise of nature, Kether imparts the gifts of life and death. It is understandable why this force is thought of as simultaneously the greatest wonder and the greatest terror!

Intriguingly, Jewish students of the renowned sixteenth-century Jewish Kabbalist Isaac Luria view the sephiroth below Kether the Crown, Chokmah, Wisdom, and Binah, Understanding, to be holy sparks that have descended to earth to be confined in shells, or according to others, imprisoned in flesh. Above all, this state of physical captivity is recognized as a magnificent opportunity to earn one's freedom to return to the Source.

Flowing out from the Oneness of Kether is the manyness of creation. Rising out of the Tree of Life's neutral Middle Pillar of Equilibrium, Kether contains the pre-material for all of existence. The Great Androgyne that Kether is contains nature's positive and negative polarities, *yang* and *yin*, or male and female characteristics, signified by the Tree of Life's two outer pillars. Chokmah/Wisdom, the Creator, or Cosmic Father, heads the *yang*, positively charged Pillar of Mercy, below and to the right of Kether. While Binah/Understanding, the Creatrix or Cosmic Mother, tops the *yin*, negatively charged Pillar of Severity below and to the left of Kether. The whirling inner vortex of Kether*ian* energy is beneath and within, supporting, holding, and upholding all outer forms. Hearing this, Carole, a student and NASA scientist, equated Kether with the electronic state, which is neither a solid, liquid, nor gas.

Moving Image of Eternity

Reiterating: Kether crowns the Pillar of Equilibrium in the present, the eternal moment, or "now," sits above and between the past and future. Plato's definition of time as "a moving image of eternity" is another fitting description of Kether's out-of-time time zone. Like Kether, time, particularly in the eternal sense (referring to before the concept of time came into being), is only partially comprehensible. Time is conceptualized in innumerable ways. I'm using the terms "eternal time," "relative time," and "biological time" signifying both the Tree of Life's activities and structure. Assembly-wise, these time frames are conjoined with the spheres of the Kether, Chokmah, and Binah as eternal, relative, and biological time, respectively. The following further couples time and the Tree's three pillars: Kether-Crown, surmounting the Pillar of Equilibrium, signifies the present. Chokmah-Wisdom, topping the Pillar of Mercy, represents the past. *Binah*-Understanding, heading the Pillar of Severity, designates the future.

Human awareness of time is our ability to distinguish which of any two events is earlier and which is later. Adding to this is our perception of an instantaneous present, continually transforming into a remembered past and an anticipated future! Qabalistically speaking: time past, the Pillar of Mercy, is replaced with the up-and-coming future, the Pillar of Severity, after moving through the present, the Pillar of Equilibrium. Human need and experience resulted in the idea of compartmentalizing time, leading Qabalists to assign specific time references to the Tree of Life.

Of course, from the universal perspective, there's no time but the present—everything happening at this very moment makes it timeless. Supporting this, Einstein wrote: "People who believe in physics know that the distinction between past, present, and future is only a stubbornly persistent illusion and that true reality is timeless." Jumping forward at least a half-century to Samuel Alexander and C.D. Broad's, "The Block Universe Theory," or Eternalism in which the past, present and future all co-exist 'now.' This cutting-edge premise likens our universe to a gigantic four-dimensional block of space-time, containing all the things that ever happened and will happen in our traditional perception of time, yet doing so simultaneously in the here and now. This concept is again reminding me of the first line of *Pattern on the Trestleboard*, "All the power that ever was or will be is here now."

Although a bit dated, I am suddenly recalling a memorable article, "Time Nothing but a Clock," by physicist George Zebrowski. Zebrowski proposed that time is an eternal container in which everything happens that cannot be comprehended apart from physical events, and that our perception of time is illusory. Simply, the perception of time may be understood as a narrow foreground of change occurring within an infinitely wide background. Because our physical bodies are continually running biological clocks, we experience time. If we could stop all clocks, eternity—a different type of time—would remain. Our knowledge of time insists that our mindsets and body clocks recognize and relate to it. Briefly, we humans have always had eternal time in the background of our lives while simultaneously adhering to time's exact and observable characteristics in the foreground.

QABALISTIC IMAGE OF KETHER: AN ANCIENT ONE IN PROFILE

Seeking to further expand their understanding, Qabalists ascribe an archetypical or classically recognized image to each sephirah. The representation of a partially visible human alludes to Kether's mysteriousness and hidden nature. The figure's incompleteness underscores the fact that the totality of this sephirah remains somewhat concealed and inexplicable. As the Most High contains maleness and femaleness or masculo-feminine energies, I opted to update the image, traditionally depicted as bearded, to be beardless and thereby to suggest a gender-neutral or non-binary individual who contains the potential for the entire garden of sexual variations.

THE QABALISTIC INTELLIGENCES:

EXPANDING, THINKING, KNOWING AND DOING

The *Sepher Yetzirah*, the ancient *Book of Formation*, also known as the *Book of Creation*, was written in about 200 BCE in Greek, as Hebrew was only used for prayer. Although originally coupled with Jewish mysticism, it became relevant to the cross-cultural study of Qabalah. A potent example of this is seen in the assignment of an Intelligence to each of the Tree of Life's ten sephiroth, which we will now be exploring.

Intelligence is the ability to acquire and apply knowledge and skills. The Qabalistic Intelligences are the forces of the one great Universal Mind or Intelligence, which through attention and intention we may come to understand and apply to our lives, to behave more intelligently! Accomplishing this expands our human intelligence, ushering us into a more open, universal way of perceiving ourselves, others, and the world. Over time, this change of perception morphs into behaving in ways that are increasingly aligned with universal and natural laws, truths, and principles. A potent example of this is seen in this statement from the United States Declaration of Independence: "All men (people) are created equal." Often, and depending on the subject, the distance between knowing and doing is a matter of time and maturation.

Tools and Powers

The Qabalistic Intelligences are universal concepts, which when grasped by the human mind and heart, become tools helping us handle life with increasing amounts of wisdom, understanding, and grace. An example of this follows. Overwhelmed with grief and concern, Rudy stood in the synagogue fervently praying for his younger brother Joel's recovery from serious radical surgery. Joel underwent an orchiectomy the removal of his testicles to stop the production of testosterone, which his case of prostate cancer cells, needs to survive and multiply. In the midst of petitioning the Most High for Joel's healing, Rudy suddenly began pondering the term "radical," used to describe the surgical procedure. Doing this expectedly opened his mind and intelligence to the Universal Mind and Intelligence, uplifting and modifying his habitual thinking.

Rudy's insight went something like this: As a member of the *Haredi*, an ultra-orthodox Jew sect, Rudy habitually announced, "As heaven is my witness, I believe in the complete destruction of Islam and death of all Muslims." Yet, due to his beloved brother's radical surgery, the door to Rudy's heart unexpectedly opened to a more expansive meaning of the word radical, and with it an understanding of the Radical Intelligence connected with Tree of Life's sphere of Severity, *Geburah*.

Suddenly Rudy recalled from his studies of the *Zohar* or *Book of Splendor*, that Geburah is *both* the fierce guardian of the righteous and loving protector of the weak and oppressed. Accompanying this he began thinking, what was for him, an extremely radical thought: while the Most High's creation and protection of the Jewish people is just, what about the rest of creation and thereby, the protection of *all* humans, who as the Old Testament states, were created in God's image. This thought unexpectedly moved Rudy to start examining his radical political views and deep-seated hatred of all Muslims, especially the Palestinians. Although not "the chosen people," yet one of the Most High's creations, perhaps they too have a right to be shielded. This marked the beginning of Rudy's departure from his extremist views.

Looking up the word "Muslim" and learning it meant "One who gives himself to God," Rudy took to integrating the idea that Muslims have as much right to divine protection as do Jews. He launched his undertaking by behaving more humanely towards an Arab co-worker and whenever he could remember, cease repeating, "dirty towel head bastard" under his breath. Rudy also started considering the value of what was for him an extremely *radical* idea: the possibility of "a two-state solution" to the Israeli-Palestinian conflict. This led to Rudy courageously talking about these ideas with close family members and friends, also fitting in with *Geburah's* Radical Intelligence.

Consider this example when exploring the Intelligence coupled with each of the Qabalistic Tree of Life's spheres. Simply, once we start pondering the principles of a sephirah, such have a way of becoming potent tools helping us live life, as one student enthusiastically put it, "Mo' better."

THE *SEPHER YETZIRAH*, NAMES KETHER,

THE ADMIRABLE AND HIDDEN INTELLIGENCE

Kether is named both the Admirable and Hidden Intelligence. Admirable stems from the verb "admire." Dovetailing with Kether, admire originates from the Latin *ad-mi-rari*, meaning "to wonder." When someone or something is admirable, such evokes amazement. The result of sensing and admiring Kether's sacred force hidden within the physical world arouses our desire and inspires us to experience it more fully.

The Admirable Intelligence is the all-pervading universal intelligence, arousing awe in those capable of beholding its workings. It is the light-and life-giving power of the One, "which hath no beginning or end." Glimpsing the miraculous transfor-mation of nothing into something through the myriad forms of the physical world is nothing short of awesome. Similarly, Hinduism refers to creation as a *lila*, the effortless, playful relationship between the Absolute reality and the possible world. Consequently, this Intelligence may be aligned with the Hindu view that creation occurred so that Divinity might amuse and admire itself by seeing itself mirrored in the spectacle of creation.

Hidden and Mysterious

Kether is also known as the Hidden or Mysterious Intelligence, embedded in the physical world. Fittingly, several Native American tribes refer to Divinity as the Great Mystery. Connecting Kether with the ideas of what is hidden and mysterious has a solid scientific basis.

According to cosmologists, visible matter comprises only about 25 percent of the total contents of the universe. Dark energy and dark matter are names given to the 75 percent of the universe that remain invisible referring to the Veils of the Absolute. Yet, this inexplicable force drives the expansion of the universe and binds galaxies together.

When something special is hidden or mysterious, our interest to know it is often kindled. This quote from Sufism's *Hadith Qudsi*, the "Extra-Koranic Word of God," attributed to the Prophet Muhammad, supports this idea: "I was a hidden treasure and I loved to be known, so I created the world." Kether, the concealed and mystifying abode of the Great Unmanifest, serves as a portal to existence and beyond. The great yogi Paramahansa Yogananda alluded to this when writing, "From that sphere where the mind cannot penetrate, God is pouring forth His (Her) essential Light—the Cosmic Intelligent Vibration that structures finite creation."

The inability to directly observe, or better yet recognize, Kether's subtle nature is actually an invitation to look deeper and longer. Recognizing the entire physical world as the outer raiments of Spirit makes the imperceptible perceptible and available to us. Getting acquainted with the power of the Hidden Intelligence offers us the potential to be cognizant of, and in an increasing number of instances to perceive life through super sensorially attuned senses, the Admirable, Amazing, and Awesome presence of the One secreted within the many—each and every person, creature, thing, place and set of circumstances in the physical world.

EXPLAINING THE UNEXPLAINABLE SPIRITUAL EXPERIENCE

Varying from person to person, spiritual experiences tend to be difficult to fully explain to others. That said, each of the ten sephroth on the Qabalistic Tree of Life is paired with a particular Spiritual Experience. Such offer us a tangible sense, or better yet, experience, of the principles of a sephirah permeating our lives, and in doing so, granting a deeper, more expansive, transcendent meanings to worldly events, personal and interpersonal occurrences—meanings which we ordinarily don't recognize in this way. Mystical-spiritual experiences are fast trains from thinking to knowing. It is for this reason that the expansion of an intellectual concept into a physical experience through sensory or extrasensory perception begins with the words, "The Vision of..." By confirming our growing knowledge of each of the Tree's ten sephroth, Spiritual Experiences are adding fuel to the fire of our life journey.

Heightened occurrences will spring up while doing mundane activities such as getting out of bed in the morning, grocery shopping, and driving. These may also be the byproduct of an altered state of consciousness resulting from meditating, praying, reading and discussing inspirational material, traveling, exercising, listening to music, viewing art, taking a consciousness-altering substance and so on.

An extremely potent combination of physical exhaustion and emotional openness resulting from giving birth to my son brought me an unforgettable incident. The Spiritual Experience of Understanding, Binah, the Great Mother Principle, is the Vision of Sorrow. Looking into my newborn's eyes for the first time, the Vision of Sorrow spontaneously arose. During those moments of intense bonding, I was filled to overflowing with a mixture of unspeakable joy and sorrow. While navigating through these powerful feelings, I actually "saw" in a fast-forward rush of time showing how my tiny baby, who was just beginning his life, would, like all physical beings and things, age and die. Within mere seconds, I *experienced* the undeniable truth that when a soul is born into a physical body, it becomes subject to nature's laws and cycles.

THE SPIRITUAL EXPERIENCE OF KETHER:

UNIFIED EXISTENCE

It is only logical that the Spiritual Experience of Kether, Unified Existence "crowns" the Tree of Life. As it states, Unified Existence is the union or reunion of the personal with the impersonal immortal spirit of life at the center of the universe. One student fittingly suggested this experience is "the jewel in the crown," terminology used to describe the most valuable part of something. Unified Existence is stepping out of time, as we know it, into the timeless universe and becoming one with it. The blissful oblivion of one's individuality and personality is the ultimate goal of spiritual practice.

Of course, if we humans genuinely knew and lived out the fact that we are one and thereby interdependent, conflicts such as war would not exist. Yet not knowing or forgetting that the totality of existence and events in the physical world are in some way unified in the greater spiritual world, brings awakening, often in the form of suffering. A certain amount of misery, aka ego-annihilation, goes along with having a physical body. When our awareness of the interconnectedness of all things is absent or denied, we can be left feeling increasingly disconnected and miserable. Unable to find an anchor or reference point for putting events into a context beyond the personal, we may find ourselves afloat in a sea of endless despair. It is understandable that this state often opens the door for addictive behaviors to enter. While these only provide temporary relief, in time, such have the potential to lead to a spiritual awakening.

Growing Ready

Unified Existence begins rooting when we grow ready to begin releasing ourselves from the chains of our "Wanting what I want when I want it," attitude. Easing up on the belief that each of us is always something all-important, we began walking the path of becoming the No-Thing important, the state of Unified Existence. This may be likened to the raindrop being reunited with the cloud from which it originated. The crowning experience of Unified Existence confirms our link with the One Reality and the perfection of life as it presently is for furthering our growth and development in every way.

Forgetting or not knowing that the totality of existence and events in the physical world are in some way unified in the greater world, we suffer. Although suffering goes along with inhabiting a physical body, when our awareness of the interconnectedness of all things is denied or absent, we tend to feel even more disconnected and miserable. Unable to find an anchor or reference point by which to put events into a context beyond the personal, we may find ourselves afloat in a sea of endless despair. It is understandable that this state may open the door for addictive behaviors to enter. While these do provide relief, such is only temporary.

One Vast Cosmic Web

This Spiritual Experience of Unified Existence imparts the certainty, even if momentary, that the same holy lamp igniting and enlivening every cell in my being, does so for the entirety of existence. From another view, herein lies the realization that individual beings and things are connected by one vast, cosmic web, any thread from which is traceable through the space-time fabric of the universe to every other thread. The Hawaiian *Kahuna* or shamans knew of these connections which they term *aka* or threads, centuries ago. However, it has only been within the last century that scientists have postulated a string or loop theory in which everything in the universe is conjoined. Receiving the certainty that we are heavenly children transforms the statement that we are made in the image of Spirit from an abstract idea into reality. Furthermore, no matter how brief an ecstatic experience of Union might be, it forever sparks the unforgettable fire of inner knowing or en-lighten-ment. While this initial experience may be short, its memory is endless.

Winnie, both a Qabalah student and longtime practitioner of Transcendental Meditation, shared the following: "The state of Being (or not being) is one of pure consciousness, completely out of the field of relativity; there is no world of the senses or of objects, no trace of sensory activity, no trace of mental activity. Herein there is no triad of thinker, thinking process, and thought; doer, the process of doing and action; experiencer, the process of experiencing, and object of experience." The state of the transcendental Unity of life, or pure consciousness, is completely free from any trace of duality.

Climbing Jacob's Ladder

Unified Existence, *Unio Mystica,* Union or-re-union with the Most High is the ultimate goal of all mystical occurrences. According to Qabalistic and other traditions, the human soul is derived from the universal soul, which may re-ascend from the physical world into the upper supernal world and this elevated state of spirit by means of dedicated intention and ethical purification. Unified Existence results in stepping out of time as we know it, into timeless eternity, blissfully rejoining our individual soul with the One Great Soul at the center of the universe. It is the state of at-one-ment with the one great organism, wherein our personality *consciously* merges with impersonality in physical death. Essentially, we are transformed from being a part of creation, into being the whole of creation.

Westerners term the experience of personal extinction "enlightenment," a momentary encounter that usually increases our hunger for it as a permanent state. Another name for the Tree of Life is, "Jacob's Ladder." St. John of the Cross, compared "the steps of the ladder" to Christians moving from darkness into light or illumination and then union, the indescribable ecstasy of personal oblivion. It is the journey of the soul from bodily sensation into divine radiance and from there to the annihilation of any separation or physical consciousness.

Kether's state of Unified Existence is known in the Hindu, Buddhist, Zen, Sikh, and Sufi traditions as *Mahasamadhi, Nirvana, Satori, Mukti, Hahut,* or "The Conference of the Birds," respectively. Here, one effortlessly penetrates the greatest mystery of life to blissfully merge with it. This quote from the *Bhagavad Gita* describes a route taken to accomplish this: "Fix your mind on Me, be devoted to Me; thus uniting yourself to Me and utterly depending on Me, you shall come to Me." Relatedly, Hasidic Jews believe that merging themselves with the teachings of the Torah causes their bodies to be "clothed" in the actions it commands, leading to *Unio Mystica.*

Post Script

Devoting ourselves to learning special rituals and studying mystical texts, teachings, and spiritual practices is undoubtedly worthwhile. However, the practical application and integration of the underlying principles of a tradition into everyday living are paramount. Walking one's talk by leading a life focused on compassionately adhering to universal laws, truths, and principles is uplifting to oneself, and through the process of osmosis, others. Of course, Unified Existence occurs for reasons beyond linear comprehension. It is essential to remember that this or any Spiritual Experience occurs when we are ripe is crucial. Anxiously seeking a spiritual experience usually pushes it further away. Bringing it on before one is ready tends to make it not stick, or may even yield tragic results. This makes me think of the careless use of a psychedelic that played a part in facilitating a client's death.

Being composed of carbon or stardust, we are already one with the cosmos. Becoming increasingly alert to this fact accelerates our focus. It also grants access to more expansive, "Big Picture" ways of thinking, feeling and doing. Having the awareness that we are more than finite humans is itself a quantum leap into the infinite. Acting on this truth as we go about our day-to-day routine and interactions, helps cement this truth into the foundation of our beings.

That is, building the critical mass of enough thoughts, words, and actions to become fully identified with the eternal in the temporal, will in Divine time result in cosmic union or Unified Existence.

ATTRIBUTES: FLESHING OUT EACH SEPHIRAH

Because each of the ten sephiroth is initially perceived as a group of intellectual concepts, the assignment of sensorially perceptible attributes and the ideas these evoke make each sephirah increasingly real and penetrable. Attributes offer the dimension of familiarity through physicality. Suggesting pictures such as the sparkle of a gem, an image of a plant, animal, geometric shape, or whiff of a scent, helps concretize abstract ideas, and by doing so, makes the intangible tangible—increasing each sephirah's intelligibility and perceptibility. Noticing any or all of these while going about our daily routines helps key us into and assists our practical application and integration of the teachings of its corresponding sephirah.

FEATURING: KETHER

NUMBER, ONE: A fitting reminder of this leading sephirah, the number one is defined as unity, uniqueness, and beginning. Number one affirms the presence of Kether, the One in all. One signifies the state, fact, or condition of being a single entity or unit underscoring Kether's main teaching that from the cosmic view, all of creation is one. Characterized by indivisibility, one symbolizes coherence, the singleness of purpose and action, as does Kether. *The Emerald Tablet of Hermes*, an ancient Hermetic text, begins with the statement, "All things are from the One." Consequently, some Qabalists use the Roman numeral "I" to symbolize the one Great Spirit of the universe, the source of all.

One is also the number of integration. Kabbalist Isaac Luria taught that we are *Tzimtzum*, shattered vessels seeking repair and wholeness, or *Tikkun*. Restoration is the conscious unification of our personality with our soul-spirit Self in Kether by living spiritually attuned lives while embodied. When we recall and act upon the inseparable connection between our actions on earth and the cosmos, we are whole or one. Luria's philosophy is further coupled with activities intended to restore and improve the planet, *Tukkun Olam*, since it is, like us, a manifestation and reflection, of the Most High..

Awarding someone or something first place is an honor. Bearing the honor of uniqueness, Kether is the one-of-a-kind archetype or prototype from which the basic substance of all in the physical world emanates. Recalling the seven planes of existence paired with the Tree of Life, wherein Kether stands alone on the spiritual plane, this fact is crystallized.

Kether is coupled with the Spiritual Experience of Unified Existence. Unification highlights the truth that everything originates from the same source, although appearing in its own unique form. There is only one Great Spirit or Universal Life Force, which takes on the forms of the many, defining unity as the continuity of one-on-one, within the One!

COLOR, WHITE BRILLIANCE: The color or achromatic shade of maximum lightness conjoined with Kether is white brilliance, which reflects all colors and is the shade from which all colors originate. Akin to Kether's functioning, achromatic colors transmit and receive light without separating it into colors. This full-on spectacle of Kether's brilliance is seen when looking at a crystal-clear prism with light streaming through. Every hue is contained in and is emitted from the prism's white light, as all of life is contained in and emitted from Kether. Intimating Kether be considered a positive reflection of negative existence, the Three Veils of the Absolute.

Hindus are known to wear white during funerals at funerals because it symbolizes purity and the fact that the person who died is freed from the illusions that come with having a physical body. Women in central and northern India are bound to wear white from the time of their husband's death onwards. This practice is used to show the world both their widowhood and unavailability for remarriage. I have found it encouraging that some women are now violating this tradition by adorning their white clothing with colorful accessories.

Of course, white is associated with purity. (We will explore this as a cultural misnomer under the color black in Binah.) The words from the hymn "Amazing Grace," stating "Was blind, but now I see," suggest the personality raising the white flag of surrender to Kether's impersonality. Similarly, the experience of seeing or walking into the "white light" of Spirit is often paired with the surrendering or passing away of the physical body, or in this instance acknowledging the supremacy of Kether's Unified Existence reigning overall.

GEMSTONE, THE DIAMOND: Originating from the Greek word *adamantinos*, meaning "unbreakable," the "diamond," reminds us of Kether's indestructible, eternal nature. Conjoining the diamond with the qualities of purity, durability, eternity, sparkle, and reflection further prompts us to recall Kether. Advertisements for diamonds promote the idea that "Diamonds are Forever," and Kether's activities are eternal. Like our ascent through the Tree of Life to Kether, diamonds are formed under extreme pressure. The unpolished diamond is black—a reminder that out of the darkness of the void comes the brilliant radiance of Kether. Despite being colorless when properly lit, diamonds emit the entire color spectrum.

Much as Kether is seeded within us, biology's carbon cycle shows it being the seed element in most compounds from which living and dead organisms are composed. Although we humans are at different places in the carbon cycle, the diamond and we ourselves are both carbon, making us "diamonds in the rough."

Although diamonds can cut anything, little can cut them. Having the ranking of "10—the hardest on the Mohs scale of mineral hardness—renders it comparable to the enduring workings of Kether. Gemologists consider the diamond superior to other gems, much in the same way that Kether reigns above the remaining sephroth. This exceedingly precious jewel emits a dazzling white brilliance containing and emitting an infinite number of facets, as does Kether—a fact paradoxical to Kether being the epitome of singularity.

The seat on which Buddha attained enlightenment is known as the diamond throne or *Vajrayana*. This is analogous to how a working knowledge of Kether has the potential to bring us to the center of the universe and thereby attaint the "seat" of fully illuminated consciousness. Related, *The Diamond Sutra* is probably the most revered text of Mahayana Buddhism. Yes, diamonds can penetrate all, and this jewel of the world's religious literature helps practitioners break through their ignorance and illusion to get to the one and only reality, Kether.

Some alternative healers occasionally recommend using diamonds along with other gems to amplify their treatments. Along similar lines, it is said that as one progresses spiritually, the calcified brain sand in our pineal gland becomes clear and diamond-like.

SCENT, AMBERGRIS: Kether, the basis for life, is paired with Ambergris, the basis or fixative that blends a combination of scents into a single scent for the world's finest perfumes. Kether is the Hidden Intelligence,and until fairly recently the true origin of the rare and expensive ambergris was unknown. Dating back about 1.75 million years, and used for more than a thousand years, this precious and pricey secretion is found only in the intestines of the sperm whale. Ambergris forms when the whale eats something indigestible, such as cuttlefish. When indigestion occurs the whale disgorges the fish, which is then surrounded by digestive substances. Such would ordinarily be considered disgusting, yet in this instance contains the exquisite ambergris. Because whales were being slaughtered by the thousands to obtain it, natural ambergris is prohibited. Aromatherapists recommend using ambergris to induce cosmic consciousness, Kether's Unified Existence.

PLANT, LOTUS FLOWER: The lotus flower has represented spiritual unfoldment and divine perfection since antiquity. This blossom has a seemingly infinite number of petals, as Kether has an infinite number of ways of expressing itself. Despite floating gracefully on the top of the water, the exquisite Lotus possesses an intricate root system buried in the mud below and through which it derives its nourishment to grow, emerge, and blossom. This may be likened to how Kether, rooted in the unseen, is the hidden and sustaining source of life that too develops and blooms simultaneously.

In Hindu yoga, the Thousand Petaled Lotus or *Sahasrara*, counterpart to Qabalah's Crown Star (that we will soon be exploring), is coupled with Kether. Similarly, the foremost mantra of Tibetan Buddhism, *Om Mani Parma Hum*, means, "Praise to the Jewel at the heart of the Lotus!" This jewel, like Kether, is none other than the precious, sacred Buddha nature living within the nucleus of the manifest world.

PLANT, BANYAN TREE: The greatly revered banyan tree, a member of the *Tillandsia* or Bromeliad family, is an air plant. Comparable to Kether, air plants seem to grow out of thin air—the non-physical world—to appear and flourish in the physical world. On reaching the ground, the majestic banyan's aerial rootlets, become like Kether, embedding themselves in whatever they touch. Further corresponding to the Tree of Life, the Banyan tree grows from top to bottom.

ANIMAL, THE FALCON: Sitting on its perch, the falcon symbolizes the great Egyptian sky god Horus, or *Heru* in Ancient Egyptian, whose name means, "One who is above." Paralleling Kether, the keen-sighted falcon remains poised in the heavens, observing life on earth impartially.

ANIMAL, THE SWAN: Hindu mythology teaches that when a swan is given milk mixed with water, it separates the two. Drinking the milk and leaving the water, the swan demonstrates transcendent wisdom, as does Kether. The swan is born black and turns white, paralleling how Kether emerges from the invisibility and darkness of the Three Veils of Negative Existence into visibility and whiteness.

The white swan has long been a symbol of spirit and purity. The Sanskrit word for swan is *Hansa*. In the Yogic tradition, a highly developed practitioner receives the title *Paramahansa*, meaning "great and pure soul" in addition to their name. This is exemplified in names such as Paramahansa Yogananda.

Vedic tradition teaches the potent mantra, Hansa, meaning, "I am That I am." Qabalistically speaking, "That" refers to the Great Spirit of the Universe, Kether. Repeating this sacred statement affirms oneness—the Unified Existence of Kether. Hansa automatically connects the practitioner with the infinite via their incoming and outgoing breaths. Listening carefully to the sound of my breathing, I'm hearing *Han* while inhaling and *Sa* while exhaling. Because we begin "repeating" this sacred vibration at birth with our first cycle of respiration, such is regarded to be our first and most "natural" mantra. Consistently reciting this powerful phrase promotes full-on identification with Kether. In closing, Hansa is equated with Kether's Word of Power or mantra, *Eheyeh*, to be explored in a bit.

MEDICINES AND DRUGS: Each sephirah is paired with a medicine and/or drug. Since these terms are often used interchangeably, many believe that medicines and drugs are the same—something that is theoretically untrue. Medicines are substances or preparations used in treating disease. An example of this would be the use of insulin to regulate blood sugar in people with diabetes. Certainly, there are times when for various reasons a medicine is incompatible with one's biology—I'm deathly allergic to penicillin, whereas a friend sickens from aspirin.

Drugs, on the other hand, are any chemical compound, manufactured in a laboratory or of plant, animal, or marine origin. These are intended to bring change in the normal functions of the body and mind and may have a positive, negative, or mixed effect as in the use of the psychoactive drugs in Psilocybin ("magic mushrooms"), Mescaline (the active substance in the Peyote and San Pedro cacti), LSD, Ecstasy, and so on. In a sense, all medicines are drugs, yet not all drugs are medicines.

MEDICINE, *ELIXIR VITAE*: Kether, the ageless, deathless, ever-lasting, imperishable representation of eternity and immortality, is conjoined with the supernatural Elixir Vitae. Because the words Elixir Vitae, meaning "medicine of life," and medicine are semantically related it is used as a synonym. Ancient alchemists identified Elixir Vitae as the miraculous, self-perpetuating remedy possessing the curative and regenerative energies to cure all ills and maintain life in a physical body indefinitely. This helps clarify why this Fountain of Youth, the immortality-giving medicine, is conjoined with Kether, the vitalizing life force that is eternally bestowing life upon the world.

Originating in ancient Egypt, alchemy and teaches that the greatest secrets of life are found by searching for the mysterious Elixir Vitae or "Philosopher's Stone." Believed to hold the life-giving power of the universe, this legendary substance is capable of restoring youth and vitality to the ill and aging. Elixir Vitae is said to contain the ability to turn base metals into gold, which in Qabalistic terms is The Great Work of transforming the ordinary, mortal human into the extraordinary, enlightened, immortal human. Accomplishing this, we become the embodiment of universal and natural laws, truths, and principles—Eternal Verities, Perennial Philosophy, *Dharma*, and so on. We become mediums capable of affecting great physical, mental, emotional, and spiritual regeneration in ourselves, and in certain instances, others.

I'll close this segment with the fitting and inspiring words of Sophia Loren: "There's a Fountain of Youth: it is your mind, your talents, the creativity you bring to your life, and the lives of the people you love. When you learn to tap this source, you will have truly defeated age."

THE SACRAMENT OF KETHER, THE CROWN, IS BAPTISM

The sacrament or ritual of baptism is known to have originated from the ancient pagan Mysteries, wherein it symbolized purification through the cleansing of the body before entering a holy place. A large basin of water situated in the temple's courtyard was used for ceremonial ablutions by the priests and priestesses, who ritually bathed themselves before putting on their sacred robes.

Ancient Egyptians recognized two symbolic baptisms: water, signifying the purification of the body through strict observance and physical regeneration; and fire, representing the illumination of the spirit and descent of consciousness from on high.

Accepting baptism as a means of washing out Original Sin is a purely religious doctrine. Qabalistically speaking, the true Original Sin is ignorance, which over time our life experiences cleanse, so that greater Wisdom and Understanding may enter. Truth purifies the mind and heart and in doing so, allows entry into the inner sanctuary of the mystery school, the sacred temple within. Although requiring differing physical behaviors, as I understand it, all the sacraments are similarly symbolic.

Hindus, Jews, Christians, Muslims, Protestants, and...

As you likely noticed from the title of this segment, I did not list Buddhism, similar to Qabalah in that it is more of a philosophy than a religion. So here goes, starting from the oldest and ending with what I know as the newest.

HINDUISM: The Hindu practice of *Namkaran* or name-giving occurs on the 12th day after birth. This ceremony includes prayer by a priest as well as music, singing, poems, readings, parental promises to their child, the appointment of "guide parents," and perhaps a symbolic action such as planting a tree, signing a certificate, or writing in a wish book. Interestingly, Hinduism has sixteen main sacraments termed *Samskaras,* ranging from conception to funeral ceremonies. Each aims at bringing practitioners closer to living in ways that benefit themselves and all humanity.

JUDAISM: Although the term "baptism" is not used to describe Jewish rituals, the purification rites in Jewish law and tradition, called *tevilah*, have similarities to baptism. Tevilah is the act of immersion in naturally sourced water, called a *mikvah*. It is repeated according to particular rules and needfulness. The act of cleansing of impurities in the mikvah is done before the Sabbath, on holy days, after menstruation, childbirth, contact with a corpse, and on conversion to Judaism. This rite aims at preventing one member of the community from contaminating the rest of the community. Its intention is to facilitate an individual's full participation in community life.

According to the Old Testament, male children are blessed, named and circumcised eight days after being born. It is only recently that the birthing and naming of female children are being celebrated and ritualized. Such are also performed eight days after birth with a joyful ceremony including blessings that are especially meaningful to her parents and other family members.

CHRISTIANITY: In Christian tradition, particularly Roman Catholicism, baptism cleanses sinfulness, or lack of holiness, into which humankind is believed born. It cleanses "Original Sin," which comes along with being descendants of the first people, Adam and Eve. This condition is different from the sins a person may commit during life.

Traditionally, baptism occurs either after birth, when one is given their name, or during conversion to Catholicism. It is the central sacrament of the messianic movement started by John the Baptist. Baptism is performed in the name of the Father, Son, and Holy Spirit or in the name of Jesus Christ.

In this tradition, there are three types of baptism by which one can be saved: sacramental baptism with water, the baptism of implicit or explicit desire to be part of the Church, by water, and the baptism of blood, martyrdom.

ISLAM: The "Five Pillars of Islam" and Islamic "Articles of Faith" are spiritually uplifting principles that form the framework of Muslim life. Such encompass the monotheism of God, the pledging of faith, and numerous vital humane, community-oriented principles. Although these do not include baptism, from antiquity mosques have had tanks of water wherein the faithful must wash their feet before entering.

PROTESTANTISM: Since Protestantism was the last of these religious groups to be founded, I have listed it last. In this tradition, baptism is a "Means of Grace." Infants and adults are "re-born" into this "saving-grace." Herein Protestants are redeemed, initiated and sanctified by the Holy Spirit. Forgiving all sins, this ritual bestows eternal salvation, including deliverance from the devil and damnation at death.

BAPTISM A LA QABALAH: Qabalistically, the sacrament of baptism is coupled with Kether's placement on the spiritual plane, rather than on the physical plane, where it usually resides. Kether is the sephirah where each soul makes its sacred contract or covenant with Spirit, Most High God/dess, etc. *prior* to its physical birth. Entering into this business-like "acceptance agreement" enrolls each signator in the school of life and gives our consent to *everything* that accompanies being born into the physical world. Signing on transpires without knowing specifics such as our race, sex, ethnicity, family situation, skills, gifts, geographic location, conditions in the world, life's potential triumphs, traumas, tragedies, and so on.

Inhabiting a human body suggests emulating the Qabalistic Tarot's Fool, by taking a leap of faith and trusting that whatever occurs is aimed at facilitating our soul's development. Life in a physical body and on the earth plane may be compared to a sailor departing for sea. Although the sailor has signed-on for a journey and is aware of the generalities of being at sea, they are unaware of the precise details of what lies ahead—weather conditions, stops along the way, shipmates, and the like.

When performed at birth, baptism is synonymous with becoming a member of a particular religious faith. However, in the instance of Qabalah, baptism takes place before birth and is conjoined with becoming a member of the community of *Homo sapiens*, the species to which modern human beings belong. There is yet another baptismal grouping specifically coupled with Kether, that of *Homo Spiritualis*, the mature souls who are *purposefully* incarnating to uplift all of creation. These humans, who to my knowledge, are born within all religio-spiritual traditions, have a clear recollection of their spiritual origin, past lives, and their soul's commitment to serving Spirit by uplifting life on planet Earth, and in doing so themselves.

"Wishing I Wasn't Born"

Certainly, there are times when life's painful, worrisome, and calamitous situations have me feeling, thinking, and saying things like, "I wish I wasn't born." When lapsing into this state, I fully acknowledge my feelings. I reconsider Kether's sacrament of baptism and the sacred agreement that I was ready to trustingly sign before being born. Naturally, in the midst of extreme mental, emotional, and physical anguish, I feel that while fully consenting to the generalities of my contract, the fine print or specifics were not disclosed, and if such had been, I might have had some second thoughts. A handful of examples follow:

Being born to physically, mentally, and emotionally abusive parents. Bodily carrying and admitting a beloved friend to the emergency room and mental hospital when he was dying from a suicide attempt. Experiencing a terrifying "back-alley" abortion. Fasting when only having enough food to feed my child. Suffering the traumas of having been raped, molested, and given a serious STD. Living with personal and professional jealousy—slandered, stabbed in the back, and knifed in the heart. Dedicating myself to raising a rejecting stepchild. Being genetically predis-posed to a crippling health problem. Certainly, I have learned and am still learning much from these experiences, which includes owning the suffering I have caused, and acknowledging the innumerable upsides to my life!

Each event has been, is now being, and will be fuel for the engine of my soul's maturation and the souls of those involved, whether they are aware of it or not. This was borne out when not long before my mother's passing while suddenly after driving her to a doctor's appointment she tearfully blurted out and apologized for beating and endlessly berating me by stating, "I am sorry for doing to you what was done to me." Her admission and apology were something I had let go of ever happening many decades before. This incident served as a powerful reminder that all things occur in Divine Time, not mine!

Despite everything, we Qabalists, akin to other traditions, teach that each soul comes into a physical body to plow the field of its continuing growth and maturation through whatever life presents. By doing this we not only evolve, we subtly encourage others to do likewise and help build the critical mass for the betterment of all. Essentially, this means knowing in every cell of our being that our soul-spirit-Self signed on to live in a physical body to the following: Derive wisdom, understanding, and compassion from our life experiences; contribute our particular abilities to the world; and remain open to learning in general and learning from others, no matter how different they are from us. In these and innumerable other ways we transform into better people and grow closer with Spirit.

Our gradually unfolding consciousness makes "traveling the path of return" more palatable, and in time, easier to chew over and digest. To summarize as have I come to know it, Qabalistic baptism is the sacrament wherein before being born on the earth plane, a soul, for the purpose of its further development agrees to "take" a body along with the entire menu of what of that soul needs to evolve. There are also those fully evolved souls who regardless of being technically "done," opt to be reborn to serve a particular group of people, cause, and the like. In either instance, all promise to unconditionally accept everything that could possibly occur while inhabiting their physical form and circumstances.

A SEPHIRAH BY ANY OTHER NAME:

ALTERNATIVE TITLES

"A rose by any other name would smell as sweet" is a popular saying from Shakespeare's play *Romeo and Juliet*. This phrase is used to state that the names of things do not always shape what they genuinely are. It also broadens the picture of what or who is being perceived and named. The practice of assigning each sephirah on the Tree of Life Alternative Titles aims at doing this very thing. My friend Elena's husband often calls her "Elena-de-Braina" since she has encyclopedia-like knowledge. On the other hand, a former neighbor was nicknamed "Catmandoo," because he compassionately tended to stray felines.

KETHER'S ALTERNATIVE TITLES

THE MOST HIGH: Originating from the ancient Hebrew root, *Elyon*, meaning, "Highest," "Sovereign over All," and "God the Highest,"—apt names for the genderless, yet all-gender Kether. Elyon is further interpreted as the directive for human-kind to "Go up, rise, and ascend."

ONENESS: Preferring non-religious, secular titles, some Qabalists use Oneness, Higher Power, Universal Life Force, and like designations when referring to Kether.

THE GREAT SPIRIT: The Native American names Great Spirit and Great Mystery, English versions of tribal languages, are identical to Kether's Universal Life Force. Two examples of this title in Sioux and Algonquian follow *Wakan Tanka* and *Gitche Manitou.*

NOTHINGNESS: Kether is synonymous with Nothingness, the cause, root, primal essence, and source of all of creation. The Arabic word *Allah*, meaning God, is inter-preted, "the One who comes from nothing." Underscoring these ideas is the Buddhist concept of *shunyata*, which Chogyam Trumpa Rinpoche defined as "nothingness, emptiness, the absence of duality and conceptualization." Nothingness is further aligned with the Void the open spaciousness and boundlessness of Kether. Fittingly, the brilliant and highly intuitive Emily Dickinson stated, "I'm nobody, who are you?"

THE ONE STILL POINT: Residing in the middle of the ebbing and flowing Primor-dial Ocean of life, Kether is the indivisible and motionless center of Existence, the One Still Point. In this sense Kether is deemed to be the center of the cosmos, from which all activities originate and dimensions emanate. This title also implies that our lives spiral around a still point, the universe, while constantly moving to and from it.

I suggest giving T.S. Eliot's remarkable, "The Still Point in a Turning World" a read. Here is an appetizer:

"At the still point of the turning world. Neither flesh nor fleshless; Neither from nor towards; at the still point, there the dance is. But neither at rest nor at movement. And do not call it fixity, where past and future are gathered. Neither movement from nor towards, Neither ascent nor decline. Except for the point, the still point, There would be no dance, and there is only the dance."

BEGINNING OF BEGINNINGS, THE WHIRLINGS, AND SWIRLINGS: The Beginning of Beginnings suggests a primary point of departure, as does Kether—whereas the Beginning of the Whirlings and Swirlings, termed *Rashith Ha-Gilgulim* in Hebrew, couples Kether with the dynamic movement following the beginning. However, before spiraling outward, the powers of the universe, and consciousness itself, are spiraling inward. Turning in is considered an act of cosmic intention. This is the universal life power's gathering of energy by first turning into the earliest, most elemental point within itself, prior to spinning, swirling, whirling, and unfurling out. These actions are sometimes compared to the winding-up, and subsequent winding-down, of an old-fashioned clock.

MONAD: Kether is singular and philosophers such as Plato used the Greek word Monad to denote "singularity." This term also refers to the metaphysician's inseparable, indivisible, indissoluble, impenetrable, completely cohesive, and indestructible unit considered both the basic constituting element of physical reality and the unseen center at the core of life. In Theosophy, the Monadic Plane is home to the Monad or Oversoul. Physicist George Zebrowski employs this terminology to designate humans who by nature exist eternally, and into whom everything that will ever occur is programmed. This idea more than implies the hypothesis that Kether contains the plan for the entire universe—everything that was, is, and will be.

THE PRIMORDIAL, OMEGA, OR STILL POINT: These titles designate the first Still Point from and to which all powers of the infinite emerge and converge. Descriptive of Kether, the Primordial Point is Reality at the precise moment of becoming real. This cosmic center crystallized in the midst of non-being contains the potentialities for all to come. It corresponds to the spiritual plane from which creation springs and designates the first order of things that began before, and is at, the beginning.

Physicist and cosmologist Frank Tipler's *Omega Point Theory*, a thought-provoking blend of physics and theology, equates the Omega Point with the Godhead. Because life goes on eternally the universe is closed, with everything in it fated to spiral to a final unifying point. Tipler likens this to the phrase from the Old Testament's Book of Revelation, "I am the Alpha and Omega," the first and last letters of the Greek alphabet. Essentially, the beginning and end states of the universe are actually singular—that being the Primordial or Omega Point.

THE EXISTENCE OF EXISTENCES: Kether, the one pure and supreme existence, is the origin and source of all other existences.

THE PUPPET MASTER, CONCEALED OF THE CONCEALED: Although having the ability to make the puppets move, the puppet master remains like Kether, concealed behind the scenes. Evoking the Hidden Intelligence, this title implies how alluring the hidden and consequently mysterious can be. It underscores the fact that all religious, mystical, and spiritual traditions have at their core some concepts beyond human understanding. Such concepts entice and hold the interest and devotion of seekers. Concealed within the seeming disunity of life is the unity of Kether.

ANCIENT OF DAYS: Describing the ageless, deathless Ancient of Days, Hebrew texts state the following: "Above the felting phases of life sat the One who remains ever the same." This title aims at differentiating between the oldest of gods, the primogenitor or firstborn of all the gods, symbolized by Kether, from the newer gods.

AMEN AND "SO BE IT": These are extensively recognized expressions of blessing, approval, relief, and solemn endorsement. Kether innately blesses and thereby approves of the entirety of what it sends forth.

LUX INTERNA: is Latin for Internal Light. This designation addresses Kether's sacred luminosity, the divine spark that enlivens and dwells within the manifest world.

LUX OCCULTA: Kether is the Hidden Intelligence, and Lux Occulta is Latin for Hidden Light—the presence of the three Veils of the Absolute hidden behind and within Kether. Although unapparent to ordinary sense perception, the Veils are the primal illuminating and enlivening principles embedded within the entire Tree of Life and thereby creation.

THE GREATER AND VAST COUNTENANCE: Qabalistic texts often note The Greater and Vast Countenance, *Anrik Anpin*, and *Macroprosopos* in Hebrew and Greek, respectively. Countenance means "face" and likens Kether's Divinity to an enormous face watching over the world. The Vast Countenance is mentioned in prayers that include pronouncements such as *Psalm 40:* "O Lord, the one who watches over us always..." The enormous heads crafted on the statuary from ancient Egypt and on Easter Island are embodiments of this concept.

This age-old notion is extraordinarily similar to physicist Andre Linde's musings that the universe and observer are inseparably coupled. Linde addresses the essentiality of having an observer perceiving the universe, without which the universe is non-existent.

THE SUN BEHIND THE SUN: According to the ancients, the physical sun was the cause of light and life. Surpassing human comprehension, these people believed the sun brought life to Earth from the mysterious heavens via their solar deities. Presently, this title describes Kether, the one radiant life force or sacred Sun *behind* our physical sun, energizing and freely sending its vitality throughout the entire solar system. The Tree of Life illustrates this wherein Kether the Crown hovers directly above the sphere of the Sun situated in Tiphareth, Beauty. An arousing Sioux Indian chant alludes to this when declaring, "Let me be one with the infinite Sun, forever, forever, forever!"

THE CROWN OF THE CREATION: This title offers a reminder that Kether, the heavens and spiritual world, reigns over and exists in the tenth sephirah, Kingdom, Malkuth, the earth and the physical world, which is really spirit in tangible form.

OVER-SOUL: Originating from 19th century New England Transcendentalism, this title speaks of the unity of creation, the one great soul, from which all souls emanate. In his essay "The Over-Soul," Ralph Waldo Emerson describes it as "the spiritual essence or vital force in the universe, in which all souls participate, and that transcends individual consciousness."

YEKHIDAH: This is the ancient Hebrew name for the one and only "indivisible" Spirit, which cannot be separated from itself.

ATMAN: This is an ancient Sanskrit term for the Supreme Self, the spiritual principle of the universe, living within everyone and everything. Experiencing the *Atman* is synonymous with Kether's Spiritual Experience of Unified Existence, cosmic consciousness, bringing moksha, the complete release from the bonds of existence.

WELLSPRING OF CREATION: Kether is the inexhaustible well of potential preceding creation. This title reminds us that life arises from the depths of the great unmanifest. It describes the set-up from which the universe bursts from No-Thingness into Some-Thingness.

THE HEAD WHICH IS NOT: This paradox is a reminder that Kether is an idea of an idea. Kether is a human concept aiming at helping us comprehend the incomprehensible, superhuman Spirit of Life.

THE UNMOVED MOVER: Kether corresponds to Aristotle's seemingly contradictory theory of the Unmoved Mover: the eternal motion of the universe is caused by an eternally unmoved mover, Kether.

IN THE NAME OF HEAVEN:
DIVINE AND ARCHANGELIC PRESENCES

In the early thirteenth century, Rabbi Eleazar of Worms penned the mystical treatise, *Sefer ha-hoakmah* (Chokmah), *Book of Wisdom*, detailing the divine and angelic presences and names reigning over each sephirah on the of Life. Fast-forwarding six centuries, the modern Qabalistic tradition regards these names to be the Western equivalent of the Eastern mantra and entitles them "Words of Power." Invoking or calling in these sacred presences with patience, persistence, and an open heart and mind will bring them forward. Manifestations come through any of our senses as well as in dreams, the words of another, and even a fortune cookie. Whether this practice is intended to bring guidance, upliftment, and comfort in trying times or to augment and help digest a sephirah's teachings is a matter of sincerely asking for what we need and then being open to receiving whatever comes our way. I have also noticed that remaining open, yet discerning, to possibilities brings more results than restricting my wants and needs to exactitudes. Of course, if success is not instantaneous, keep at it—all things in Divine Time!

THE DIVINE PRESENCE OF KETHER IS, *EHEYEH*

The ancient Hebrew people were taught that there's only one source of life, no matter what face and shape it wears. When Moses, Jesus, and the prophets of antiquity asked the presence instructing them, "Who's telling me what to do?" the answer was *Eheyeh*, "I Am That I Am," The One and The Only Indivisible Self. Eheyeh is also referred to in texts as "All That was, is, and shall always be." Eheyeh is the cosmic, completely pervasive, "I Am." Invoking Eheyeh is affirming that no matter wherever we are and whatever is happening, a power greater than ourselves is there, too. To invoke Eheyeh is to affirm that no matter where we are and what is happening, a power greater than ourselves, is there, too.

"Listen Humanity!"

Moses received the Ten Commandments on Mt. Sinai proclaiming, "Hear, Oh Israel, God is One, and Our name is One." (In Hebrew the word "Our," rather than God, was used to accentuate the fact that creation originates from the One, which contains the positive and negative polarities, what I often refer to as God/dess and Most High. This holy proclamation of unity, known as the *Shema* (written phonetically as *Sh'ma*) means, "Listen." The Shema is a call to attention that I interpret generically as, "Listen humanity! Everything that has, now does, and will exist originates from Me, and is Me." This interpretation acknowledges creation's sacred source, and thereby its innate holiness.

The principles of the Shema were further encoded into Judaism with the first of the Ten Commandments, "Thou shalt have no other gods before me." Qabalistically speaking, this statement accentuates and affirms the importance of putting the Most High, God/dess, Great Spirit, at the forefront of our lives. We interpret this as being firmly rooted in heaven while living on earth. Doing this emphasizes the essentiality of carrying out our worldly duties and obligations with this attitude, rather than setting what is "spiritual" apart from the physical. It is being aware and respectful of the mystical embedded within the mundane. When separating spirit from matter, we are invalidating and denying the magnificence of the material world and our own self. Being rooted in heaven while living on earth is embodying the heartfelt assurance that whatever we think, say and do is spiritual work. Qabalists relate to this as pledging to live in accord with universal and natural laws, truths, and principles, the Eternal Verities, and so on, encoded within the Tree of Life.

Spiritualized Senses

The Shema and First Commandment further indicate and underscore the primary Qabalistic principle: recognizing the indwelling presence of the Divinity, in all people, places, things and situations at all times. Personally, I relate to this as perceiving the events of day-to-day living through "spiritualized" senses. For me, doing this rests on knowing, believing and trusting that the fruits of my actions will benefit my evolution and perhaps the evolution of the "collective" humankind and planet Earth as a whole. It is the pathway to fulfilling my greater needs through my lesser wants.

A Buddhist practitioner and Tree of Life student likened this to living the Dharma. In this state, we are consciously accountable to and regulated by our Buddha Nature, that of living in ways that will liberate ourselves, and all sentient, feeling beings.

ANGELOLOGY, SEXY ANGELS, AND THE TREE OF LIFE

While it is true that angels have both male and female names, they belong to the unearthly order of beings, which is genderless. When appearing in the Bible, angels were perceived as male. This plus the fact that traditional culture refers to as angels male, and rarely female, kindled my curiosity. Sleuthing around revealed that the gender designation of angels is a result of the English translation word for "angel." In Ancient Greek and Medieval Latin, the go-to languages for English, the word angel stems from the male noun, *angelos*, as opposed to *angelas*, signifying femaleness. In addition, the gendering of angels is a consequence of translators being predominantly male *plus* the longtime linguistic practice of automatically using male pronouns when designating creatures and ownership. (Thankfully, this archaic practice is in the midst of changing!)

Going still further back in time, I learned that Angelos is a translation of the Hebrew, *Malak*, and Arabic, *Malaikah* meaning "Messenger of God," a term used for both males and females, yet more particularly for denoting females! While quite a mouthful, my favorite designation is "supernatural intermediary," a term originating from several authenticated canonical sources and a reminder that Spirit encompasses all sexes.

THE ARCHANGELIC PRESENCE OF KETHER IS, *METATRON*

The term Archangel designates to the head or chief angel. There are ten archangels; each one of these and their minions, or assisting angels, reign over one of the Tree's ten sephroth. Metatron meaning both "servant," and "an instrument or tool that mediates and guides," presides over Kether. This archangel is focused on sustaining humankind by facilitating a connection between the earthly and heavenly realms. Metatron accomplishes this by communicating with the human spirit through our sense or "super sense" of intuition.

Although Metatron is named in the Talmud and mystical Hebrews texts such as the *Merkebah* or "Work of the Chariot," more often than not, Metatron is only referred to as "an angel" in the Old and New Testaments. This first of the ten archangels is called the King of Angels, Prince of the Presence, Divine Face, Chancellor of Heaven, and Lesser *Yahweh*. Metatron is the angelic presence mentioned in *Exodus 23:21* of whom it is said "...and hearken unto his voice; be not rebellious against him...for My name is in him." Considered a personification of the Hebrew's *Yekhidah*, or One Self, Metatron is believed to have the ability to give humans the full-on awareness of Kether. As mentioned in Hebrew apocalyptic writings, some scholars state Metatron was the angel who visited St. John in the New Testament's *Book of Revelation*.

Holy Living Creatures

Presiding over Kether, Metatron is chief of the uppermost Angelic Order of Holy Living Creatures (*Chailoth ha Qadesh* in Hebrew), counterpart to the Christian Seraphim or "fiery serpents." The Holy Living Creatures are uninterruptedly surrounding and protecting the throne of the Most High. Sacred art depicts these angels as an eagle, lion, bull and human with two or three pairs of wings and fiery red faces. Fittingly, this grouping is referred to as the "angels of holy fire" and the "fire of fire." Able to appear as a pillar of fire, Metatron is said to have been the presence within the burning bush and to have handed the Ten Commandments to Moses on Mt. Sinai. The *Zohar* or *Book of Splendor* designates Metatron both as the teacher to Moses and guide to the Hebrews during their Exodus from Egypt.

Legends further tell of Metatron giving Qabalah to Adam (who, in Qabalistic terms, signifies humankind) with the goal of guiding our conscious, step-by-step return to the Garden of Eden. This idea reiterates the ancient Kabbalistic concept of Tikkun Olam, "Repair of the World." Essentially, each human is spiritually obligated to participate in healing and improving the world and, thereby returning it to its harmonious state,.

The word Qabalah is sometimes defined as "to receive" and "from mouth to ear." Metatron is believed to be the inspirational messenger-guide charged with transmitting the wisdom teachings encoded within each sephirah to those with the ears to hear.

Enoch and Metatron

"The Ethiopic Book of Enoch" is found in the *Apocrypha*, texts that were deleted from sanctioned versions of the Bible. Despite this, references to the Patriarch Enoch as a direct descendant of Adam and the father of Methuselah appear in both the Old and New Testaments. After living 365 years Enoch ascended to heaven "in a fiery chariot." This is translated to mean that Enoch's faith and wisdom earned him (like Elijah, Jesus, and the Virgin Mary) the right to go to heaven in his physical body and immortality.

After his ascension, Enoch became a "watcher angel," charged with "watching over" and guiding human affairs. *Genesis 5:24* states "And Enoch walked with God, and he was not; for God took him." This suggests why Enoch is sometimes called Enoch-Metatron. Interestingly, Koranic lore often conjoins Enoch with the Prophet Idris, who also arose to heaven in his flesh and blood form.

OF GODS AND GODDESSES: MYTHOLOGY AND QABALAH

Qabalists believe that creation emanates from the One, meaning we perceive the One, the source of life, in the entire spectrum of bodily forms and names. Fittingly, and as mentioned, many Qabalists are practitioners of Henotheism. Henotheists believe in one Supreme Being or religion without denying the possibility and validity of others. Holding this attitude throws open the door to acknowledging and incorporating the pantheons—gods and goddesses—to people cross-culturally. Fleshing out the intellectual concepts presented by a sephirah in a variety of physical shapes and sizes is a potent means of deepening our comprehension and assimilating its teachings. Clothing a sphere in such also holds the potential to help us perceive its principles within ourselves and others. Please note: Athough some of the deities listed in this and other sections are not perfect fits, they had enough traits to qualify under their respective heading. Lastly, due to innumerable and at times confusing differences, I was unable to list the exact times of these deities' origins and appearances sequentially. Thank you for understanding!

MYTHOLOGY AND KETHER:

GENDER-NEUTRAL, PRIMORDIAL SOURCES AND PRIMARY ORIGINATORS OF LIFE

The primordial ocean is a category that appears in the mythology of numerous cultures. Although intermittently challenged, it identifies Kether with the theory that life began from a "primordial soup," the earliest ocean in which, before creation, were the seeds from which all living things would sprout and grow. Such aligns Kether with the abstract, androgynous, non-binary, gender-neutral, and primary originators of life: those beings who brought livingness out of nothingness from the highest of heights and deepest of depths. They are the self-created, self-perpetuating, all-inclusive makers of every deity.

EGYPTIAN

NUM: In the beginning, there was nothing except watery chaos. Num is the deification of this Primordial Ocean, the self-created, fluidic abyss in which, before the creation, were the rudiments of every living thing and creature. Like Kether, Num is an abstract intellectual concept.

ATUM OR TUM: Emerging from the self-created deity Num, came the "Hidden One." The Ancient Egyptian priesthood taught that before creation occurred within Num dwelled a "spirit still formless," who carried the sum total of all existence. The name, Atum, is derived from the root meaning "not to be" and "to be complete," fitting the all-inclusiveness of Kether.

Atum was later personified as the sun before rising and before setting, and was re-named Atum-Ra meaning "Hidden Sun," forging a link with the ancient Qabalistic alternative title, "The Sun behind the sun."

PTAH: Much in the way that the impersonal Kether lacks distinct features, Ptah is portrayed as a featureless mummy. The cosmic egg and life were birthed when the Ptah opened its mouth. Ptah was the sovereign Deity and originator of life in Memphis and like Kether, headed a triad of deities.

ASSYRIO-BABYLONIAN

APSU: Myths originating from this region tell of the primordial Apsu, a deep chasm or abyss filled with a fusion of sweet and salt water that surrounded and embraced the earth. During this period, the earth was thought of as a round plateau encircled by mountains. Sitting on top of the mountains rested the vault of heaven, which floated on the waters of the Apsu. From the Apsu came the springs, which broke through the surface of the earth. From these waters, gods, and then the rest of creation came to exist.

GREEK

RIVER OCEANUS: Similar to both the Apsu and Nun, the early Greeks imagined that the immense God, River Oceanus, formed a liquid girdle around the universe. Having neither a source nor an outlet, this genderless deity gave birth to the waters flowing from the earth. Homer speaks of River Oceanus in the Odyssey as "the essence of all things, all rivers, the entire sea, all springs and deep wells, even the Gods."

CRONOS: The cosmogony of the Orphic religious cult of ancient Greece prominent in the 6th century CE (Common Era is aligned with AD) refers to Cronos as the First Principle—Time. Because Qabalists ascribe the beginning of time to Kether, the Greek deity of Time, Cronos, is fitting. Although distinctively male, his act of devouring his children may be likened to how Kether both exudes and then absorbs everything it has created back into itself.

ROMAN

SATURN: Saturn, meaning "Son of Night" is the Roman counterpart to Cronos. Although little is known of this deity's origins, Saturn is believed to have been self-created and self-perpetuating. While Saturn, like Cronos, is traditionally portrayed as male, his qualities of self-creation and perpetuation conjoin him with Kether.

EAST INDIAN

PARA BRAHMA-BRAHMA: Akin to other deities, Para Brahma is dual-aspected. Its first aspect is the Para Brahma. Para Brahma, meaning what is "beyond" Brahma and its source, is the attributeless, indescribable, indeterminate, indefinable Source of Life. This deity signifies the omnipresent soul of creation and the spiritual principle *behind* the moving parts of creation, Brahma. The actual process of creation, Brahma, may be likened to Para Brahma exhaling—resulting in the projection of the Life Force outwards from Kether into the orb of the next sephirah, Chokmah.

NORSE

BURI: Akin to Kether's manifestation out of nothingness, Buri, said to be the first of the Norse gods, appeared out of the ice.

TOLTEC, AZTEC AND MESOAMERICAN

OMETEOTL: Regarded as the most powerful deity of the ancient Aztec pantheon, Ometeotl is omnipotent, omnipresent, and omniscient. Like Kether, Ometeotl reigned as the predecessor of the gods and all creation. This ancestral head or progenitor of the Aztec deities and founder of nature's dualities is also portrayed as a binary god, the male-female pair and polarities of nature, Ometecuhtli and

Omecihuatl respectively. We will explore these fascinating deities under the spheres of Wisdom and Understanding, Chokmah and Binah respectively.

OF VIRTUES AND VICES:

Existing within the world of nature are the positive and negative polarities. The ancients related to these in terms of the behavioral extremes of virtues and vices—or positive and negative personality traits manifesting in excessive or deficient behaviors. While these represent polar opposites, it is essential to recall that there are also shades of grey, i.e. the process of growing out of or into a particular vice and virtue.

At the inception of this system, related to alchemist Ramon Lully's theory of Astral Medicine or Lullism, there were only seven planets. These became both the seven planetary virtues and seven deadly sins. (This paradigm was later presented in Dante's *Divine Comedy* and Spenser's *The Fairie Queen*.) Correspondences to the remaining three sephroth ruled by Uranus, Neptune, and Pluto evolved over the 19th and 20th centuries.

Modern Qabalists regard the virtues and vices of character strengths or attributes and character weaknesses or detriments to be related to maturities and immaturities. While categorizing behaviors in such terms is black-and-white thinking, a pattern that Qabalists tend to avoid, much may also be learned from making such distinctions regarding these traits.

Giving it some thought, our strengths hold the potential to help us overcome our weaknesses or vices. Whereas our weaknesses, when causing us enough pain and destruction, offer the opportunity to tap into and further develop our strengths or virtues. Of course, strength may deteriorate into weakness and weakness may transform into strength. Here are examples of how such might manifest: One of the virtues of the fourth sephirah, Mercy, is generosity. When flawed, generosity may be used to control others. The vice of the sixth sephirah, Beauty, is pride. When sound, pride is the state of recognizing and celebrating the Most High within oneself and others.

The willingness to acknowledge the existence of the mature and immature facets of our personality holds the gift of motivating us to become increasingly accepting and compassionate towards ourselves and others. (Certainly, doing this tends to include getting help to modify and change our attitudes and behaviors.) When we become open to facing the fact that we have an immature behavior pattern or "vice," we also open to developing its opposite "virtue" or mature side. Kether's position on Tree of Life's Middle Pillar suggests the value of finding a middle ground between extreme behaviors. Plato's writings on ethics named moderation as the greatest virtue, underscoring this fact.

Keeping Our Feet on the Ground and Ego in Check

When I catch myself thinking that I'm better than someone else because I'm enacting a particular virtue, I cue myself into remembering that, as a human being, I have the potential to develop its opposite or vice. Doing this helps contain my "holier-than-thou" attitude, and keeps my feet on the ground and ego in check. My behavior also reminds me to consider that I have probably been, or may again be, where the person I am now judging or feeling superior to stands.

Virtues build and raise our Self-esteem. These are thoughts, words, and actions, which preserve, elevate, celebrate, and so on, our own or another's sacred Self. Genuinely virtuous behaviors, those not done for show or to impress others, are done for the sake of feeling uplifted by engaging in benevolent works and service, also because we desire to refrain from "acting out," that is, enacting our particular frailties or weaknesses.

Vices bring some type of short-term satisfaction, yet also undermine and lower our self-esteem—as giving in to an immature personality trait is synonymous with relinquishing our ability to be self-regulating. Vices are the thoughts, words, or actions that demean, degrade, and shame. Vices hurt others and those enacting them. Yet within pain lies the potential for healing and maturation. That is, we arrive at the place wherein we have had enough—whether such is harming ourselves and/ or genuinely experiencing how our behavior is injuring others. Reaching this crossroads, we have the opportunity to surrender to the compelling need for change, no matter what doing so entails. This means compassionately seeking out the skillfulness needed to terminate, rather than propagate, misery.

Reconciling Opposites

Reading over the list of vices and virtues it is worthwhile remembering, as shown by the examples of Mercy's virtue, Generosity and Beauty's vice, Pride, described above, that these are *not* completely black-or-white issues. Over time, I've learned to liken them to the ancient Hermetic Principle of Polarity, which explains the various shades of darkness and light and the reconciliation of opposing forces like so: The entire manifest world is made up of positive and negative poles. The difference between things that are diametrically opposed, such as light and darkness, hot and cold, and virtue and vice is a matter of *degree*. Every set of opposites may be reconciled.

The universe is continuously shifting and balancing itself out—and, and we, as part of the universe, are doing likewise. Consequently, every positive or negative action contains the potential of bringing its opposite into play. Centered behavior is the result of finding a balance between two extremes or polarities.

The willingness to acknowledge the existence of the light and dark, the positive and negative aspects of our personalities with their accompanying vices and virtues, or better said, strengths and weaknesses, have the potential to make us increasingly compassionate towards ourselves and others. Holding this attitude makes us increasingly capable of mitigating detrimental behavior patterns. After facing the fact that I had the dark "vice" or immature behavior pattern of over or co-dependence, I became open to developing its opposite light "virtue," independence. However, after years of enacting independence, I suddenly "got" that the grey middle ground between co-dependence and independence, interdependence, was for me the wiser and healthier option. These underscore Kether's positioning on the Pillar of Mildness and the importance of equilibrium.

Kether's Virtues of Completion and Attainment

Kether is situated on the spiritual plane coupled with the virtues of completion and attainment of The Great Work. Traditionally, *magnum opus*, the Latin term for The Great Work, designates the completion of an individual's most important work of art, music, literature, and so on. However, Qabalah-wise, this term refers to the practice of automatically applying and integrating the universal and natural, laws, truths and principles offered by Tree of Life study to our daily routine. Living in this way leads to completion and attainment: the unification of our personal self with the universal Self. This harmonious blending of opposites results in freeing us from the cycles of birth and death.

Despite this lofty goal, we are already more than familiar with the virtues of completion and attainment. I vividly recall showing my son the importance of completing his cycles—whether it was putting away his toys after playing and receiving a sticker or putting his dishes in the sink after eating and getting dessert, doing these simple things eventually translated into him completing work-related projects and attaining feelings of self-satisfaction and professional recognition.

Kether is seated in the present also known as the now, eternal moment, or timeless time. Ancient alchemical texts state, "Without Completion, there is no Attainment." Completion is the act of finishing something in its entirety, which leads to experiencing attainment.

As basic and ordinary as it might seem, I'm presently experiencing both completion and attainment by being focused on what I'm *now* doing—entering each letter of every word into this Word Document. This behavior is in stark contrast to anxiously dwelling on the thousands upon thousands of letters and words it will take to finish this chapter, let alone this book. It is in this ordinary self-styled way of completing each word, sentence, paragraph, and page that I'm experiencing Kether's virtues of completion and attainment and planting seeds for more complex acts. Furthermore, the systematic completion of this *magnum opus* is simultaneously serving as a model for The Great Work of integrating the Tree of Life's teachings into my life. Undertaking this project, regardless of whether anyone reads these words or not, is slowly expanding my awareness to experience the mystical forever present in the mundane.

An Organic Process

Completion and attainment of The Great Work is an organic process that naturally progresses over time, which is in the eternal sense, limitless. It becomes effortful when we are either unaware of how to behave or resist doing so. In either instance, the feedback we receive in the form of pain and misery has the potential to be educative. Reaching this juncture, we may make an effort to learn how to behave differently or recall where we were off track and self-correct. Of course, we may keep repeating our behaviors until we become so distraught we become ready to grow and change.

Of course, we are already united with the eternal; such is merely a matter of expanding our limited perception to consciously "realize" and internalize and live by this fact. This cues us into why this state of awareness is termed Self-Realization and, when ready to be absorbed back into Kether's oneness, God-Realization. The most exalted levels of consciousness are always available; recognizing this fact is part of our developmental process. Traversing our particular highway of life to Kether is "The Great Work," spoken of since antiquity. Our slowly expanding ability to identify with and be at one with the One, this disambiguated reality is what facilitates the completion, and thereby attainment, of The Great Work.

The Vice of Abstention

Sitting on the spiritual plane, which contains all possibilities, the Qabalistic tradition does not assign Kether a vice. Giving it a bit of thought and reflecting on my own life, and my occasionally impassioned push for enlightenment, the virtues of completion and attainment can certainly transform into vices. A spontaneous, lively discussion with a group of advanced students about Kether and spiritual development, explored how these virtuous behaviors may in excess, become unhealthy obsessions.

While we cannot possibly abstain from this evolutionary process, and may even seek to accelerate its workings, those who fear change may effort to avoid or block spiritual emergence—touched on under the Grade of Ipsissimus—and its sometimes temporarily disconcerting facets like retro and precognitive insights and the bodily discomforts of sleeplessness, tics, itching, and restlessness. Because we are essentially spirits wearing skin suits, this maturation process is part of the scheme of things and continual from birth—some traditions believe it also occurs before and from the time of conception.

Like breathing, spiritual growth is inherent to having a physical body. Of course, how aware, involved, or obsessed we are of this natural, developmental progression is something else. Essentially, we best abstain from frenzied striving—driving ourselves, and possibly those around us, to distraction while pursuing the Qabalah's Holy Grail. That said, I vividly recall quite loudly and repeatedly celebrating an uncontrollable itching on my arms, shoulders and upper back, thinking it was a sure sign that the hours of breathing and meditation exercises, aimed at making my Kundalini rise, were working. As it turned out, I had accidentally picked up a case of poison oak while walking off-trail in the woods of Northern California in January! This was both a humorous and potent reminder of the fact that while I can aim to be more aware of what think, say and do, spiritual growth proceeds in its own time, not mine.

Ignorance, Forgetfulness, and Egotism

In addition to fear, abstaining—aka refraining from integrating spiritual principles and practices into what life presents—stems from not only fear, but genuine ignorance, normal forgetfulness, denial of such truths, excessive egotism, and so on, all of which are part of the evolutionary process. A potent example of this may be seen in the statement attributed to Machiavelli's *The Prince*: "The ends justify the means." Since the beginning of human history, groups varying as widely as hunter-gathers, scholars, prominent religious figures and world leaders have enacted this idea. Those knowingly behaving in this way and the possible consequences of their actions are either denying, or perhaps *genuinely* unaware of the reprehensibility of their actions.

Examples of vice may be seen in uncompromising ideologues that advocate harming other living beings and the planet itself for financial gain. While some claim to be doing this in the name of betterment, such ideologies tend to regard the world to be random and spiritless and put such a world first. A few instances of the ends justifying the means follow: wealth by way of slavery, political power through assassination, and improvement of the human race via genocide and Eugenics. A more specific and somewhat contemporary example of this thinking may be seen in former President Donald Trump's statement, "Make America Great Again," and his subsequently repealing the Fair Play and Safe Workplaces Executive Order, which ensured that federal contractors comply with worker protection laws before receiving government contracts. Comparing the aforementioned to humane and universal standards show how, in the least, such are the product of immature thinking, while in the most, warped or malevolent thought.

Although these outlooks, actions, and their results block and distort expansive thinking and doing in the short run, abstention is what over time ushers in (often not gently) awareness and openness to a greater reality. Because of my certainty that all come from the One, I'm slowly, yet surely digesting the verifiable fact that my ignorance, blind insistence, resistance, and the like, are in fact moving me (and us) towards completion and with it, attainment. Eventually, whether we go kicking and screaming, dancing and singing, or some special combo, we will all arrive at the same end.

POWERING-UP: MAGICAL-MYSTICAL SYMBOLS, TOOLS, TALISMANS, AMULETS, AND SIGILS

Segueing into this topic is a bit of history. Neo-Platonic offshoots of the earlier works of Hermes Trismegistus such as Finocian and Enochian Magic made offerings, used incantations, and designed various charms inscribed with planetary glyphs to draw particular virtues and repel their vices. This practice was actually reminiscent of the ancient Egyptians imbuing the statues of their gods and goddesses with the power to do likewise.

Aligned with what we have been exploring with Attributes, Alternative Titles, and Mythology, this section continues expanding and "fleshing out" the concepts offered by each sephirah, with yet another opportunity to make these teachings tangible, and practicable. Magical-mystical tools, talismans, amulets, and sigils marked with relevant characters, names, astrological signs and more, have been used as empowering, uplifting reminders and protectors, in most cultures throughout human history. Certainly, many of these are already in use—e.g. the six-pointed Star of David appearing in synagogues and the *Sri Yantra* of Tantric Yoga. These are also crafted and personalized by the wearer, a friend or enemy, wiseone, teacher, shaman, priest or priestess, and so on, to carry a particular combination of symbolism and empowerment. While in the making, these are imbued with prayers, words, mantras, and other messages that subtly remind the bearer of the skills and mindset needed to support one holding a particular attitude or the accomplishment of a specific, activity, state of mind, or goal.

Objects are worn, displayed, or hidden, put in a special place, used in rituals, and the like. Wearing a golden-colored heart-shaped pendant or lamen (such are typically worn over the heart), as a reminder of the sphere of Beauty, Tiphareth prompts me to open my heart and look for some modicum of Beauty in situations wherein I might initially perceive only ugliness. Powering-up offers the subtle, or not-so-subtle, cues to attend to, apply, reinforce, and energize the Qabalistic teachings these articles represent.

Now let's move on to de-mystifying the sometimes mystifying, yet useful sigil. Originating from the Hebrew, *segulah* is something that protects a person from harm and action leading to a change in one's fortune or destiny. The Latin *sigillum* translates as a pictorial seal or signature of a deity or spirit. Sigils are found in the *Book of the Angel Raziel* or *Sefer Raziel HaMalakah*. Along this line in medieval ceremonial magic, sigils were identified as a mystical symbol signifying the various beings—demons, angels, and the like, which the magus would invoke for assistance. While writing their Enochian Keys, alchemists John Dee and Edward Kelly used sigils when invoking help from their guide, the Archangel Gabriel.

Norse and Celtic runes are excellent examples of sigils. I recently explored several Sigil-based Tarot decks. Alternatively, we may take a hint from Trina, a dedicated Qabalah student, and customize our own. Each sigil is comprised of an intricate blend of several symbols and/or geometric figures, letters, and other shapes, charged with a very specific meaning and purpose. These often take the form of seemingly nonsense words. The sigil URNOWCATGW posted on the face of my computer, subtly reminds me of my ongoing dedication to enacting Kether's Virtues of Completion and Attainment: You Are Now Completing and Attaining the Great Work. Consider conducting an experiment with the following to become increasingly aware of Kether, or any sephirah's, virtues and vices.

THE CROWN: Signifying royalty, and Kether, the crown of the Tree of Life, is the royalty of the Most High, Power Greater than Our Self and so on. Works of art sometimes conceptualized the crown as a halo, a universal symbol of holiness, a fitting match for Kether.

When needing to further remind myself that I'm always in the process of the Completion and Attainment of The Great Work, I wear a crown-shaped hairclip.

THE POINT: Much as Kether is defined in geometric terms as "dimensionless," the point has no specific attributes other than location. The alternative title, "Beginning of Beginnings," more than suggests a point of embarkation. Viewing matter through an electron microscope, it appears as little points of light or atoms.

THE DIVINE SPARK: Fittingly, Kether is symbolized as the Divine Spark jump-starting the fire of life burning throughout the universe. This leading sephirah ignites processes required to manifest the physical world. The Hebrew or "flame" alphabet as it is called originates from the letter *Yod*, which is shaped like a spark.

THE LAMP: This symbol is meant to us of Kether's and our own holy inner light, the radiant undifferentiated cosmic energy that sources all creation. Kether's incandescence is an ocean of limitless light, the boundless, eternal light preceding manifestation. The barest experience of Kether ignites the inextinguishable lamp of inner illumination. This mystical state purveys an awareness that defies description, yet through which we may perceive the world lit by cosmic luminosity. In all synagogues, the *ner tamid*, a special lamp that burns unceasingly over the holy ark, signifies this same eternal light.

During the eighth century, a Sufi mystic named Rabia lived in Basra, Persia. As a child, her parents imbued her with the importance of valuing the sacred. Although orphaned and sold into slavery, Rabia never lost her faith. She fasted during the day when attending to her chores and prayed unceasingly during the night. One night while in deep meditation, her master unexpectedly awoke. Awestruck when seeing a lamp above Rabia's head, suspended without a chain illuminating the whole house, he freed her the next morning.

THE *YIN-YANG* OR *YANG-YIN*: This symbol represents the entire universe, which is composed of the complementary cosmic forces of *yin*-darkness and *yang*-light, manifesting in nature's positive and negative polarities. Although this symbol's true origin is unknown, it was found as early as the Neolithic period in about 3400 BCE.

THE SWASTIKA OR COSMIC PINWHEEL: Cosmologist Carl Sagan suggested that in prehistoric times a comet came so close to the Earth that the jets of gas streaming from it were "bent" by the comet's rotation, leading to the adoption of the swastika as a sign of heavenly power. Seen in artifacts far back as 1000 BCE, the currently emotionally charged swastika is a fitting glyph for Kether's designation as the "Beginning of the Whirlings and Swirlings."

Both an ancient universal and religious icon, the swastika is found almost everywhere in the world. Its name originates from the Sanskrit *svasti* meaning "well-being", "life" and "good luck." Looking carefully, this cross-cultural symbol is actually an equal-armed cross with slightly twisted ends. That is, the hands of the swastika's arms are bent at right angles in either a clockwise or a counterclockwise direction. Because its hands point above and below with Spirit residing at its center, the swastika may be likened to a "cosmic pinwheel," signifying the cosmos in motion. The shape suggests both the balancing of opposites and a point at which the infinite and finite touch.

Origins and Meanings

Some groups make a sharp distinction between the swastika's turning—right meaning life and left meaning death. Linking Kether with this icon, Qabalists pair the swastika's clockwise, right-turning direction with the winding up of the cosmic creative cycle, while the counterclockwise, left-turning direction is its unwinding of spirit into matter. The glyph's neutrality and potential to spin in either direction further align it with Kether's potential for positive and negative electrical charges and movement.

One of the swastika's most prominent origins was the Aryan culture that lived in Iran and the Northern Indian subcontinent, wherein the right-turning swastika was linked with *Shakti*, the sacred life force that generates the world. Having to pay reparations for damage to France and the United Kingdom during the First World War brought severe economic depletion and shame upon the German people paving the way for Hitler's rise. The superstitious Nazis distorted the right-turning swastika, by turning it left and in this way reorienting it to bring forth the power to destroy and conquer their oppressors.

Interestingly, the left-turning *sauwastika* is used in Tibetan Buddhist rites and culture, wherein it is known as the *manji*, or "whirlwind." Although turning leftwards, it shares the same positive meaning as the right-turning Aryan symbol. However, history reveals that the Tibetans employed its left-turning powers for protection and to rout invaders.

The Hopi Indians term the swastika as *meha*, representing the four directions, as well as the great powers of cosmic law and nature. Their prophecies speak of a time when human-made laws will intrude so negatively into the Hopi (and human) way of life, that it will set off the meha, the activities which will bring about monumental planetary cleansing and purification, yet ultimately restoration. This further aligns meha with other traditions wherein its clockwise motion meha creates, while its counterclockwise motion destroys.

THE SPIRAL: The spiral glyph reminds us that the involution and evolution of life, the downward-receding, and upward-approaching spirals, start and end on the spiritual plane with Kether.

THE *VAJRA*: Tibetan Buddhist scepter, wand, or Vajra, is held by the Dalai Lama and other monastic leaders, signifying unified consciousness, the human mind that has evolved beyond duality to experience Kether's same nature. Vajra means both "unbreakable" and "diamond" in Sanskrit. This sacred implement is said to be the embodiment of the great Tibetan Buddhist mantra, *Om Mani Padme Hum*, translated as "Praise to the Jewel in the Lotus!" Chanting this mantra while trekking in dazzlingly bright sunshine of the Himalayan Mountains of Nepal suddenly had me imagining the cosmic jewel of Kether shining out from the center of the lotus flower of all existence.

ASTROLOGY AND QABALAH

Qabalistic Astrologers

The Franciscan monk and astrologer Francisco Georgi was deeply influenced by the early Renaissance work of Pico Della Mirandola, the first Christian scholar to master the Jewish mystical theology of Kabbalah. Mirandola, a prominent member of the Medici's Platonic Academy, was also touched by Lullism, the teachings of Ramon Lull (discussed under Virtues and Vices), who had been inspired by studying ancient Greek astrological treatises. Giorgi, in his Cabalistic (this spelling of Qabalah denotes the Renaissance Christian-oriented Cabalists) work of 1525, *De Harmonia Mundi*, couples the Christian angelic hierarchy *with* the sephroth and seven, then known planets. He proposed that heavenly influences descend into the angels and sephroth over which they preside, and in that way to the various planets and physical world.

In Giorgi's system, like those of his predecessors Mirandola and Lull, *all* celestial influences are considered helpful to one's spiritual development. Rather than being at the mercy of the planets and luminaries, Qabalistic astrology aims at suggesting ways for practitioners to become conscious co-creators, who work along with these heavenly forces.

Law of Synchronicity

As a student of esoteric astrology, I regularly call upon this art and science—the influence of the heavens upon human affairs—to broaden my understanding of myself, others, and the Tree of Life. As I know it, the study of astrology is essentially a belief in the Law of Synchronicity, parented by the science of sub-atomic physics, which proposes: "All events are tied together in an unbroken wholeness." In metaphysical terms, this may be summed by the statements: "Microcosm (the small, physical world) reflects Macrocosm (the great, spiritual world), macrocosm reflects microcosm" and "As above, So below; As below, So above." Alternatively as stated in the Old Testament and verified by science, humankind and all on earth are comprised of the same elements as the heavenly bodies—or in the words of the visionary songstress Joni Mitchell, "We are stardust."

Qabalistic astrologers call the planets the Seven Inner Stars, the Western counterpart to the Eastern chakra system. They likewise report that these Stars function within us much as the planets do in the heavens. The planetary assignments of each sephirah indicate the celestial energies streaming into and influencing the human personality. This inter-relationship further suggests how the planets affect not only our individual temperament and activities; these have a natural effect on earthly events and the universe that surrounds us.

In summary, each sephirah on the Qabalistic Tree of Life has an astrological counterpart suggesting how our understanding of it has the potential to enhance our understanding of astrology. Over the years, I have had several professional astrologers as students; they claimed that Tree of Life study greatly expanded their skills. I found it more than interesting to discover that Abraham, father of the Jewish people (who some say authored the Qabalistic "Book of Formation" or *Sepher Yetzirah)*, is known to have been a practicing astrologer more than 4,000 years ago in the city of Ur.

ASTROLOGICAL CORRESPONDENCE TO KETHER:

NEPTUNE, THE UNIVERSE *FINALLY* COMES THROUGH!

Mentioned earlier, the entire Universe, *Rashith Ha-Gilgulim*, or the Beginning of the Whirlings and Swirlings as it is translated from Hebrew, corresponds to Kether. To this concept, we will now add the planet Neptune. Although it is somewhat easy to grasp how Kether is described as a spinning vortex of energy containing the entire cosmos, its connection with the planet Neptune is somewhat puzzling.

When the Tree of Life was first conceived, millennia ago, the three outer planets Uranus, Neptune, and Pluto, a dwarf star or exoplanet with a very "eccentric" orbit, were undetected. With the discovery of these spheres (beginning in the 18th century), the ancient Chaldean system of astrology originally linking planets with all but the spheres of Kether, Chokmah and *Da'ath* with the Tree of Life need to be updated. Essentially, the universe had finally come through with heavenly bodies for each of the ten sephroth!

Neptune, Uranus and Pluto are associated with impersonal activity as are the Crown/Kether, Wisdom/Chokmah and the generally little explored, Knowledge/Da'ath, respectively. In addition to the fact that the first sephirah, Kether, emanates the second, Chokmah, similarities between Chokmah and Uranus and Da'ath and Pluto have led numerous Qabalistically-oriented astrologers to this new ordering. The longer orbits of the outer planets imply the profoundness of the planetary cycles being internalized. Requiring more time, or divine time, for incorporation is coherent with these planets' qualities and our human nature. Resultingly, Kether, the farthest sephirah from human cognition, is matched with the activities of Neptune, the farthest planet (Pluto is a dwarf star) from the Sun.

Bridging the Gap

After seriously contemplating the alternatives, I decided to match Pluto with Da'ath. Da'ath or Knowledge is the "Invisible Sephirah" situated on the Tree of Life's Middle Pillar at the gap or "Abyss," between Chokmah/Wisdom and Binah/Understanding. Although the connecting point between the worlds of spirit and matter, and considered by some to be the fourth sephirah in the Supernal "Triad," Da'ath is regarded as "invisible" by Qabalists who don't recognize it among the sephroth. Of this, the ancient Hebrew writings state, "There are only ten sephroth, not nine and not eleven, but ten." Yet, as with most things, there are other ways of viewing Da'ath's invisibility and activities. Positioned below Kether on the Middle Pillar, between and slightly under the energies emanating from Chokmah and Binah, it functions as their intermingling and meeting point.

In the biblical sense, "Knowledge" refers to sexual union and Da'ath is the result of the coupling of the Cosmic Father, Chokmah with the Cosmic Mother, Binah. Da'ath/Knowledge is the sephirah within the Supernal Triad where the patterns from the spiritual and causal planes of existence are coalescing into their particular bodily forms. This makes Da'ath the cosmic birth canal, through which the offspring conceived from the union of nature's positive and negative polarities, Chokmah and Binah, are born, into the flesh-and-blood world. Do we make less of Chokmah and Binah because they are not physically perceptible? Of course not! Likewise with the sphere of Da'ath.

Hovering between the unseen and seen worlds makes Da'ath a bridge. While this idea is getting a tad ahead, the workings of Da'ath may be likened to the womb-like function of *Yesod*/Foundation that occurs on the astral plane, just above the physical world in Kingdom/Malkuth.

NEPTUNE, GOD OF THE GREAT WATERS

Neptune, or *Rahav* in Hebrew, was named after the Roman god of fresh water, who controlled winds and storms. He was later merged with the Greek Poseidon, to become the god of earthquakes, and all bodies of water—streams, lake, rivers, seas and oceans. Fittingly, traces of methane gas in its outermost regions cause Neptune to appear a watery share of blue. Kether is the great cosmic ocean of unmanifest life, the pure and formless ground of being, from which creation and manifestation wash onto the shores of the manifest world.

The ingredients for the physical reality flow out of Kether's primal soup. Speaking of which, soup lovers know that there are innumerable kinds of soups, made of an almost endless variety of ingredients, making each unique. Along this line, on September 15, 2021, astronomers at the Harvard-Smithsonian Center for Astrophysics in Cambridge, Massachusetts, released new evidence related to the "cosmic soups" surrounding stars, from which distant exoplanets such as Pluto and beyond, form. These cosmic soups are a mix of chemicals in protoplanetary disks; the rotating flat and circular spheres of dense gases surrounding young newly formed stars, which are the birthplaces of planets. Astronomers have now mapped out the ingredients—the chemicals in five different protoplanetary disks—in extraordinary detail. They found that, just as with the culinary favorites on Earth, no two cosmic soups are exactly alike!

Inspiration

Much as Kether is the inspiration for all existence, Neptune, also the Roman god of storms, is the planet most connected with the intuitive, soul-felt urge to turn inwards for comfort and a reality orientation when the seas of life become stormy. This is affirmed by the planetary symbol of the sea god Neptune's trident—a waxing crescent hovering over the Christian or "crucifixion" cross. Together this glyph underscores our innate yearning for liberation and the tests and trials arising on the pathway to Kether's Virtues of Completion and Attainment.

Astrologically, Neptune is termed the transpersonal aspect of Venus, making it the uppermost rung on love's evolutionary ladder, what Rastafarian Bob Marley sang of as, *One Love,* "One love, one heart. Let's get together and feel all right." Venus is related to desires and attachments that are personal, limited, selfish, and conditional. On the other hand, Neptune is coupled with the devotion that is spiritually attuned—limitless, selfless, and unconditional. Accordingly, this planet highlights the development of unreserved, ever-expanding, divine love/Agape, in contrast to Venus' reserved, human love/Eros.

No matter how strong the tides of emotion are, Neptune's characteristics in their most developed state surpass individual preferences to say and do what is universally best, as does Kether. Venusian energies hone in on what is esthetically pleasing on a person-to-person basis. Yet, Neptune, like Kether, guides us to attend to the fact that every part of creation is inherently beautiful and perfectly placed in the greater scheme of things. Underscoring this is the fact that Alchemists view water to be the universal solvent, which, like Neptune, functions to cleanse and dissolve individual differences to benefit both our whole person and planet.

Suffering and Revelation

Neptune is further conjoined with spiritual ideals, cosmic consciousness, mystical, visionary experiences, and mind-expanding substances. (The difference between psychedelic and hallucinogenic drugs: Hallucinogens are a large, diverse group of psychoactive drugs that produce altered states of consciousness, whereas psyche-delics are a subclass of hallucinogenic drugs that can produce an apparent expansion of consciousness.) The aforementioned Neptunian qualities offer the awareness that inspires us to honor our spirit-bound obligation to distinguish truth from falsehood and engage in selfless service, which may require sacrifice, suffering, and in extreme instances, martyrdom. Suffering has the potential to remind us of the part of our baptismal contract that obliges us to live by universal and natural laws, truths, and principles; neglecting this, we suffer. Misery is a natural response to being human when life does not turn out as planned. Yet, from Kether's expansive view, distress aims at clarifying and redirecting our passions, attitudes, and behaviors to grow increasingly discerning, in this way increasing our awareness and ability to bypass needless torment.

Despite cues to do otherwise, I allowed myself to fall in love with someone who initially showered me with longed-for affection, fun, and friendship, yet slowly revealed that he subconsciously more than disliked women. When I became a target for those unresolved feelings plus frustration around his career and refusal to partic-ipate in couples counseling, I ended the relationship. Although the suffering that accompanied doing this was difficult to bear, the reward of honoring and caring for myself more than validated my decision. Oh yes, along with my own introspective journey, a confirming revelation of the situation occurred through the assistance of a psychedelic taken under professional supervision.

Neptune is also linked with self-undoing, whether through self-loathing, belit-tling others, escapist behaviors, knowingly buying into illusions and self-delusion, and the like. This state includes giving oneself up to consciousness-contracting, mind-numbing substances and activities such as alcohol, drugs, gambling, overwork, sex, and so on, to temporarily lift our spirits, suppress or repress painful feelings, and so on. Here too may arise the shock that comes from awakening to what we honestly are doing. Eventually, our behavior functions to inspire us to surrender our personal self, to more fully attend to our soul spirit Self. That is, we live from the perspective that every particle of the finite contains the infinite.

Compassion for All

The workings of Neptune symbolize the possibility of emerging from the deepest and darkest of wells with an increasingly compassionate attitude. Emergence opens the way for heightened inspiration, intuition, and creativity thereby enhancing the goal of living by our spiritual values. Accompanying this state may also include the use of consciousness-expanding medicines to further throw open the doors of our hearts and minds. Enlarging our perspective of life and our place in it leads to involving ourselves in activities aimed at benefiting all of creation. These ideas are summed up in the refrain to the charity song, *We Are the World*, by Michael Jackson and Lionel Ritchie:

"We are the world,
We are the children,
We are the ones who make a brighter day, so let's start giving."

Yes, Neptune tends to represent the crossroads in our life journey wherefrom we naturally begin expanding our solo identification with our personality and physical body, to realizing it as a potent means through which to know our Soul, Spirit Self. This state is stepping out of the world and time as we know it to re-enter the world and time with a *Reality* orientation. That is, we aim to penetrate life's illusions to perceive what is genuine.

MAKING THE GRADE: TRAVELING THE GRADED TREE OF LIFE

"Grading" or assigning competencies for mastering the principles of each sephirah on the Qabalistic Tree of Life, is both a fascinating and worthwhile carry-over from the mystery school tradition. This arrangement was originally created to provide aspirants with a map of how spiritual maturity progresses through the Tree of Life. These also offer criteria by which to review and reflect on our strengths and weaknesses as well as to consider what tests and trials may lie ahead. Yet, despite the best of intentions, this system has the potential to deteriorate into a form of spiritual one-up-man-ship, a pitiable way of lauding power over others. (Certainly, such practitioners are revealing their true state to those with "the eyes to see.") Gaming aside, the graded Tree of Life aims at laying out the general characteristics and abilities required for and resulting from digesting the teachings of each sephirah. It attempts this by offering us ten models for assessing our maturation.

While explaining the graded Tree of Life in class, a student asked,"Is it possible to be working in more than one sephirah at a time?" Because we are multi-faceted people living in a world pulling our time and attention in myriad directions, engaging with more than one sephirah simultaneously is pretty much guaranteed.

Involution-Evolution

Each of the ten chapters of the book contains a section laying out one of the ten grades of the Tree of Life. Experimenting with the Suggestions for Practical Application and Integration then offers the chance to become increasingly skillful and increasingly aware of each grade's proficiencies.

Before exploring spiritual development through the Graded Tree of Life, further clarification is needed. This book begins in the spiritual world in Kether and ends in the physical world in Malkuth. For the most part, spiritual evolution as outlined by the system of grades *begins* at the bottom of the Tree in the physical world, in Malkuth, and *ends* in the spiritual world at its top in Kether. To my knowledge, the reverse of this only occurs when a highly evolved, enlightened soul consciously chooses to be reborn with a specific purpose such as bettering life for a specific group or for the entirety of planet Earth. (Of course, bettering life for one group in time, directly or indirectly, uplifts all.)

From another view, involution—the descent and transformation of a soul into a personality and physical body living in the physical world—*begins* on the spiritual plane in Kether and *ends* on the physical plane in Malkuth. Evolution the ascent and transformation of a personality and physical body into a soul inhabiting spirit body *begins* on the physical plane in Malkuth and *ends* on the spiritual plane in Kether. Reaching Kether, the matured soul transmigrates or reincarnates into a new body repeating the process over and over again "till cooked."

A common aspect of involution is that once born, we tend to forget our past lives. Remembering occurs when evolution and awareness begin dawning, and then, only *if* recollection is necessary. (Of course, there is also therapeutic exploration.) Grasping the workings of the Graded Tree of Life is assisted by a belief in reincarnation. For those more scientifically oriented, an attention-grabbing, scientifically-based alternative to reincarnation known as epigenetic genetic inheritance, to be explored in later chapters, may prove worth investigating. But for now, this theory asserts that a parent's experiences, in the form of epigenetic tags, and memories resulting from both environmental and psychological stressors such as toxins, pollution, and anxiety, can be transferred from one ancestor to another. Lacking these or similar views tend to make the Graded Tree's progression somewhat more difficult to fathom.

An Alternative: Experiencing Past Lives in Present Time

I had a fascinating and educational foray learning about the power of past life regressions or "reveries" from a highly knowledgeable and skillful woman named Phyllis Krystal and her daughter Sheila. The key principle I learned was that helping others link present traumas and difficulties to another lifetime, even if what is called up regarding a past life is the byproduct of imagination, still has the potential to bring awareness, improved health, and healing.

An example: Despite being an excellent swimmer, Sol was unreasonably terrified of drowning in the ocean. In the process of doing "reverie" work, Sol discovered that his dread was the result of a "past life," in which he was a young Haida Indian. Sol recalled being out on a whaling expedition in his beautifully painted (he described it in some detail) red cedar log canoe, when he was knocked unconscious and drowned after a swipe from the creature's tail capsized his boat into stormy seas. Doing this, plus post-session "homework," which included consulting his doctor, helped Sol overcome his fear. He even considered learning to kayak on the Monterey Bay with his teenage daughter.

Engaging in this process, I clearly understood that even if what surfaces in a reverie is imaginary, the intuitive associative process that ensues presents something concrete to attribute today's upset and trauma to, and thereby has the potential to lessen and dispel it.

An Organic Process

The Graded Tree of Life, coupled with the Qabalistic Mystery school tradition, offers us as tree travelers a way of gauging our ability to apply the teachings of the Tree of Life to solving the many mysteries life sends our way. This remarkable glyph outlines the evolution of an ordinary human into an extraordinary human—beginning in Malkuth, the physical world, and ending in Kether, the world of spirit. Malkuth is translated from Hebrew as, "Kingdom" and is given the Alternative Title of "Bride." Despite this, Malkuth, like Kether, sits on the all-inclusive Middle Pillar and is the sephirah signifying the entire physical world. It is for this reason I prefer referring to Malkuth as, "the Royalty or Realm of Spirit embodied in flesh." For brevity's sake, I will also use "Kingdom."

As with physical growth and development, spiritual growth and development is an organic process that we each grow and develop through, whether we are fully cognizant of it or not. Our initial awareness of awakening spiritually may result in feelings ranging anywhere from fear and disequilibrium to extraordinary joy and elation. Yet, as we begin trusting, welcoming, and celebrating our increasing recognition of the mystical embedded in the mundane, our responses become more moderate. Certainly, our initial spiritual emergence and blossoming tend to increase our hunger and impatience for enlightenment. Essentially, with the passing of time, we become progressively more confident that we are *always* on the path to more expansive states of consciousness. As the eighth statement from the *Pattern on the Trestleboard* affirms, "I look forward with confidence to the perfect realization of the Eternal Splendor of the Limitless Light."

Please note: When writing about the Graded Tree of Life there is a general tendency to externalize and futurize the accomplishment of each grade, which did not ring completely true. After much contemplation, and as part of my way of rein-forcing the inevitability of our complete ascent of the Tree of Life, I became inspired to write the segments for each grade as if we have met or are in the midst of meeting its qualifications. Giving it some thought, this is something we are already doing, in our perfectly-imperfect ways.

Patterning and Re-Patterning Ourselves

The Tree of Life comes into existence from top to bottom, beginning in Kether and ending in Malkuth. However, ascending the Graded Tree of Life—like grades in school—starts with learning the basics in Malkuth, and ends with mastering these in Kether. When discovering a sphere, I suggest contemplating the characteristics and proficiencies coupled with its grade, noting those that presently apply in one form or another, and considering those ahead. Accompanying this is the essentiality of remembering the truth that everything comes to fruition in infinite or Divine time, not my time.

Each grade on the Tree of Life is conjoined with a sephirah and statement from Paul Foster Case's *Pattern on the Trestleboard*. A Trestleboard is a table on which an architect does their design work. Paul Case was a Mason, and Masonic tradition terms the Most High, Spirit or Divinity, "The Grand Architect of the Universe." In this sense, the *Pattern on the Trestleboard* is both a universal and personal blueprint for evolution. Its ten statements or affirmations are encapsulations of the teachings encoded within each sephirah that came to Dr. Case during meditation. (I have been inspired to adjust these slightly over the years.)

The Pattern opens with this statement, "This is the truth about the Self. All the Power that ever was or will be is here now!" In my experience and that of others, this brief declaration actually emits the eternal, omnipotent, omniscient, and omnipresent vibration of the entire Tree of Life. It goes on to use the word "I"—personalizing and transforming what comes next into sacred assertions. One student, a former Marine, nicknamed the Pattern "My Mission Statement," and each Grade became a "Rank." Repeating these lines is a potent way of affirming the fact that we are Trees of Life. Repetition of the Pattern functions as direct instructions *and* subtle suggestions to our conscious and subconscious minds.

THE QABALISTIC GRADE OF KETHER:

THE *IPSISSIMUS*

Approaching the system of Grades in reverse from how it and evolution typically occur, we are starting this road of our Tree of Life travel from Kether. Stationed on the neutral Middle Pillar is Kether's Grade of Ipsissimus, which translates from Latin as "One who is their Self," or "Most Selfness," the maximally conscious, or superconscious state of awareness while embodied, the superlative of "self," and the epitome of "Self-ness." While Kether, the highest point of the Tree of Life, appears dizzying when looking up, we have descended from and are ascending back to this wellspring of life. An Ipsissimus has the heartfelt certainty that all life events are springboards for seeking out and upholding what is genuine. Inherent to living in this way, *Ipsissimi* (the plural of Ipisissimus) automatically recall that we are exactly where we need to be to fulfill our part in our Baptismal contract.

In Raja Yoga Ipsissimi are known as avatars, the conscious descent of Spirit with the aim of helping others evolve and achieve this end by example. An avatars is born with mindful control over the five senses—sight, smell, taste, touch, and five functions of the body—speaking, eating, reproducing, eliminating, and moving, and five elements—earth, air, fire, water, and ether. These souls are unique as they are omniscient or all-knowing—innately possessing infinite awareness, wisdom, understanding, and insight.

Again, rather than putting the attainment of each grade like a distant star, far into the future and beyond reach, I have proceeded to describe each grade as if we are already in the process of meeting its qualifications—which, fact, is so. Doing this further reinforces the developmental processes involved in this journey.

We Tree-Climbers

Over time, we tree-climbers achieve a cellular awareness or knowledge of Kether's Admirable, Hidden Intelligence, Spiritual Experience of Unified Existence, and Virtues of Completion and Attainment. Ipsissimi know we are physical embodiments of the first declaration from the *Pattern on the Trestleboard*: "I am a center of expression for the One Divine Will to express itself, which eternally creates, sustains, and transforms the universe."

Achieving Unified Existence or at-one-ment with the Spirit of Life pulsating beneath the manifest world, the veil of illusion has been lifted. Union with Divinity is what some Hindu and Buddhist practitioners refer to as Tantric yoga. Hindus more specifically term it *Sachchidananda*, Bliss Absolute, and for Buddhists, Nirvana. Christian mystics term this *Unio Mystica*, Mystical Union, the state of being in which unqualified peace and harmony reign. Whatever the name, an Ipsissimus exemplifies the first of the Old Testament's Ten Commandments, "Thou shalt have no other gods before me." This means committing ourselves to place the Qabalah's universal and natural laws, truths, and principles front and center since these are the revelation and embodiment of Spirit. Doing this translates into identifying and treating every facet of life as our spiritual practice. It is having absolute trust that in both the beginning and end, all is One. This is suggested by the heartfelt words of the Baal Shem Tov, "Let me fall if I must. The One I will become will catch me."

Maturing into knowing in every cell of our being that all physical circumstances are sacred in essence and origin, we automatically respond to whatever occurs in daily with this certainty. Along with this, we Ipsissimi are completely devoted to fully participating in the ancient concept of Tikkun Olam, the repair and healing of the world as a byproduct of repairing and healing ourselves. We are completely committed to serving Spirit in the guise of creation, and in this way remain focused on the One. Ipsissimi are living embodiments of the words to the following prayer from Sri Sathya Sai Baba:

"O Lord, take my hands, and let them work incessantly for Thee;
O Lord, take my soul, and let it be merged in One with Thee;
O Lord, take my mind and thoughts, and let them be in tune with Thee;
O Lord, take my everything, and let me be an instrument to work for Thee."

Beyond the Ceaseless Ebb and Flow

Certain that life is a combination of situations, the Ipsissimus has transcended dualistic thinking. This means easily perceiving the positive polarity present within negative situations and the negative polarity present within positive situations. The result is living in a physical body and world, yet not being thrown off-center by its ceaseless ebbs and flows—or if being so, immediately rebounding. Being re-habituated by sacred awareness denotes that we are active participants in the ever-changing dance of life and have this brand of input into the human evolutionary process. This state is akin to Kether's self-perpetuating gods and goddesses who are forever improving the entirety of what they create.

It is essential to underscore the relationship between Kether's Spiritual Experience of Unified Existence and the Grade of Ipsissimus. Life in the physical world demands our moving between the positive and negative polarities. In the prolonged state of inactivity and perfect equanimity wherein our male and female sides are in complete masculo-feminine accord, the Ipsissimus is free from duality. Here the blissful union or reunion of our soul with its source occurs, making it synonymous with physical death.

Raja Yoga terms this *Mahasamadhi*, the state of perfect equanimity wherein we consciously decide to leave our body and return to the great source of life at the center of the cosmos. This act is only possible once the yogi or Ipsissimus has achieved God Realization or *Nirvikalpa Samadhi*. A student of Dzogchen Tibetan Buddhism added that at this stage of development some lamas will manifest the Rainbow Body or body of five radiant lights substantiating that they have transcended all suffering and have attained a state of complete union with the universe. Herein we recognize and experience our oneness with all. As the soul's cycle is over, there is no question of rebirth. Note the prerequisite state to this experience is Samadhi, entering and exiting the state of oneness at will. This capability is explored under the Grade of Magus in the next chapter: Chokmah, Wisdom.

We Ipsissimi are unceasingly centered in Spirit. Perpetually able to find greater spiritual-mystical meaning in whatever is before us provides us with a surer sense of the bigger picture and our ultimate well-being in even the direst situation. While editing this, the tragic mass shooting of nineteen children and two teachers in Uvalde, Texas occurred. What sustains an Ipsissimus when experiencing or learning about this and other catastrophes is the fact that while horrific these are undoubtedly assisting the evolution of consciousness. Spirit uses whatever means necessary to mature us. Ipsissimi understand and actively participate in the truth that until enough people agree upon and advocate for a remedy, these and other problems will persist and often worsen until the critical mass for change occurs. Essentially, at this level of awareness, the personal goals of each Ipsissimus are automatically aligned with the universal goal aimed at evolution—the benefit of all creation.

The Practical Mystic

In 21st Century terms, Ipsissimi have grown into the Crowning experience of being full-on practical mystics. The practical mystic has developed soulful longing and commitment to applying the spiritual precepts of the Qabalah (or any such system) to the multiple facets of life. We have developed the desire, willingness, fortitude, and ability to habitually identify the Most High, God/dess and so on, ever-present in the physical world. Ipsissimi live out the Crowning truth that the only difference between what is mundane and mystical is knowing or fully recognizing in every cell of our being that all that transpires in life originates from the One Reality. We perceive the totality of life events through spiritualized senses and the chores of everyday living as spiritual practice. This attitude is the reference point for all of our thinking, communicating, and doing, with the aim of interpreting and responding to whatever is transpiring both personally and universally.

Anonymity, Sacrifice, Endings, and Beginnings

While not driven by personal ambition, we Ipsissimi may appear like people who are, yet without clinging to a particular outcome or being opposed to making the sacrifices that reaching a goal demands. Not wanting to appear different from others, or be given any special status, an Ipsissimus lives in as much anonymity as is possible. Consequently, we refrain from revealing our elevated state of awareness unless doing so is the *only* way to assist others. Living simply and ultimately teaching by example, we are sincerely humble about any accomplishment-—never thinking of ourselves as anything other than an extension and helper of the One Doer. Furthermore, it is only when an Ipsissimius by necessity exhibits extraordinary attitudes and behaviors that their freedom and desire to go unnoticed, is lost.

Experiencing Divinity as mother, father, sister, brother, lover, and friend, Ipsissimi may have few relationships yet feel loved without condition. When necessary, we will sacrifice our life for another human, creature, or cause. Ipsissimi avoid *intentionally* harming another unless doing so is aimed at protecting and aiding the weak and oppressed or in certain instances, a matter of our own life and death. If and when others feel hurt, angered, and so on by what we are spiritually obligated to say and do, we understand that such stems from their immaturity, which gives way to misperceptions, misinterpretations, and the like.

After developing only a minimum of bodily identification, we are at any time ready to die and become part of the great void in the center of the cosmos. Yet, because Kether is coupled with the Baptismal contract, at death an Ipsissimus may opt to be reborn, or as the military term states, to "re-up" in order to continue serving.

Rapture and Madness

From a different view, individuals living in the state of rapture associated with mystical exaltation, an Ipsissimus may be inaccurately considered mentally ill. Those exhibiting enrapt behavior are referred to in some esoteric traditions as Masts (short for Masters) and Holy or Blessed Fools. A closer examination finds that those making such evaluations lack a genuine understanding of advanced spiritual emergence and the behaviors that fall outside of the realm of the norms described in an examiner's educational or life experience. Because there are those who are truly ill and a danger to themselves and others, the need for updated diagnostic tools and perceptive abilities is essential rather than quickly labeling, medicating, and institutionalizing. Writing this reminded me of the practice of trepanning, drilling holes in the head of one great saint to release his "evil spirits."

With a deeper understanding of what the mystical experience is, we discover people so exultant that they were judged insane when speaking or writing about their interactions with Spirit, God/dess, celestial messengers, the sudden enliven-ment of an idol, photograph, or visitation from an angelic presence, patron saint, the Blessed Virgin, Jesus, and so on. The Archangel Gabriel dictated the *Koran* to Mohammad by way of nightly visitations, bringing inspiration to millions. There are also accounts of Ipsissimi so "blissed-out" that they lose track of such as their body's need to eat and have to be lovingly fed in order to remain alive. It is only within the last several decades that the concept of "spiritual emergence," rather than the traditional determination of psychosis and other illnesses, has been validated.

HEAVEN ON EARTH: OUR INNER STARS

The Qabalistic Tree of Life keeps reminding us that we are stardust by way of the ancient Hermetic axiom, "As above, so below. As below, so above." That is, whatever happens in the heavens, on the spiritual plane, is reflected on Earth, on the physical plane. Taking this a step further, according to the increasingly familiar idea of Tikkun Olam, whatever repair and healing is occurring on Earth is reflected and occurring in Heaven. As mirrors of the cosmos, we humans are microcosms of the macrocosm, little likenesses of the big world. Bearing this in mind, Qabalists refer to the planets and luminaries as Inner Stars. These Western counterparts to the Eastern chakra system signify the inner personal presence of the outer impersonal heavenly bodies. Although non-physical, their existence is acknowledged by most mystical-spiritual traditions—Hinduism, Tibetan Buddhism, Taoist yoga, and alchemy—as well as the fascinating experiments with Kirlian photography.

Each planet or Inner Star emits universal electromagnetic currents. All living creatures have a subtle etheric body and a gross physical body. An invisible elec-tromagnetic cord joins the heavenly energies to the etheric centers in our physical bodies. This non-physical energy body holds the patterns, which form our flesh-and-blood body. While these Stars do not originate in our physical bodies, they do exert and influence upon them, an vice versa.

A growing number of holistically oriented physicians propose that disease can originate in the etheric body. Healing modalities such as Biophoton and Chiren ther-apies have been developed to help rectify this damage. Furthermore, some studies correlate disease and illness in our physical organs and secretory systems and imbal-ances in the Stars conjoined with these organs and systems. The Seven Inner Stars act like a bridge between our subtle and gross bodies. As with the functioning of our flesh-and-blood body and its systems, our Inner Stars are interrelated. Consequently, if one Star is out of alignment, the others are likely to be misaligned.

Humanizing the Tree of Life

When humanizing the Tree of Life, the three pillars of Mercy, Severity, and Equilibrium correspond to the spine as follows:

- The Pillar of Mercy, the positive right male or *yang* channel, or yogic *Pingala*.
- The Pillar of Severity, the negative left female or *yin* channel, or yogic *Ida*.
- The Pillar of Equilibrium, the neutral central channel or *Shushuma* that balances the other two.

The Universal Life Force, Holy Spirit , Chi, Ki, Fohat, or Kundalini, spirals up and down the spine in and through the Qabalist's equivalent to the chakra system, our Seven Inner Stars.

Before moving forward, please note that when we look at the Tree of Life from the *outside*, Wisdom, Mercy, and Victory are on the right, and Understanding, Severity, and Splendor are on the left. However, when slipping inside and *becoming* the Tree of Life, this reverses. Simply, the sephroth on the right side of the Tree shifts to our left side, and the spheres on the left side of the Tree are now on our right.

KETHER, THE CROWN STAR
OR THOUSAND-PETALED LOTUS

The sacred energy center or Star associated with Kether the Crown of the Tree of Life is the Crown Star. It corresponds to the *Sahasrara* or thousand-petaled lotus in the Hindu chakra system. When considering this summit of human consciousness, I find it invaluable recalling that we, like the lotus, develop out of the mud and murky waters—life's trials and tribulations—to in time blossom into magnificent flowers.

The Crown Star is the conduit to energies *both* to and from the personal. It is the gateway exiting from and entering into sublime unity. The direction depends upon whether one is beginning or ending physical existence. Generally, descending the Tree of Life from spirit into matter is involution-from disembodiment to embodiment, whereas ascending the Tree from matter into spirit is evolution-from embodiment to disembodiment. The exception to this being when a fully-evolved soul chooses to enter a physical body for a specific purpose such as freeing the slaves.

This Star is paired with the pituitary gland, the master gland that controls all other glands by secreting the hormones directing growth, metabolism, and reproduction and connecting to the central nervous system via the hypothalamus.

Signifying the One Transcendental Consciousness, our connection with the infinite, the Great Spirit of Life descends and ascends through the Crown Star. This is why Qabalists label Kether, the Crown of the Tree of Life, "The One Still Point," the sphere wherein our immortal soul either emanates out from into physical form, resides between lives, or is reabsorbed into Oneness. The result of "being Divinity" elevates individual perception to the domain of the sacred, blissfully obliterating any individuality.

Fitting to Kether, the Crown Star is the nucleus of pure spirit and undifferentiated consciousness. Such is coupled with the final stage of spiritual evolution, Unified Existence, the unequaled, transcendent state of cosmic consciousness or divine bliss wherein we have earned our freedom from karma and thereby the cycles of death and rebirth. Analogous to the Hindu and Buddhist states of Mahasamadhi and Nirvana, all desires, suffering, and sense of a personal "I" have been extinguished. At this juncture, the interrelationship between all beings and life events is crystal-clear. Perhaps this is what then-Scientologist Leonard Cohen meant when asking in his song *Famous Blue Raincoat*, "Did you want to go Clear?"

THE PALATE REFRESHER:
HOMEPLAY SUGGESTIONS FOR THE PRACTICAL APPLICATION
AND INTEGRATION OF EACH SEPHIRAH

Naturally, after feasting on the other courses come digestion and assimilation. These segments focus on the immeasurable value of putting the universal and natural laws truths, and principles explored through the teachings of each sephirah into practice. Doing this aims at the self-improvement gained by intentionally and repeatedly applying these illuminating and Self-centering concepts to our thinking, feeling, and doing.

Homeplay encourages and supports the important step of enacting what we have been studying to improve our lives. The Homeplay Suggestions for Practical Application and Integration, included in each chapter, are aimed at inspiring the day-to-day use of the teachings of Qabalistic Mystery School tradition, to solve the mysteries of life! This means taking the tools offered by each of the Tree of Life's sephroth and enacting them to uplift, repair, and restore ourselves, and as a possible byproduct, others and the world around us—enacting the concept of Tikkun Olam.

Homeplay expands our ability to perceive the mystical embedded within the mundane. Yes, practice does make perfect! Repetition boosts our ability to handle whatever life presents with ever-increasing grace, compassion, Self-knowledge, and satisfaction plus the benefit of perceiving the perfection at the heart of life's imperfections.

Introducing: Life's Greatest Teacher, Try See!

Learning about a sephirah is one thing, whereas putting our learning to the experiment of applying these principles to our thoughts, feelings, and actions and thereby learning even more is, as my vaudevillian grandmother Sadie would say, occasionally neighing laughingly in the process is, "a horse of a different color!" Homeplay aims at encouraging the integration of what we have been studying into our lives. I decided to begin each chapter on a sephirah with "Personally Speaking," illustrating how the teachings have inspired and continue to inspire me. To round out the picture, each Homeplay section is followed by "Student Experiences." These describe when, where, and how class members have taken the Suggestions I offer and others they create, to the test of "try see." Taking this ancient, yet ageless, wisdom a step further by integrating it into day-to-day living, we are transforming the mundane into the mystical and the mystical into the mundane.

Experimenting with these exercises as well as dreaming-up others is a priceless way of chewing over, digesting, and deriving nourishment from the sumptuous feast the Tree of Life serves up. This is precisely why I entitled this book QABALAH FOR THE 21ˢᵗ CENTURY: *LIVING* THE TREE OF LIFE. As generations of test-takers, we know how easy it is to forget what we have memorized, as compared with the application of theories to life situations as these are occurring. Reading parenting theories in his child psychology class paled in comparison to my student calling these up when he was on lockdown during COVID-19 with his five-year-old twins.

Lastly, sharing our experiences, the practice of what some groups term "giving testimony" is essential to the continuation and deepening of both our own spiritual journey and possibly inspiring others to do similarly. The key to keeping a philosophy or system alive is demonstrating how well it works—be it Qabalah, Homeopathic Medicine, Hatha Yoga, Tai Chi, or the latest computer app. Confirming the workings of Qabalah by testing it out, we help keep that system and its attending forces vital and grow wiser in the process. Neglecting to do this is a reminder of the Zen proverb stating "A donkey carrying a pile of holy books is still a donkey!"

THE PALATE REFRESHER:
HOMEPLAY SUGGESTIONS FOR THE PRACTICAL APPLICATION
AND INTEGRATION OF THE CROWN, KETHER

1. Apply the scent of ambergris (synthetic, of course) and wear white as I experience the Grade of Ipsissimus, "one who is most their Self," conjoined with Kether. Consider the following before, while, or after taking action:
    *Putting my relationship with the Great Spirit, Most High, God/dess, a Power greater than myself, and belief in Qabalah's universal and natural laws, truths, and principles at the forefront of my life. *Seeing and increasingly experiencing myself as a non-binary or masculo-feminine being. *Growing into automatically identifying with Spirit in situations in which I would have previously identified solely with my personality. *Reminding myself that everything I perceive with my senses is a facet of the Eternal. *Taking a more expansive or cosmic point-of-view (aka "the high road") in an instance where I was in the midst of doing or considering doing otherwise. *Mulling over a way that I am stepping up and playing God/dess by participating in Tikkun Olam, the repair and healing my immediate surroundings or community. *Seeking out what is Real, and then enacting it by being most my Self, in the midst of a confusing or troublesome situation. *Becoming increasingly aware of the essential spiritual nature of myself, others, my surroundings, and all daily interactions. *Glimpsing the fact that every part of the physical

world is a manifestation and reflection of the spiritual world. *Performing selfless service and offering its outcome to Spirit. *Noticing one way in which Spirit, the Most High, God/dess is aiming at upgrading life on planet Earth. *Experiencing myself functioning like a precision tool in the hands of a master artist.

2.   What comes next has the potential to facilitate my experience of Kether, the Crown, by experimenting with the following:

Feel the Tree of Life's Middle Pillar against my back as I take several long, deeply relaxing and centering breaths. Next, send a grounding cord or root down from the base of my spine into the earth and up from the crown of my head to root in the heavens as I do this. Continue by sensing my breath spiraling up and down these roots as I breathe. Slowly bring myself into the sphere of Kether by doing such a: Imagine showering or surrounding my body in a translucent white veil, the hue of the sphere, and inhaling the scent of ambergris. Invoking Kether's divine and archangelic presences by calling out or chanting their names, listed below under number 18. Summoning the support of the sphere's mythological deities—gods and goddesses—or bringing the associated flowers, plants, and animals into my mind and imagination. Enacting the aforementioned or whatever else I imagine relevant that will help me to kinesthetically, mentally, emotionally, and spiritually experience myself in Kether. I might also focus on my Crown Star, as this is where Kether touches my astral body. Now experiment with the following:

Kether heads the Tree of Life's neutral Middle Pillar in present time. The key to comprehending this somewhat incomprehensible sphere is nurturing the healthily detached, centered, neutralized state of Equanimity that is also termed Witness Consciousness, Mindfulness, and Insight. It is bringing myself "to center" by focusing on the Tree's Pillar of Equilibrium in the midst of life's unending changes. Doing this helps me to more accurately "observe," and thereby better interpret and understand the past and present events occurring in my life and the world around me. Such contributes to doing what I am able to accept whatever now is, plus plan for a future of conscious choice, rather than one of unconscious chance.

A.   After centering in Kether, proceed to contemplate a puzzling situation, first with my usual personality-oriented positive and negative feelings and evaluations. Then, slipping into impersonality, the neutralized, Self-centered state, consider that "this is how Spirit is presenting itself to me" and re-viewing the situation. Notice what I proceed to think, feel, or imagine: relieved, uplifted, concerned, sad, angry, optimistic, cautious, calm, uncomfortable—any and all of which are acceptable. Experimenting with this is giving me the opportunity to experience what is transpiring both personally and impersonally.

Please note: the aim of this exercise is to give myself the chance to acknowledge what now is, and in doing so, to open the way to a more expansive perspective and insight as to moving forward with maximum integrity. By allowing my thoughts and feelings to be as they presently are, I am also sowing the seeds of acceptance and a change for the better.

Next, reflect on what it could be like to apply this equilibrated, Spirit-centered point of view to situations when I am in the midst of these occurring. While the cultivation and perfection of this meditative, equilibrated, and insight-oriented Ketherian attitude or view takes time and practice to master, it is of inestimable value along the way. Such empowers me to acknowledge and surrender to the perfection of the Greater Reality—and from this calm, neutralized state to make decisions that I will be much less likely to later regret.

B.   Seek what is Real! After positioning myself in Kether, Crown of the Tree of Life, experience Ketherian awareness by identifying all I am sensing—hearing, smelling, seeing, touching, thinking, and feeling as Spirit, Divinity, God/dess.

C.   Experiment with walking in a beautiful place while repeating Kether's Divine Name Eheyeh: Eh-hay-eh, "I Am *That* I Am." Doing this affirms my oneness with the Great Spirit of the universe, Kether. This practice also goes for calling-in Kether's archangelic presence, Metatron: Met-ta-tron, Servant of the Most High.

Alternatively, if you prefer remaining seated in the sphere of Kether, repeat the ancient Sanskrit mantra *Hansa,* which also means "I am *That* I am." Again, That refers to the Great Spirit of the universe, Kether. As explained earlier, the repetition of Hansa automatically begins at birth with our very first cycle of respiration: inhaling *Han,* and exhaling, *Sa,* making it our inborn and natural mantra. While these do mean the same in English, you might prefer the sound of one—or use them in different circumstances.

Or, after imagining myself in the sphere of Kether, begin verbally or mentally repeating Hansa, while inhaling Han, and exhaling, Sa. "I am *That* I am." Reciting Hansa aligns and solidifies my identification with the One Reality Spirit within and without.

3.   Kether is known as both the Admirable Intelligence and the Hidden Intelligence, the holy unseen universal consciousness embedded in all of creation, which arouses admiration, veneration, and awe whenever it is recognized. Mull over answering one or more of the following:

*In what area of my life is the wonderment of the Most High, Spirit, God/dess, a Power greater than myself, coming increasingly to my attention?
*How am I being, or might I be, more respectful of the One Great Spirit

hidden within myself, another, a particular set of circumstances and/ or everything now surrounding me? *Have I suddenly recognized the cosmic process concealed within what I initially thought to be drudgery, bothersome, or upsetting? *What experience is moving me to acknowledge the truth that all physical people, creatures, things, and events are spiritual in essence and origin?

4.   The Spiritual Experience of Kether is Unified Existence. Consider reflecting on the following:

*Have I unexpectedly encountered the unity existing between the cosmos and myself? *Did a sense of Kether's existence bring me the momentary experience of at-one-ment with Spirit while handling a disagreeable person or upsetting situation? *Although I am living in a male or female body, am I experiencing myself as a non-binary or masculo-feminine being? *Could I be feeling eased by knowing that every event and interaction occurring in my life and in the physical world is unified with Spirit? *In what way am I reminding myself that the little, personal pictures of my life experiences cannot in Reality be separated from the big, impersonal picture of my life? *Am I growing increasingly aware that all of creation originates from and will return to Unified Existence? *Is art, music, dance, the scent of springtime, the taste of a tree-ripened apricot, hearing children laughing, watching a sunrise, feeling a newborn's skin, and the like moving me to experience the One Reality? *Have I experienced the many aspects of the physical world like facets of a diamond, sparkling out from Kether's oneness?

5.   Ponder applying the foremost teaching of Rabbi Israel Baal Shem Tov, "I set the Eternal before me always," (*Psalm 16:18*) to the vicissitudes, of day-to-day living. For example, The Baal Shem teaches that equanimity is achieved when we receive criticism with the same response with which we receive applause. Make a note of what happens when I apply this teaching:

6.   Kether's Sacrament is Baptism. When or if I find myself thinking, feeling, or saying, "I wish I wasn't born," experiment with the following: Write out or talk out my distressing thoughts and feelings. After examining my upset, proceed to do whatever is needed to center myself such as enacting letter A from exercise number 2 above. From this Spirit-centered place of Kether's Oneness, consider the baptismal contract I agreed to before being born. Doing this offers me the opportunity to recall the terms that came along with "signing on" to experience living in a physical body and world. It presents the chance to recall and contemplate the overriding truth: that although I was uncertain of the specifics—my race, sex, ethnicity, family situation, skills, gifts, conditions in the world, life's triumphs, traumas, tragedies, and so on—I was then certain that whatever resulted from these and other details would be necessary to my spiritual evolution and contribution to

life on planet Earth. Observe any shift from my personal view to Kether's impersonal Spirit-centered view:

7.   Contemplate the following in relationship to Kether:

"The net of heaven has large meshes and yet nothing escapes it."
Lao Tse, *The Simple Way*

"Let me fall if I must. The One I will become will catch me!"
Baal Shem Tov

"I'm nobody, who are you?" Emily Dickinson

"And I will give unto thee the keys of the kingdom of heaven: and whatsoever thou shall bind on earth shall be bound in heaven: and whatsoever thou shalt loose on earth shall be loosed in heaven."
Matthew 16:19

"Let me be one with the infinite sun, forever, forever, forever."
Sioux chant

"I am without beginning, without end, older than night or day, younger than the child new-born, brighter than light, darker than darkness, beyond all things and creatures, yet fixed in the heart of everyone. From me shining worlds flow forth, and to me all at last return."
Paul Foster Case, *Book of Tokens*

"Let thine eye be single." Unknown

"I am the Alpha and Omega, the beginning and the end, the first and last."
Revelation 22.14

8.   Create a personal statement that affirms my relationship with the Crown of existence such as: "I recognize and accept the Spirit of the Universe as the Source of my life and all that being born into my body, family, community, country, and planet Earth at this time involves." My personal statement is:

9.   Acknowledge, explain, or list a way in which I embody, or would like to better embody, this line from the *Pattern on the Trestleboard*: "I am a center of expression for the One Divine Will to Express Itself, which eternally creates, sustains and transforms the universe."

10.   Have a Crowning Experience. When in the midst of daily living I find myself feeling attacked and confused by interruptions, unplanned changes, delays,

broken promises, new information, interpersonal conflicts, and so on, ponder doing what follows.

After taking several deep breaths, surrender to what is occurring by saying something similar to: Thank you, Spirit, God/dess, Most High, Supreme One, for all that is happening and the thoughts and feelings these are stimulating within me. I am making peace with this situation by my expressing acceptance of what the Universe is Crowning and empowering me with. Although I am not fully understanding what is happening and am confused, sad, angry, frustrated, and the like, I thank you anyway. I am certain there is something for me to gain from the situation at hand—such as trust, patience, praying for guidance, etc. Note what shift results:

11. Kether heads the Pillar of Mildness seated in the now, present time, or eternal moment. Ask myself the following:

    *Although I would rather be elsewhere, how might I best go about focusing on where I presently am? *Is there an activity or non-activity that could assist me to be in the here and now? *Could living in the moment be a means of avoiding what I must do tomorrow or owning yesterday's behavior? *In what ways would a personal or professional relationship benefit from participants being fully present? *What can I do when I am feeling too tired, hungry, upset, overwhelmed, etc. to remain present with others? *Is my decision to eliminate distractions helping me to now focus on planning for a better future?

12. Kether is coupled with the Virtues of Completion and Attainment. Ask myself: What goal, project, or dream am I now involved in *completing*, and what satisfaction am I looking to *attain* by doing so?

13. Light cannot exist without darkness. Kether is coupled with the idea of a void or emptiness, the result tending to be the disruption, fading away, or disappearance of life as we have known it. Tibetan Buddhism refers to this state as the bardo. Traditionally, this refers to the condition of the soul between death and rebirth. For our purposes, it is the time between the dissolution of an old reality and the birth of a new one. It may be likened to some of what occurred during the COVID-19 pandemic.

    Observe: *In what area of my life—work, career, family, love relationship, health, am I feeling as if, "the rug has been pulled out from under me"? *What void or emptiness am I presently facing? *How might I benefit from accepting and surrendering to, rather than fighting, the empty space now in my life? *How am I mourning my loss? *What unforeseen benefits might the cosmic reshuffling of the deck of my life be offering me, and in doing so, perhaps others? *Am I extending reminders of the "Big Picture" to myself to ease the disorientation, fear, sense of loss, upset, or disappointment, I am now encountering? *What suggestions, if any, might I offer another who is undergoing a similar experience?

14.   Kether is astrologically conjoined with both the entire Universe and Neptune or *Rahav*. Neptune symbolizes the "higher-octave" or more refined, spiritually oriented qualities of Venus. Much as Kether is the inspiration for all existence, Neptune is the planet most connected with turning inwards for divine inspiration and is associated with dreams, fantasies, illusions, and disillusionment, consciousness-contracting and-expanding substances. Kether signifies the gift of life and Neptune is coupled with the sacred gifts life brings as it presides over impersonal or transpersonal love, mystical and visionary awareness, and abstract thinking—as well as the ultimate aim of lovingly submerging the personal self so that the impersonal. Self may emerge. It is further aligned with the sacrifices inherent in honoring my spiritual ideals and obligations and the misery that results from doing otherwise.

Explore how the planetary influences of Neptune are being activated in my life by asking myself the following: *Might there be a spiritual gift I am yearning to receive? *How is mystical-spiritual study and practice inspiring and freeing me from unnecessary suffering? *What do I hope to gain by engaging in or ceasing to engage in martyr-like behavior? *Could I be consciously suppressing or unconsciously repressing a painful experience, and why might allowing it to surface be liberating? *Am I noticing that doing what is personally best is becoming increasingly aligned with doing what is universally best? *Is there a behavior or attitude that am I being challenged to sacrifice in the name of fulfilling a sacred obligation? *To whom or what am willingly surrendering my time and energy? *Has a dream or mystical experience caused a long-submerged goal to surface? *In what situation was I automatically more identified with my soul spirit Self and less with my personality? *What revelation or fantasy could be that of a visionary who is ahead of their time? *How am I dealing with my tendency to depend on numbing substances such as certain drugs and alcohol? *What expanded reality or illusion am I nurturing through consciousness-expanding medicines or psychedelics? *In what area of my personal or professional life am I feeling motivated to serve another person, a group, cause, etc., or suffer a guilty conscience? *How is deepening my spiritual practice rescuing me from drowning in the sea of illusion? *What am I hoping to gain by engaging in or ceasing to engage in martyr-like behavior?

15.   Experiment with placing the teachings and practices of my spiritual path as the main reference point for all interactions and occurrences in my life for three minutes-use a phone or set a timer. Consider increasing the amount of time by one to five-minute intervals. Notice how all of my needs and goals are gradually boiling down to one: alignment with the Tree of Life's universal and natural laws, truths, and principles, aka the Eternal Verities or Perennial Philosophy.

16.   Reflect on ways the plants, gems, creatures, mythological figures, or other symbols coupled with Kether may serve as helpful reminders to improve my

life by applying and integrating the teachings of the Crown. For example: I have positioned a yin-yang at the Crown of my computer, which I call The Chariot or Victorious One. This potent, attention-getting symbol reminds me to be victorious by remaining centered on what is Real in the midst of the positive and negative energies continually streaming through cyberspace into my email box.

17.   What attitudes or behaviors might I adopt to better engage with the physical world and circumstances of my life to become increasingly aware that the entire physical world is Spirit temporarily embodied in skin suits? Where in my personal or professional life am I consciously doing heavenly service while living on Earth? Who is setting an inspiring or discouraging spiritual example for me? In what ways is the example of how I am living suggesting to my children and/or others to behave similarly? In what situation(s) might I become more of a conscious participant rather than a bystander who is feeling subjugated to, or victimized by, my circumstances?

18.   Passionately call out and in Kether's Divine and Archangelic Presences to help me become more attuned with, and live out the teachings of Kether, the Crown sephirah. Kether's Divine Presence is: Eheyeh (E C F C Eh-eh-hay-eh, I Am *That* I Am. Kether's Archangelic Presence is Metatron (G# E D A G Me-ta-tr-on-on), Servant of the Most High.

19.   Give myself the priceless gift of expanding my comprehension of the Crown and Qabalistic Tarot's minor arcana by laying out and reflecting on the Four Aces as follows: Contemplate how *each* card symbolizes the Crown's/Kether's attributes:

- The Admirable and Hidden Intelligences.
- Spiritual Experience of Union with the Most High.
- Sacrament of Baptism.
- Virtues of Completion and Attainment.
- Astrological Counterpart of Neptune.
- The Qabalistic Grade of Ipsissimus, "One who is their Self."

THE DESSERT:
AFFIRMING, CONFIRMING,
AND INSPIRING STUDENT EXPERIENCES

Welcome! After reading through the general Suggestions for the Practical Application and Integration of each sephirah you are ready for what comes next. The
following are the results of class members taking the principles of Kether to heart, by
applying and thereby integrating these suggestions, as well ideas of their own, into
the challenges, tests, and trials of life in the 21st century. When returning to class,
they shared what took place when *Living* the Tree of Life. Each student's Homeplay is
followed by a few of my comments. Now here goes:

■ "Brad and I own and run a car repair shop and are parenting his two teenagers
half-time," shared Lorinda. "I can't tell you how much it helps that we're actively
involved both with this school and with a meditation teacher and daily practice
for a number of years. Since learning about Kether, Brad and I are noticing that
the line between our spiritual practice and work in the world is blurring.

Like most folks, we've separated our spiritual practice from our daily
work and family obligations. Studying Kether has been helping us get that
there's *really* no difference, only our attitudes. It's all the same! Everything is
our spiritual practice! Reflecting on this after politely sending a more-than-
difficult, continually dissatisfied customer on his way, Brad and I agreed that
everything we do is spiritual practice when we think it is! Courteously walking
this man to his car after giving him a small refund helped us to experience this
priceless truth."

*Wonderfully insightful, Lorinda. You and Brad are definitely assimilating
the basic underlying principle of mysticism-—there's nothing but Spirit.
Mystics make the Divine One their all and everything, and by doing
so, cultivate an intimate relationship with their Source. In other eras,
practitioners from both the Eastern and Western mystical traditions
endured great physical discomfort, even self-torture—practices the likes
of self-flagellation with whips, piercings with nails, extensive fasting—so
that their bodies would become purified and more appealing vessels
for Divinity to enter. A notable exception to this was Buddha, who,
after putting himself through tremendous deprivation realized, when
weakened by hunger, how essential good physical health is to spiritual
practice. It taught him, and then others, the value of moderation in
all things. Buddha actually embodied the ancient hermetic-Qabalistic
principle: "Equilibrium is the basis for The Great Work."*

*Qabalistic Mysticism greatly values and teaches Equilibrium and
the all-pervasiveness of Spirit by way of the Tree of Life's Middle Pillar
and sphere of Kether. Unlike earlier forms of this system, it does not seek
to eliminate all worldly things, including our physical body, in order to*

know Divinity. Qabalah teaches that Spirit is embodied in every atom and aspect of the physical world. The contemporary study of the Tree of Life offers the opportunity to perceive the presence of the Most High in the entirety of daily life and physical existence.

■ "I'm presently doing some freelance editing for a book publisher in Seattle and working on my poetry and music in my spare time," shared Elle. "Although I want to be living just as I now am, I was raised to be very security-conscious. If my mother only knew I don't have health insurance, she'd go ballistic! Anyhow, since beginning our work through Kether, I've been noticing something unusual. Here I've gone and set up my life to have time to play music and write, but haven't felt the muse.

Earlier this year I felt inspired to volunteer to bring animals from the SPCA to visit elderly shut-ins and also signed up to help at the HOSPICE project. Then, out of the blue, both of these organizations got in touch and presto, my free time was no more! At first I felt concerned, but suddenly I got inspired to start writing again.

Every time I see one of my clients from either the HOSPICE or SPCA projects, I feel united with the universe. The times I get to spend with these folks make me feel that I'm being used as a divine instrument. Okay, I do sometimes forget and start thinking it's me deciding what I should be doing. Eventually, I come around to the truth that it's *really* the One True Self guiding me. I'm using the personal statement: 'I'm an instrument (like my bass) of the One.' Doing this is helping me to be more trusting of the journey I'm taking with my creative undertakings, is bringing me genuine peace of mind *and* a sense of security."

It sounds as if you are touching on the spiritual experience of Kether, Union with the Most High. Your community service is underscoring that everyone and everything is interrelated. You're having the direct knowledge that the physical world and all it contains is, in spite of its divisions and boundaries, actually is a seamless and inseparable whole—a conclusion that mystics and saints throughout the ages have experienced, and lived by.

■ "Taking some extra time to really look at, be present with, the trees, plants, and flowers and feeling their Real nature, I've been experiencing more and more about Kether. Listening to the birds singing in the morning while dressing for work, I'm sure Divinity is present," shared Catherine, the manager of a dental office and a family person. "Looking at our Homeplay assignment last week, I honestly didn't connect much more other than what I just shared. Then I began thinking about my husband and how his attitudes about spirituality and God are really challenging me, and how much I want to understand the truth about this challenge. Okay, Adrian isn't even the slightest bit interested in knowing about what I'm learning in class, or even what I believe in. He's completely closed, and I can't figure out why. When I've asked him, he'll answer somewhat sarcastically, 'I'm happy that you're going to class.' Although I know he knows there's something greater going on, he refuses to discuss it or belittles what I'm saying. Almost every time I try to share something I've discovered or ask him what he thinks of it, we end up arguing.

His roots are in Greek Orthodox Church, yet as he's gotten older he stopped attending church. He's now maintaining: 'You're born. You die. And that's pretty much it.' Hearing this really drives me nuts. He claims not to believe in a spiritual side of himself or anything, but I know it's there. I experience it in the way he cares for animals. You should see how he fed and nurtured an injured Robin. He's another Saint Francis! Yet, he doesn't recognize good qualities in himself. If anything, he disavows almost everything he does. And more than that, it HURTS when he comes at me with his negative attitudes and judgments about my spiritual beliefs. I honestly want to figure out the Real nature of this challenging and to be real, *very* upsetting situation, and how to meet it. It's creating this awful, awful distance between us."

I get how upsetting your situation is, Catherine. If you think about it, accepting another, especially our significant other, who believes much differently than we do and is causing others upset, specifically you, as a result, is one of the greatest issue we humans face. Throughout human history, so much blood has, and unfortunately continues to be, shed over differences in ideology, religious and otherwise. Perhaps this might give you something to consider with regard to Adrian. I congratulate you for wanting to come to terms with it.

It's important that you continue getting your needs for spiritual validation and camaraderie met in groups such as this one, and the dream group you've been participating in for years. Although it certainly doesn't take care of what you can and cannot share or discuss with your husband, it does give you outlets...and inlets.

Your experience seems to be somewhat common in a long-term relationship, wherein people grow and change. Might knowing that your husband does have a spiritual side, although he doesn't identify it as such, give you any relief? Certainly, his put-downs are hurtful. Are you telling him that it hurts? Then again, is it possible that you're unwittingly pushing your spiritual agenda on him? Might finding more joy in the things that you agree on help balance out your upset? I recall you telling us about your mutual love of gardening, cooking, reading, biking, and raising your children together. While doing this will not fully make up for your needs, or should I say your wants, it might be worth a go or two to focus on your commonalities. Of course, having the willingness to recognize when outside help is needed is also worth considering.

I'm wondering what it might be like for you to experiment with giving him complete permission to be exactly as he is and believe as he does. In other words, shifting into Kether's state of neutral, and acknowledging

that what your husband's saying is true for him. After all, these are his
beliefs. You have your way of perceiving life, and he has his. You're asking
about the Real *nature of the situation, which could well be accepting*
the fact that you have somewhat differing realities. The difficulty often
arises when we want to make others, especially those close to us, see
things as we do.

■ Aisha, a busy courtroom reporter, shared the following: "Because I was sick
on and off since New Year's, I've been moved to observing the *Shabbat* (Jewish
Sabbath) alone, rather than with others as I usually do. After bathing, I dress in
a pure white robe, Kether's color. Doing this, I've come to realize that there is
something about putting on white and the idea that the Sabbath is a pure and
holy day. For me it's become a time when, after lighting the *Shabbos* candles
at sundown on Friday night, I'm not watching TV, answering the phone, or
working until Saturday at sundown. Instead, I'm spending my time regenerating
by doing yoga, meditating, listening to sacred music from the *Sephardim* (Jews
from Spain), eating lightly and reading uplifting books.

My new Holy Day was inspired by exploring Kether, as well as by my deep
need to explore from whence I come. I've been kind of dabbling in a number of
different paths, yet this very simple observance is giving me a peaceful feeling
like none other so far. There's something simple, yet unique about wearing what
I'm calling Kether-white, that makes everything I do after dressing different. It
gives me the feeling of separation and purification from my often all too hectic
work schedule. I just love it! My new practice actually helps me jump back into
my work world feeling more prepared for hearing, recording and being more
tolerant of whatever's going on in the courtroom. And that's *really* something!"

What a beautiful and uplifting experience, Aisha! How wonderful to be
giving yourself this time. By lovingly disciplining yourself to do this, you
are moving forward into the week spirit-centered, a state that is surely
touching, even if subtly, those around you.

■ Kelvin, an electrical engineer, told us how he became aware of Kether in himself,
others, and his environment. "Having studied Zen Buddhist meditation,
I found myself inspired by our class work with Kether to do some walking
meditation. I kept focused on my breathing and being present with each step.
First, I looked at all the things around me, then started taking each one back
in my imagination to where they truly came from back to their pre-atomic and
atomic states and then to the state of light. (It was almost like taking peyote,
something I did with a shaman in Mexico in what now seems like *light* years
ago-Ha!) I was entranced by everything from the concrete on the sidewalk to
the clouds in the sky!

Envisioning the world around me breaking down to its most elementary
state immensely helped my understanding of Kether. By doing this, I realized
how much I want to spend more time seeing my life in its *true* Light. I tend

to get so lost in my routine that I mindlessly forget that Spirit is present in everything! Simple as it sounds, actually doing this reminds me of the old saying, 'Not seeing the forest for the trees.'"

Both the concepts of Unified Existence and the number one are conjoined with Kether. Usually, we're taught to view the material and spiritual worlds as being separate and disparate. In addition, some exoteric or traditional religions encourage practitioners to separate spiritual practice from life practice, rather than perceiving their innate interconnectedness and unity. It's so inspirational knowing how you are combining the teachings of Kether with your Zen meditation practice. (I have the sense that your Zen teacher would smile.) Doing this not only unifies the material and spiritual worlds but also brings out the commonalities between the philosophies of Qabalah and Buddhism. Remembering, as you did, that all that is, is in some way unified with the Great Spirit of Life, living on planet earth becomes more comprehensible and doable.

■ "I started off doing our Homeplay thinking I'm never going to experience Kether" began Ri, a pediatric nurse. "Then suddenly, I'm involved in doing some forgiveness work around my relationship with my sister, Dana and through it, I got to what I believe is Kether's Vast Countenance.

My mother's death last year forced my sister and me into a closer relationship after decades of physical (she lives in another state) and emotional distance. Because my mother lived just a few miles away from me, she asked me to handle everything around her dying and death. She also decided to appoint me as the executor of her will, in which Dana and I are named as beneficiaries.

Well, it's been six months since my mother passed and my sister is getting extremely, and I mean e-x-t-r-e-m-e-l-y, impatient about getting her share of the estate. Her angst has brought me to fully recognize that Dana always tends to be in a hurry while I always tend to be in a slow, sometimes too slow for Dana, mode. It makes sense that my sibling feels frustrated and is having difficulty understanding why the finances haven't all been pulled together by now. Despite the fact I do update her regarding probate, it's nowhere near enough. Although she has the lawyer's contact info, she keeps pestering me. I've actually received a couple of extremely angry letters from her. Each time I've gotten a letter, I've practiced something I learned when attending a death and dying seminar. I send mercy to myself for the hurt and anger my sister has been directing my way and mercy to her for feeling so upset.

Being one-hundred percent honest, Dana's letters have stirred up a tremendous amount of pain and anger in me. I've finally come to realize that I feel this way because I'm not being loved the way I'd like to be loved, and that's probably, how she feels. I'm not taking care of things the way she'd like to have them taken care of, and neither is she. It's an agonizing situation for us both.

Reaching up to Kether for inspiration through the Homeplay suggestion to, 'set the Eternal before me always,' I got to know my sister more fully. Raising my awareness, I experienced Dana as both a hurt little girl and in a much bigger way as a divine spark. This is what I meant when I started out by stating, 'I experienced Kether's Vast Countenance.' I can't tell you all how this beyond-the-beyond, awesome opening helped to take the sting out of the misery that keeps being passed back and forth between us.

I honestly wanted to run away from knowing the truth about what was going on. Feeling trapped and desperate forced me to reach beyond myself. It inspired me to become willing and then able to take the greater or vaster, as in the Vast Countenance, view of our situation. I also called upon the archangel Metatron, the Servant of God, while walking home from a friend's house last Saturday afternoon. Doing this opened me to realizing how perfect, healing, and Self-serving, in the big picture, what's occurring between my sister and me actually is. Hey maybe if I move a bit faster, she might move a bit slower."

The disharmony between you and your sister has certainly been fostering quite a growth spurt. All that's been happening around your mother's passing is functioning as the catalyst for much growth, and I'll add, harmony, over time. Receiving insight as to how your personalities differ—being the impatient and patient ones—and what you might do about it, is amazing. It's no coincidence that Kether is sometimes known as the Amazing, aka mind-blowing Intelligence. That is, one's immature mental and emotional constructs are shattered. It's a blessing that you've come to understand the relationship between you and your sister with some needed objectivity, and in doing so, love. It looks like this situation is moving both of you towards Kether's Middle Pillar or middle ground.

■ "Although what was going on began through an unusual set of circumstances, thanks to Kether, I was better able to put my spiritual work first and foremost," began Noah, an up-and-coming author. As you've been hearing, I'm in the midst of negotiating with a few companies for the rights and publication of my new book. After a month of negotiating with this one company, I realized that I don't trust them. I then became completely certain I'd be making a big mistake signing with them.

I was set on formally withdrawing my manuscript when I suddenly became very concerned about plagiarism. The publisher's been almost too excited about my ideas and I'm sensing they'll be less than happy finding out that I don't want 'to sign on the line.' Actually the more I began thinking about it, the more real the potential for plagiarism became.

So I went to talk with the legal assistant at my Writer's Union. She offered me some very important suggestions regarding what and what not do about my concerns. This woman also pointed out that there are some aspects of the situation, which are now definitely out of my hands. (Poop!) Essentially, it's not a matter of whether or not I inform them that they can't copy the format or the specifics. If they're intent on proceeding, all they have to do is have their editors alter the manuscript in little bits here and there. What's making my situation more complicated is that I'm in California and they're in London and going to court out-of-county would be pricey, to say the least.

I wrote the publisher a formal letter withdrawing my manuscript and with it enclosed a very carefully worded addendum requesting that they 'refrain from copying format nor specifics.' Doing this is a professional way of letting them know I'm aware that I've opened myself to being plagiarized. My notice advises the publisher that they'll have big trouble with me should they try to copy my work and therefore best think twice (or thrice) before doing so.

Well, what to do next? Somehow, even after filling out the necessary documents, I didn't feel 100% done. Suddenly, it occurred to me to turn to my spiritual tools and so I started thinking about our assignment to apply and integrate the teachings of Kether. After lighting a candle in my lotus-shaped candle holder (Kether's flower) and inhaling some ambergris (synthetic, of course), I called in the divine and angelic presences of Kether, Eheyeh and Metatron for guidance and inspiration. I held my manuscript and legal papers to the publishers up to heaven and said, 'I've done everything in my power to protect this work and myself. I've made my best decision. I know that there's some greater force at work within the situation and in me. I trust in the power of this force of the Most High. It's now up to you! Amen! So mote it be! I Surrender!'

I sent everything off the next morning and began following up on other publishers. Because Spirit clearly has precedence over everything, I'm fully committed to putting Spirit first. Thank you, Tree of Life! Thank you, Kether! Thank you, class!"

> *It appears that you've been engaging with the virtue and sometime vice of Kether, attainment and abstention, respectively. You've attained the awareness that you are not fully in charge. You also realized that to have abstained from taking action could have hindered your work even further. By consciously taking direct action and calling upon every means you had available, including a sincere request for the great power of Spirit to intervene, you are turning a potentially disempowering situation into an opportunity for both universal and personal empowerment. Congrats are surely due, Noah!*

■ "I didn't have time to do my Kether homework when awake, so I did it in my dreams," began Marcie, a breast cancer survivor, and almost full-time single parent, hesitatingly. "I've been drowning in day-to-day stuff while needing to get into my studio and be more creative. With my ex working more and more time out of the country, I'm needing help with basic stuff like driving my children to their various activities, looking after my rental property, cooking and food shopping. Over the past week, I've been especially exhausted.

So, before going to sleep two nights ago, I focused on my Crown Star, where Kether connects to my body, imagined myself being showered in white light, and fell asleep. Then what do you know? I dreamt about a smiling young man named *Vishnu* reaching out and hugging me. (I don't recall any more of the dream but that.) While I'm not at all connected with Hinduism, I immediately wanted to know more. It turns out he's a deity of restoration, preservation and protection. I noted what the link said and here it is: 'Vishnu is ever-present within all things as the intrinsic principle of all and the eternal transcendental self in every being.'

My dream emphasized that healing, and searching for, honoring, and preserving my true Soul-Spirit Self is what I need to be doing more of right now. So I'm feeling inspired to make the time to experience myself aside from all the hats I'm wearing. One perk of my situation is that I have some extra money, which means I can get help with the genuinely nonessentials—finding a property manager for the rental, hiring someone to drive my children to and from their many activities, signing up to have some healthy, tasty prepared meals delivered, buying groceries online and so on. I'm completely sure the children will appreciate relating to someone other than 'grumpy mom,' and eating cooking other than mine. Delegating this work will help me become more able to feel myself and remain focused on what is really my most important job, healing."

As you know, Kether is the cosmic intention behind creation. In order to be creative, we need time to explore creative possibilities. It seems as if you're getting a strong message to establish this type of environment in which to do this, for the well-being of yourself and your family.

In the Hindu epic The Mahabharata, *Krishna, is an Avatar the human embodiment or incarnation of the god Vishnu, who instructs his pupil Arjuna, a reluctant warrior, to do his sworn duty to himself, and thereby others. This is an extremely potent metaphor regarding the importance of realizing your "job description" and fulfilling it to the best of your ability.*

Might Vishnu's restorative and protective presence appear to point you in the direction of being a warrior by courageously eliminating, killing-off, or better yet re-assigning, your energy-depleting roles and honoring those that uplift you? Doing this promises more quality time with your children, creativity and increased good health. It sounds as if you're being guided to act in the name of and in-behalf-of, the sacred Spirit within you. Consider creating a personal statement and using aligned self-talk to further reinforce your goals.

CHOKMAH, WISDOM

FATHER OF ALL LIVINGNESS, KING OF KINGS, CREATOR AND LIFE POWER UNLIMITED

THE APPETIZER: PERSONALLY SPEAKING

While reviewing my newly revised Homeplay questions for Wisdom or *Chokmah*, pronounced Hoke-ma, a few afternoons before class, one nearly jumped off the page: "In what area of my personal or professional life am I being given the opportunity to move up the evolutionary scale by using the Wisdom received from a past experience to perform a new task?" I sensed that I'd soon be doing this. So, when a call came from my literary agent, offering me the chance to participate in a possible "prime time TV series," featuring tools such as the tarot, astrology, runes, and *I Ching*, my intuition was validated.

It wasn't long before I was flying to Los Angeles for a screen test at Paramount Studios. Although I felt genuinely excited about the prospect of presenting the Qabalistic Tarot to such a wide audience, I also knew that what I do isn't mainstream. As my travel date approached, I received an email outlining the show's format. Instead of presenting the Qabalistic Tarot as an ancient tool used to facilitate change in a way that doesn't resemble "fortune telling," I was asked, better yet *told*, to present it, as barely one step above that of a circus sideshow. While discussing my concerns about doing this with my agent, he persuaded me to proceed by planting the idea that I might somehow elevate the proposed format. Wanting to maintain the relationship with my agent and knowing how important it was for his agency to be represented, I allowed myself to be quasi-convinced.

The evening after I arrived in Los Angeles, I met with the show's producers and other participants at a festive "on-set" mixer. When the execs shared that they knew nothing about the Qabalah and Qabalistic Tarot, I shared a few of the basics. Obviously disinterested in what I communicated, they quipped, "Just like Madonna!" then laughingly changed the subject before I could answer. Rather than push against the tide, I recognized that although they were presently closed to further information, they might at some later date, recall what I'd shared. (I later joked that these "gentlemen" would have been better listeners had my neckline been lower, my skirt shorter, and I a few years younger.)

Knowing my audition was set for seven the next morning, I set the alarm for 4:30 so I could have plenty of time to bathe, do yoga, meditate, and eat. Acknowledging I had very little personal experience or Wisdom with the Hollywood scene and that I was mildly attached to the idea of being "the person" to present the tarot to the world at large, I focused my meditation on asking that universal Wisdom enter my heart and mind to illuminate the wisest way to handle what might lie ahead. Almost immediately, images of my teachers Paul Foster Case and Ann Davies appeared in my mind's eye (the third eye being the Inner Star or chakra coupled with Chokmah-Wisdom). After this vision passed, my mind became flooded with light, reminding me that one of the foremost symbols of Wisdom is a lightning bolt. I knew in a flash that had no choice other than to be true to the teachings of Ageless Wisdom as these have been passed on to me. This was also a reminder that Wisdom is situated in the past, time-wise. This meant playing the part accordingly during the screen test. So, instead of embodying a hyperactive psychic fortuneteller, I wisely let go of any desire to be in the show and followed my regular protocol of asking for divine guidance, drawing out a client's impressions of cards, then gently, yet firmly adding my perceptions and suggestions.

It was fun to get costumed and made up for my sequence. At one point, I felt like I was about ten years old playing dress-up with my girlfriends. Remembering my childhood and again that Chokmah is paired with the past; I started laughing so hard that the makeup artist had to stop applying my lipstick. Walking down the hallway from the dressing room through the darkened studio onto the brightly lit set, I felt a slight rush of adrenaline.

Once seated, I was presented with my visibly nervous client Tamara, a stunning young woman whose first words to me were "I'd look better if I'd gotten more sleep last night." After assuring her that she looked beautiful, I explained that we would begin with a short meditation both to quiet and center our energies as well as to focus on her question. Despite being told that the producers were "very interested in seeing how you set the scene," they noisily chattered in the background while we did exactly that.

Relaxed, Tamara thankfully forgot about the camera and concentrated on the cards. Together we entered into a state in which time is irrelevant. Consequently, rather than working with the three people as scheduled, I broke the rules and worked only with Tamara. Annoyed, the producers ordered the sound techs to unplug us. Despite this, I left the set fully satisfied that I had co-created what was best for both my client and the Qabalistic Mystery School Tradition that I steward.

While leaving the stage, I could hear Tamara giving the producers glowing comments on what we had accomplished. Catching up with me on the way to the dressing room, she threw her arms around me and tearfully whispered, "I got so much working with you, and I'm really hoping you get the part." As it turned out I didn't get the part my agent had me audition for, but I did get the part Chokmah/ Wisdom directed me to get, that of keeping it Real and perhaps subtly inputting the show's producers. By doing this, I preserved both my integrity and the integrity of Qabalistic Tarot's Wisdom as it has been entrusted to my care.

True to the Homeplay question, the situation was a chance for me to move up the evolutionary scale by doing a new task. That task was about knowing myself well enough to realize that I required sage input to decide how to most honorably proceed with this unique opportunity. Opening myself to Chokmah's Wisdom, I expanded my personal Wisdom resulting in my ethical and graceful participation.

THE ENTREE:
GENERAL INFORMATION AND SYMBOLISM

CHOKMAH IS THE HEBREW WORD FOR WISDOM

Chokmah, again pronounced Hoke-ma, means Wisdom in Hebrew. The English word Wisdom is derived from the Old English *wis* and Latin *dom*, which means, "to know" and "God," respectively. Intriguingly, the Old Testament refers to "knowing" or "having knowledge of" as carnal knowledge, suggesting that Wisdom is an ecstatic state of intimacy with Spirit and thereby the ability to understand things that others cannot. According to Moses De Leon's thirteenth-century *Zohar,* or *Book of Splendor,* this "knowledge" speaks of the holy union between Wisdom and Understanding, Chokmah and Binah, as a glorifying of the male and female principles and of their union the path through which the Most High's love enters the physical world.

The dictionary defines Wisdom as "the personification of the Divine will (the Logos) with respect to the creation of the world." This brings to mind the words of St. John: "In the beginning was the Word, and the Word was with God, and the Word was God." (*The Gospel According to John, 1:1.*) Additionally, references to the Word in ancient Vedantic (Indian) and Koranic (Islamic) texts are aligned with the command, "Be!" and Chokmah is conjoined with the forward thrust to generate the totality of creation.

Synonyms for Wisdom are sagacity, knowledge, judiciousness, prudence, perception, insight, astuteness, discernment, intelligence, acumen, penetration, comprehension, and enlightenment. This list is reminding me to mention that the teachings of Qabalah are related to Gnosticism in that it is free of dogma. Beginning in the first century CE, Gnosticism broke away from rigid beliefs of Judaism, Paganism, and the then-blossoming Christianity—all of which required intermediaries of one form or another.

Gnosticism is derived from the Greek word *Gnosis,* meaning "knowing." Gnostic practitioners bypass go-betweens in favor of Self-Knowing, seeking wisdom and insight from contact with the Holy Spirit within. Lucy, a student of Gnosticism, affirmed this when sharing the following: "Studying the Gnostic teachings, I learned that it's the consequences of my behavior (when I pay attention) that are teaching me to make wiser decisions and moving me along my path to Wisdom."

Ability and Intention

The idea of Wisdom suggests a data bank of universal and natural spiritual laws, truths, and principles that has been built up throughout time—what Qabalists call "Ageless Wisdom." Such may also be termed the Wisdom of the Ages, Eternal Verities, and Perennial Philosophy. Wiseones are living libraries or again, data banks of the aforementioned. Because Wisdom is accumulated intelligence that has been tested and tried, it implies the ability and intention to choose to support and maintain wiser and wiser ways of thinking and doing. Wisdom stems from assimilating what has gone before and its relationship to the present.

A particularly relevant synonym for Wisdom is a revelation, the disclosure of hidden knowledge that is aligned with divine will and truth. In its most expansive state, Wisdom implies knowing how to act in universal accord with the best of intentions. Such is aimed at doing what is beneficial for all concerned in all situations. Of course, there are times when what the wise say and do is initially puzzling and downright uncomfortable, yet as we grow increasingly attuned and knowledgeable, these become clear.

Learning from Living

Although many have tried to do so, Wisdom cannot be bought or sold; it manifests only when we are ready to receive it. I have noticed that confusion helps to set the scene into which Wisdom enters. After my seventeen-year-old basketball-playing neighbor unwisely attempted to exit a sporting goods store carrying a pair of Steph Curry Nikes stuffed into his baggy pants, he was promptly stopped and arrested. Spending time in juvenile hall offered him the chance to "wise up" and consider ways of earning the money to purchase the shoes. That said, our actions bring about the physical, mental, and emotional instruction—agony, ecstasy, and everything in between, which eventually culminate in Wisdom. These may result in "wising," when someone compassionately, ideally without being attached to what then happens, offers missing facts or information to another in obvious need. Wisdom is the intelligent application of learning from living.

Wisdom is reaching a meaningful conclusion after carefully evaluating a given set of circumstances. Simply, the class put two and two together and learned... Wisdom is having the expertise to act in universal accord with the situation at hand. It is serving as a medium for applying spiritual or universal Wisdom or knowingness to earthly situations. It is not accidental that the name of the most ancient Hindu scriptures called the *Vedas* translates from Sanskrit as, "Truth" and "Wisdom."

The open-minded state of Wisdom encourages and allows our One Wise Self to live through us. *Kings 5:9-10* states, "The Most High gave Solomon wisdom." Intriguingly, while the Greek Orthodox Church depicts Jesus as a baby in the arms of the Virgin Mary, he is shown with the face of a grown man, symbolizing his innate Wisdom. I regularly find myself cherishing the fact that some people and groups in today's predominantly money-oriented world still measure one's wealth by their Wisdom.

Actively Receptive

Chokmah's receptivity intimates the innumerable mythological, religious, and mystical-spiritual references that equate Wisdom with the feminine principle. Having an actively receptive attitude is a prerequisite for Wisdom to enter.

Essentially, Wisdom arises only when we are ready to *receive* it. From this comes Wisdom's linkage with the numerous goddess of spiritual wisdom such as the Greek Sophia. Scholars say King Solomon's marriage to Holy Sophia is spoken of in the Old Testament's "Song of Songs." On this note, the Greek Deuterocanonical book (not included in the Old Testament), *The Book of Wisdom 9:8-11* tells us that Sophia instructed Solomon in building the great temple in Jerusalem. Solomon is said to have put her in the form of the ancient Semitic Mother Goddess, Ashtoreth, inside the completed temple.

When mediating between two mothers fighting for ownership of the same baby, Solomon wisely put himself into a receptive position with the certainty that he would know how to most wisely proceed. His decision to cut the baby in half and give each mother "her share" proved to be genuinely astute. Rather than seeing her newborn killed, the true mother gave the false mother the baby, leading the King to award the giver the infant. In this sense, Wisdom may be the unification of opposing forces for the benefit of all concerned, whether they are cognizant of it or not.

Movin' on up the Evolutionary Ladder

Psychologically speaking, Wisdom has to do with how we problem-solve. It is the act of defining an issue; determining, whenever possible, the cause of it; identifying, prioritizing, selecting possible solutions; and implementing what we judge to be best. Essentially, we accumulate Wisdom by living life. When belittling myself for not doing something perfectly, I am able to relax and recall my grandmother's wise words, "Be patient, little one. You live and you learn."

On a slightly different note, the wise have the innate responsibility to dispassionately share their Wisdom, without being attached to others paying attention to it. In this sense, Wisdom means possessing the attitude of an experienced gardener planting seeds—some sprout and grow, while others do not.

Qabalists perceive three types of Wisdom—universal, collective, and personal. As we mature spiritually, our thoughts, feelings, words, and actions become increasingly aligned with universal Wisdom. Inherent to the evolution of consciousness, both personal and planetary, is applying the Wisdom we have to ascend the evolutionary ladder. That is, after mastering one situation, which requires incorporating what we have learned, the need to know more arises to help us become wiser.

Notion and Knowingness

Kether, the Crown, is questing for some notion of the Divinity, God/dess, Supreme Spirit, and the like. Chokmah or Wisdom, on the other hand, is seeking and receiving the knowledge by which to live in closer alignment with that Spirit. Living in Wisdom is being increasingly conscious of our thoughts, words, and actions. It is possessing the awareness, desire, and ability to satisfy our deepest desires while simultaneously living by our spiritual ideals. I find it comforting to know in my heart of hearts that eventually—in what I call Divine Time—each human will mature to the point wherefrom we become compelled to seek out and enact universal Wisdom, despite what the consequences of doing so might be. (While best, it is not always easy going against "the crowd.")

In closing, Wisdom may be conceptualized as a blessing, sometimes in deep disguise, from on high. Such is what wise parents aim to teach their children and what sages intend to impart to their students. Through knowledge and the Wisdom that grows from it, we learn how to better perceive ourselves and interact more consciously with the world around us. Wisdom is a priceless key to the door of living a genuinely more fulfilling life by opening our minds to the great teacher, of life experience.

CHOKMAH IN PICTURES

The Hebrew word for Wisdom, Chokmah, is comprised of the letters *Cheth, Kaph, Mem,* and *Heh*. As suggested under Kether, some of Wisdom's most profound meanings may be understood by meditating on the tarot's imagery. Once again, these images were derived from meditations on the Hebrew alphabet: Cheth means fence—the Chariot card. Kaph indicates a grasping hand—the Wheel of Fortune card. Mem signifies water—the Hanged Man card. Heh denotes a window—the Emperor card. Before proceeding, first consider contemplating the imagery and symbolism of these cards with regard to Wisdom, first. My meditation revealed the following:

The Chariot Card and Hebrew Letter, Cheth

The Chariot's corresponding Hebrew letter Cheth, meaning fence refers to an enclosure that functions both as a protective and defensive barrier between what is inside and what is out. I am wise when I am not fenced in by superficial evaluations of good and bad. The card reminds me of my innate and sacred marriage to heaven plus the Wisdom of maintaining healthy boundaries. Yet, from another view, the card suggests the Wisdom of acknowledging my intellectual limitations and being open to judiciously venturing beyond what my senses, emotions, and biology are moving me towards accepting as wise.

The Wheel of Fortune and Hebrew Letter, Kaph

The letter Kaph, denoting a grasping hand coupled with the Wheel of Fortune, prompts me to remember that wherever I am in my life cycle, I have the opportunity to reach for Wisdom and benefit from all my life experiences. Doing so holds the potential of encouraging me to behave intelligently and co-create fortunate outcomes from the circumstances the wheel of life is continually generating. Essentially, to decide which actions and attitudes are wise to propagate and which are wise to terminate. I am wise to perceive the Wisdom encoded within unfortunate circumstances.

The Hanged One Card and Hebrew Letter, Mem

The Hanged One and its corresponding Hebrew letter Mem, water, implies that when rooted in heaven, Self-reflection sometimes reveals that the wisest action is the reverse of what I have been taught by my family, peers, culture, and society-collective Wisdom. Essential to the development of Wisdom is becoming progressively more attached to above, while living on earth, below.

The Emperor Card and Hebrew Letter, Heh

The Emperor and letter Heh, window, underscores the value of consciously opening myself to the light of Wisdom while in the midst of daily life. The card is conjoined with the sense of sight, a reminder that it is wise to train myself to see the Wisdom embedded within all of my experiences. Doing this I open the window of my mind, to the fact that everything that occurs in the physical world has the potential to contribute to my evolution and that of humankind.

LOCATION, LOCATION, LOCATION:

CHOKMAH'S PLACEMENT ON THE TREE OF LIFE

Kether, the Great Androgyne, is the absolute cosmic unity from which the positive and negative, masculo-feminine polarities of Chokmah, Wisdom and Binah, Understanding are born. Chokmah is the second sephirah or emanation on the Tree of Life within the Supernal, Divine, or Heavenly Triad. This energetically tangible projection of Kether heads the Pillar of Mercy and signifies the past, time-wise.

Situated on the causal plane, Chokmah's role is to create an effect in Binah. Chokmah is the principle of divine reason and order, the Word or Logos that stimulates and ushers the universe into being. In doing so, it brings us to consider the first of the Tree of Life's paired sephiroth, Chokmah and Binah, which may be likened to two sides of the same coin. Although appearing to be separate, they are inseparable. These two sephiroth are like two friends who never part, and their unification produces the life flow that sustains the physical world. Notice how these spheres co-exist at the same level within the Supernal Triad. Again, the Cosmic Father Chokmah receives his potency from the Kether above, and cannot do anything but respond to the Cosmic Mother Binah's seductive force field. This interaction shows Chokmah and Binah to be the primal, underlying co-creative energy behind and within all forms. In the simplest sense, Wisdom stems from Understanding what has gone before and its relationship to the present.

Chokmah is perception attained through the quick primal flash of mind, the spark of genius and vibration of creation, whereas Binah involves labor and contemplation. Binah functions to expand, analyze, and synthesize the elements of intuitive thought. Therefore, every idea sown by Chokmah has a period of gestation in Binah's Understanding, which readies it for outer exposure or life.

The Thickening of Matter

Kether symbolizes the present and Chokmah signifies the past. With the passing of time, evolution starts gathering the particles composing life as we know it. Alternatively, Chokmah is the impregnating seed, and Binah is the vessel in which the seed receives its form. This cooperative process slows down molecular movement, resulting in the "thickening" or densification of matter that eventually congeals into tangible forms. In the obscure Hindu myth, the "Fire Mist," a sea of milk is churned by the Creator, and out of this churning comes the solidifying forms of stars and planets—in effect the nebula theory of modern astronomy. According to astronomers, the "Fire Mist" is composed of the primordial hydrogen atoms from which matter aka the physical world originates.

Tendency

The best way to describe the causal plane is tendency—the inclination to be or behave in a certain way. From the natural attraction occurring between the spheres of Chokmah, Wisdom, the Creator, and Binah, Understanding, the Creatrix, the positive and negative polarities of Cosmic Fire and Cosmic Water, emerge the rest of the Tree of Life, and life. While the entire physical world emanates from the mating of Chokmah and Binah on the causal plane such are actually spawned by Kether, on the spiritual plane—making them conscious co-creators. This interrelationship is encapsulated by the Sanskrit word *arohati* meaning both "to be" and "to grow."

From another angle, act of cosmic copulation touches upon the quantum physics-flavored Anthropic Cosmological Principle. While the analysis of this principle lies outside the field of exact science, as a philosophical premise I find it exceedingly thought-provoking. It asserts that the laws of physics have been specifically designed and fine-tuned to ensure that life arises to permit its existence to continue. This principle further contends that because we observers exist, the Universe exists in such a way that *allows* us to come into existence!

Pater Matters

As abstract as it might seem, Kether is pure Isness, while Chokmah is pure Beingness. We make things from pre-existing materials, yet Spirit made something out of nothing when manifesting the stars and planets. After Chokmah, the Paternal Crown of Creation and Father of Matter projects all the life-giving potential received from

Kether above into Binah, the Maternal Crown of Creation and Mother of Matter, finitizes it further, by bestowing it with its particular *neshama*, divine nature or soul. While these parallel forces appear opposing, they are inseparable. The vigorous drive of Chokmah's vibrant fire of life or *chaiah*, to unite with Binah's actively receptive and formative principle, brings forth life, as we know it. Chokmah's positive polarity and substance projects, stimulates, and enlivens Binah's negative polarity and substance— resulting in a sublimely productive interchange and synthesis of energies. While all does originate from Kether, it is in the aforementioned way, that Chokmah is the true beginning of every creative cycle.

Creation: Intangibility into Tangibility and Back Again

Creation is a word signifying the process of objectification, or the flow of invisible forces into visible manifestation. Science has proven that because energy is the movement state of mass, and the movement of mass cannot be created or destroyed it simply changes from one form to another, Creation is not technically the beginning of anything. It is eternally existing forces assuming temporary patterns or forms. These patterns remain for a certain time and then dissolve, disappearing back into invisibility only to reappear at another phase in this cycle. Theologically speaking, creation is the formation of a perceptible universe under the direction of universal or cosmic intelligence, termed God, God/dess, Divinity, Spirit, and so on. In this sense, creation is the incarnation of the supreme principle that builds the form of the world, exactly as the incarnating human spirit builds its body. Consequently, the physical world is the body of Spirit subject to growth, maturity, and decay, just as the human body is subject to these shifts. This makes the creation process the release of intangibility into tangibility, followed by the release of tangibility into intangibility.

Intention and Attention

Whether it is the Godhead intending to create the manifest world, or the human mind intending to produce a work of art or breakfast, the process is identical: setting the intention to create, followed by the attention to actually creating. It makes sense that genuine mystical-spiritual traditions regard all forms of creativity to be sacred. This concept is exemplified in the use of modern languages, such as when we speak of creative "inspiration," the act of drawing in a breath. Chokmah draws in the life force from Kether, which then starts shaping reality and bringing new ideas to the world. Paul Case's *Pattern on the Trestleboard* says of Chokmah, "Through me, its unfailing Wisdom takes form in thought and word," intimating that the Divine Mind is so powerful that anything it thinks, is.

Rounding this out, *The Zohar*, or "Book of Splendor," describes creation in this way: "The Source, Kether, gives forth a current of supersensory energy, Chokmah, which turns into a sea, Binah, whose waters flow from the sea into seven channels, the remaining seven sephiroth of comprised of ebbing and flowing sensory energy. Essentially, each sephirah has both incoming and outgoing energies-runs on an alternating current.

Made By Mind

Among other philosophies, Qabalah proposes that the world is made by the mind, sustained by the mind, and destroyed by the mind—whether this is the one great impersonal mind or one's personal mind. Therefore, in the ordinary sense of reality, nothing exists at all; everything is comprised of "mind stuff." If you think you live in the world, think again. You live in your mind, which lives in the one great mind. This concept calls up mathematician, physicist, and astronomer James Jean's idea that; "The universe begins to look more like a great thought than like a great machine."

Time Past

Chokmah is situated in time that has passed, which may influence the present and future. An Old English proverb sums up the past's relationship with Wisdom as follows: "It is easier to be wise after an event." To reiterate, time may be categorized in numerous ways: among them are eternal, relative, and biological time. Chokmah is relative time, the non-spatial continuum in which events occur in apparently irreversible succession from the past to the present and into the future. Relative time helps us to understand, and perhaps analyze and improve upon, a creative endeavor—or any endeavor—from beginning to end. Another example is seen in Chokmah's correspondence with the sphere of the planets, luminaries, and zodiac whose orderly and repetitive movements help us refer to when events occur, and how these are related to others.

Feedback Loops

I find it fascinating that some quantum physicists propose that the universe is built like a feedback loop in which we humans may input and reconfigure the present, future, and to some degree, the past. Awareness of this concept definitely piqued my interest to know more. Feedback loops are natural occurrences wherein the output of a system resulting from an action, biological or otherwise, moves that system out of or into equilibrium. For example: when the output from an action amplifies a system, such as in the ripening of fruit and the contractions occurring during childbirth, a positive feedback loop occurs. Conversely, when the output from an action quiets or inhibits a system, as in the regulation of blood glucose levels and sweating, a negative feedback loop occurs.

Similar to football's "Monday Morning Quarterbacking," feedback loops are always aimed at improving whatever is being examined. Reading different historical reports of an identical event, e.g. the Supreme Court deciding the 2000 Presidential Election between George Bush and Al Gore or the necessity of bombing Hiroshima and Nagasaki to end World War II, offers examples of this potentially mind-expanding, Wisdom-engendering concept.

Of course, energy from feedback loops is also utilized to circle back and measure quality. Such may then function as input to create something better—whether it is a new and improved cell phone, electric car, or suitcase. (I am delighted to have the latest suitcase with multiple wheels that easily move it in any direction!) While exploring Wisdom, I would like to propose experimenting with directing the dynamic life force generated by a feedback loop inputted with some of the detrimental environmental activities that have occurred. I am quite certain that the data would direct us to wisely amp up Chokmah's dynamic life force, aka building the critical mass necessary to increase the health and well-being of our magnificent planet and its inhabitants.

QABALISTIC IMAGE OF CHOKMAH: A BEARDED MALE

Please note: although the ancient archetype for maleness, this Qabalistic image may signify someone of any sex who is predominately male-identified. This brings me to mention one of the very few female pharaohs, Hatshepsut, who as part of ruling for over 20 years wore a beard. Hatshepsut's surviving statues and paintings portray her with a male body and a false beard.

The bearded male has long symbolized not only Wisdom but also Father God or "Lord of Lords." Males in particular cultures, such as the Amish, are not permitted to grow beards until they are married. Here, the bearded man signifies the male who has matured and proven his manhood and potency, versus his unbearded or *untested* counterpart. The words test and testes, come from the same Latin root as testicle. This *attests* to the fact that in many cultures the pubescent descent of the testes along with beard growth proclaims biological manhood, yet not Wisdom. This is a reminder that Wisdom is the by-product of living and learning.

Lastly, one group of students became creative with this image. Together they envisioned Chokmah's Bearded Male to be Santa Claus, placing the gift of Wisdom on the Tree of Life!

THE SEPHER YETZIRAH, NAMES CHOKMAH,

THE ILLUMINATING INTELLIGENCE

Again, each Qabalistic Intelligence is a means of describing the powers of the Universal Mind, which, through the development of our human minds or intelligence, become a force or tool through which to behave with ever-increasing amounts of intelligence and integrity. The Illuminating Intelligence cues us to recall that when we invite the light of greater awareness into our minds, we are increasingly able to think, speak, and act with increasing amounts of Wisdom.

Chokmah, the sphere of Wisdom, is the Illuminating Intelligence. To illuminate is to fill with light, shed light upon, enlighten, and make clear. This action verb suggests the current that flips on the light of the Universal Life Force within creation. This Intelligence or power asserts that the manifest world is imbued with the sacred light of Spirit. It conveys the mystical meaning of the first chapter of *Genesis*: "And God said, 'Let there be light' and there was light." Illumination allows us to see what Kether's Hidden Intelligence obscures. That is, if I enter a darkened house, its contents are invisible, yet when I switch on the lights, its contents become visible and distinguishable from one another; in this sense, we have the first step of the creative process.

Someone who is especially wise has been seen to actually emit and spread the light of Wisdom. One who is filled with this light, and radiates it is sometimes called an *illuminati*. (Please note there is no relationship to this modern elitist group other than by its name). I cherish a photo of the Indian Saint Sri Ramakrishna actually emitting light while engrossed in chanting the name of *his* beloved Divine Mother, Kali. From such phenomena comes the term en-lighten-ment, one who is endowed with deep spiritual knowledge or Wisdom. As you may have experienced light is contagious. When someone is radiating light it spreads outwards to uplift others. Furthermore, whether we are cognizant of it or not, lighting a candle when beginning a ritual intimates the intention to connect with the Illuminating Intelligence.

Because Chokmah is also the sphere of the planets and luminaries, it is worthwhile considering photosynthesis along with the Illuminating Intelligence. Essentially, without sunlight, there would be no food and thus no life on planet Earth. This fact deems us humans and all of creation children of the sun's Illuminating Intelligence. We are enlivened, grown, and sustained by the light of the Illuminating Intelligence, which has downloaded the hidden and most admirable light of Kether.

The Illuminating Intelligence in Action

Here is a small example of the Illuminating Intelligence in action. Almost every time I met with my dear friend Cora, who has a somewhat dark sense of humor, she would make caustic remarks about life and me. Although I knew she was joking, my feelings were at times hurt. I was faced with what I thought to be my only choice. I could continue enduring her behavior and do my best to laugh, or I could spend less time with her. Contemplating the situation, I suddenly realized that both options kept me in the dark! Along with my realization, I was zapped with the inspiration to turn on the lights. (Ah ha, the Illuminating Intelligence!) I "got" that I needed to ask her about her comments.

The next time we met for a walk I took a deep breath of inspiration and asked, "Each time we meet, you make sarcastic comments about my life, which quite honestly hurt my feelings. Please tell me if I've said or done anything to upset you, and if so, what?" Doing this resulted in an apology from my friend, and her tearful admission that she felt jealous of the fact that I was then in a long-term relationship, something she had been unable to maintain.

My question and Cora's answer led to an exchange that ended up with her waving her arms while emphatically stating, "I'm a serial monogamist who would be a polygamist—if I could be!" She went on to joke that she presently would not want to be with *any* of her former flames "even if they were alive, divorced, straight or otherwise available." While sharing a wonderful hug, she tearfully expressed her appreciation for me caring enough about our friendship to share how I was feeling and ask her to explain her sarcastic statements. Thanks to being courageous and caring enough to act on the Illuminating or "Zapping" Intelligence, our friendship deepened.

THE SPIRITUAL EXPERIENCE OF CHOKMAH:

THE VISION OF THE MOST HIGH FACE-TO-FACE

Chokmah's Spiritual Experience is the Vision of the Most High Face-to- Face. The classic medieval tale of the pure and perfect Sir Galahad's attainment of the Holy Grail clearly and movingly describes this experience and then Kether's state of Unified Existence. "He had but glanced within when a violent trembling seized his mortal flesh at the contemplation of the spiritual mysteries. After expressing gratitude to heaven that he can, 'see revealed what tongue could not relate nor heart conceive,' Galahad completes his quest and dies."

The Old Testament offers other references to this type of occurrence when describing how, after Moses descended from Mt. Sinai following his face-to-face meeting with the Most High, he was so filled with the Illuminating Intelligence, or the Glory of the Most High, that he covered his face. Moses did this to quell people's conviction that they would die from beholding such heavenly radiance.

The belief that no human may gaze upon the face of the Divine Countenance and not be drawn into personal oblivion—Union with the Most High—and live is widely held in many traditions. Yet reading the writings of the German Christian mystic and poet Mechthild of Magdeburg (1209-1299) gives a somewhat different perspective. Mechthild's poetry states that because of her burning love and longing to see God, she experienced *Visio Dei* (Vision of the Most High Face-to-Face). It is further written that after seeing God face-to-face, her thirst was not quenched and she continued longing to be united with God in an "undivided condition." In the final minutes before her death, Mechthild is said to have experienced the *Unio Mystica*, Kether's Unified Existence, and left her body in a state of absolute bliss.

Cognitive Dissonance

Although what follows will likely evoke a certain amount of cognitive dissonance, Qabalists don't have to find the Holy Grail, ascend the holy mountain, or participate in stringent esoteric practices to come face-to-face with Divinity. All we need do is to look into a mirror and be open to knowing that we are actually seeing God/dess, enlivening our body. We are gods and goddesses made manifest! Alternatively as one of my teachers quipped, we are Godlings!

Taking this a step further, Wisdom is our evolving ability to view all life presents us as reflections of divinity, and along with it, the opportunity to behave wisely. In reality, we are beholding the face of the Most High in the guise of such as our ex-spouse, uncooperative child, difficult co-worker, closed-hearted boss, corrupt politician, naughty pet, racist neighbor, the driver who cuts us off, the neighbor's cat lying in wait for birds eating at the birdfeeder, and so on. While this may be a tall order, each offers the opportunity to perceive Spirit's presence. By doing this, we apply and expand our personal Wisdom as well as call forth universal Wisdom to help us rise above our erroneous personal and/or collective Wisdom.

Fascination, Dread, and Disorientation

We have been conditioned from birth (or before) to view ourselves as separate beings, a state that has its advantages and disadvantages. Envisioning the Most High Face-to-Face is a direct result of reconditioning ourselves to begin sensing ourselves, others, and the world around us as Divinity in manifest form. There is, however, a mixture of fascination and dread coupled with the possibility of experiencing this perception. These feelings are usually linked with fearing death or personal oblivion of our body and ego when facing Reality. Yet, eventually, a compelling desire for this sublime state comes to prevail.

Certainly, fearfulness also stems from seeing *through* whom we believe ourselves to be, to the being we, in fact, are. Experiencing such ecstasy causes a disorientation, that is actually, a reorientation, in which we temporarily lose our personal identity, yet simultaneously gain the ability to identify with Spirit Supreme. The altered state of impersonality, the cosmic consciousness from which one reenters their physical body, evokes great apprehension outside of mystical-spiritual circles. However, those who evolve to encounter it become capable of bringing needed Wisdom to the world.

FEATURING: CHOKMAH

NUMBER, TWO: Mathematically speaking, when referring to the number one, Kether, there is no subject or object. Extending the concept of one, the number two sephirah, Chokmah, brings the possibility of seeing the object perceived from the subject's point of view.

Two is synonymous with duplication, interdependence, reflection, and creativity. Like Roman Number II, Chokmah is a mirror image of the One. This number illustrates the activities of Kether and Chokmah to be interdependent, as are the activities of creation with the Chokmah and Binah. Inherent in number two is the idea of dynamic splitting and multiplying. "And God said: 'Let us make man in Our image, after Our likeness'..."(*Genesis 1:26)*. The activity of Chokmah splits off and projects itself out from Kether to manifest the physical universe, which is carried a step further via Chokmah's symbiotic relationship with Binah.

Qabalistic numerologists equate two with revelation, a synonym for Wisdom. This signifies that whatever appears to us in the world is an unconcealed sacred duality because it originates from the One. It further implies how the number two is the dynamic aspect of number one.

Wisdom has the dual qualities of receptivity, projectivity, and thereby inter-dependence. Chokmah is receptive when it functions as a reflection of the primal up welling of Kether's life force, projective when it responds to and extends this force to meet Binah's magnetic receptiveness, and inter-dependent since it cannot actualize itself without the instigation of Kether and Binah.

COLOR, GREY: Grey has long been associated with the ideas of neutrality, maturity, and its byproduct Wisdom. Wisdom is the open-minded state of adopting a neutral attitude; therefore, it is not surprising that the "neutral" color grey is linked with this sephirah. The achromatic Grey, like Wisdom, unites the opposites of black and white, Kether and Binah, respectively. Being a combination of black and white, grey suggests how our dark and light experiences have the potential to make us wiser.

The terms "grey head" and "grey beard" are used to signify Wisdom. Genuine Wisdom arises we are seasoned enough to let go of our pre-conceptions to examine what is before us as objectively as humanly possible. Similarly, when demonstrating mental superiority, one is said to be using their "grey matter." Finally, grey clouds usually indicate rain and the fertility that follows.

GEMSTONE, THE STAR RUBY: When the ruby—sometimes called the King of Gemstones to compliment Chokmah's kingship—is cut in a rounded form, it often exhibits a six-rayed star in the center of its dome. The rays always appear white regardless of the color of the stone, intimating the fact that Kether dwells within all of creation. The ruby is the color of the blood of life, which is set flowing in Chokmah. Because of its warm color, ancients believed this stone imprisoned a holy glowing spark (Kether), which would not dim or extinguish until the earth itself died.

Although not the star ruby, the Old Testament's *Book of Proverbs 8:11* and *20:15* contrasts rubies and Wisdom: "For wisdom is better than rubies, and all the things that may be desired are not to be compared to it." "There is gold, and a multitude of rubies: but the lips of knowledge are a precious jewel."

Of course, I *must* mention the magical ruby slippers gifted to Dorothy by Glenda, the Good Witch of the East, in the movie *The Wizard of Oz.* Along with them, Dorothy was also given the message, "Now you will always know how to get home." This event may be seen as a metaphor for the development of Wisdom that eventually leads homeward to Kether.

GEMSTONE, TURQUOISE: Egyptian, Tibetan, Nepalese, Navajo and other Native American peoples have long regarded turquoise as the "sacred sky stone," descending to earth from the heavens above. These groups, among others, use turquoise for its spiritual powers to protect wearers and facilitate creative problem-solving. History states that the Egyptians first mined turquoise in the wilderness of the Sinai Peninsula. This suggests how Wisdom may be found by courageously venturing and willfully digging into the unknown.

SCENT, MUSK: Musk, the basis for many perfumes, is the scent conjoined with Chokmah. Derived from the Sanskrit, *Muska* means testicle or scrotum. This substance or pheromone found in a gland located within a testicle-like pouch on the stomach of the male musk deer is excreted to attract and excite females—hence its connection with the potent, archetypically masculine energies of Chokmah.

Like ambergris, musk is primarily used as a fixative in perfumes, suggesting how the vibrant energies of Chokmah project the Life Force that will *fix* the life forms within the sphere of Binah. Musk is presently used solely in synthetic form,

PLANT, THE BODHI OR PIPA TREE: This species of fig is often called the "Tree of Wisdom or Enlightenment." It was under the branches of this tree that Prince

Siddhartha sat and became the Buddha. Prince Siddhartha changed his soul contract from that of a Prince who had all things, to that of a Wiseone who had all Wisdom. Upon receiving Chokmah's Illuminating Intelligence, he also received the potent ability to share the Wisdom teachings he had received with others.

PLANT, AMARANTH: Amaranth is a Greek word that means "unfading and eternally beautiful." The mythical amaranth flower is considered one of the central symbols for immortality, as it is alleged to never wither or fade. This description may also be applied to Chokmah, since its power never diminishes and Wisdom retains its beauty forever. In addition, the Amaranth plant grows upright like corn and explodes into hundreds of thousands of pods when ripe, forming a kinship with the perpetual cosmic ejaculations of Chokmah.

The abundant and life-sustaining Amaranth plant is a complete protein. The Aztec Indians believed it hold supernatural energy and power and used it in their many rites and ceremonies. As part of Hernando Cortez's inhumane conquest, enslavement, and attempt to force Christianity upon the Aztecs, he prohibited the eating and worship of Amaranth.

ANIMAL, THE EAGLE: Known as "King of the Birds," a symbol of male dominion, strength, bravery, freedom, and power, the eagle is paired with Chokmah. Believed to fly higher than almost any other bird, the eagle signified divine majesty to the ancients. Eagles are said to be the only living creature that can look directly into the sun (an ancient symbol of divinity and a reference to the Vision of the Most High Face-to-Face) without damaging their eyes.

Called "Champion of Heaven," the eagle is often shown bearing a thunderbolt, a symbol of Chokmah, the Godhead and God Zeus, in its talons. Welsh legends tell of the bird carrying the souls of brave warriors to heaven. In ancient Sumer, the eagle brought children into the world and carried departed souls to the under-world. Although the eyes of this magnificent bird may see in both directions, it looks straight ahead. This reiterates how, like true Wisdom, this creature sees beyond life dualities to consider it from a wise perspective that encompasses the One Transcendent Reality.

It stands to reason that the eagle presides over the East, the seat of Illumination on the Native American Medicine Wheel. Furthermore, this majestic bird is said to usher in "the Word" of the Great Spirit, as does Chokmah. Similarly, the Prophet Elijah, who is said to have called down fire from heaven and rose to heaven in a fiery chariot, is said to have appeared as an eagle.

The eagle has long been identified with the concept of divine fatherhood, fertilizing divine motherhood and the world of nature. Finally, the Egyptian hieroglyphic for the Sun is the eagle, and the Moon is represented by the owl. These links remind us that Chokmah is the sphere of the planets and luminaries on the Tree of Life.

ANIMAL, THE OWL: This bird has signified Wisdom since antiquity. A sage or wiseone is often depicted carrying an owl on their shoulder. Able to move its head 360 degrees, this creature intimates that Wisdom arises from the ability to perceive life from many points of view. Because owls have superior nocturnal vision, they hunt at night. This practice reminds us of the fact that the pursuit and attainment of Wisdom often ask us to penetrate the darkness of ignorance. Wisdom is coupled with comprehension or grasping; the sharp-taloned owl and eagle have the ability to seek and tenaciously hold onto what they are seeking.

MEDICINES AND DRUGS: COCAINE: Cocaine is the food, medicine, and super-stimulating and numbing (thus addictive) drug linked with Chokmah. Please note I am aiming to present a broad perspective on the use (positive, negative and in-between) properties and ancient role of cocaine as a mystical-spiritual sacrament.

As a food, coca leaves contain a significant percentage of the minimum daily requirement of vitamins and minerals needed for human survival. This is partially why it became incorporated into the diet of people in areas such as the Amazon and Andes, where a full complement of foods are often unavailable or difficult to obtain. Coca is also a potent appetite suppressant, allaying the pain of hunger and providing needed physical energy to those in regions where slowly metabolized proteins are scarce.

Another of coca's qualities that promote addiction is its ability to stimulate mental clarity; with respect to the sphere of Wisdom, the clearer the mind, and the wiser the individual. As cocaine excites the central nervous system, it also produces euphoria and at times hallucinogenic experiences. This explains why it has been used to promote the altered states inherent in certain shamanic rites for perhaps thousands of years. Certain Mexican and South American Indian tribes ritualistically gave coca to their human sacrifices to sanctify the act. Such was likely meant to raise their awareness above the physical and ease their fear of pain and death.

Because cocaine's numbing and arousing effects can increase male and female sexual pleasure by prolonging the duration of both penile and clitoral erections, it is linked with Chokmah's virility and potency. I guess you might say cocaine is the original Viagra and Ristela!

In Sir Arthur Conan Doyle's short novel, *The Sign of Four*, Sherlock Holmes comments on his own, and in doing so Conan Doyle's, use of cocaine: "I suppose that its influence is physically a bad one. I find it, however, so transcendently stimulating and clarifying to the mind that its secondary action is a matter of small amount." It is not surprising, then, that in the Western world cocaine is considered more *psychologically* than physiologically addictive. In addition to providing only mental clarity, cocaine is so energizing that it can make its user feel supremely powerful and competent while under the influence; hence its connection to Chokmah's supreme physical and mental potency.

My one and only adventure with cocaine went like this: My next-door neighbor offered me a line of "Snow White," when she saw me setting up to rototill the garden one warm and sunny early spring morning. By day's end, I had tilled the large garden plot, swam a mile in the early afternoon, phoned a few friends, prepped and cooked dinner, and if that were not enough, wrote a brief outline for a talk I was going to give in a few weeks, and enjoyed tantric love-making before going to sleep! Although the experience made me feel like Wonder Woman, to omit the "crash," and the fact that my body ached and I felt pretty much "brain-dead" for several days afterward, would be too much of a "Give Coke a Dance" commercial.

THE SACRAMENT OF CHOKMAH, WISDOM, IS COMMUNION

Paralleling how the paired sephiroth share the same plane and Seven Inner Stars on the Tree of Life, they also divvy up the sacraments, which with regard to Chokmah and Binah is Communion. Father Chokmah sends out the *non-specific* imperceptible universal forces originating from Kether, which Mother Binah then conceives, gestates, and gives birth both to the *specific* shapes of perceptible creation and the sephiroth below the abyss or Tree of Life's spiritual plane. The fleshy forms or bread of life that Mother Binah delivers as the physical universe are the result of her Holy Communion with Kether through Father Chokmah's fertilization with the wine of his life force.

Intimate Exchange

The Latin root of communion is *communionem*, meaning mutual participation, sharing, fellowship, or partnership. Communion is synonymous with intimate exchange, the sharing of thoughts, feelings, and experiences, inter-communication, petitioning, communing, closeness, togetherness, mutual acceptance, and rapport. Fittingly, practitioners of Judaism are taught from childhood to actually speak with God daily. Muslims worship and bow to Mecca, and thereby the teachings of Allah, five times each day. The Universal Life Force descends from Kether on the spiritual plane into Chokmah on the causal plane. Nature's positive polarity in the form of Cosmic Father Chokmah then projects himself out to commune with, and have "knowledge of," his soul mate, Cosmic Mother Binah. This Holy Communion or cosmic intercourse is what brings the world into being.

Soul Food

The practice of regularly communing with Spirit through prayer and meditation, rituals, teachers, guides, groups, and so on is ancient. One student described this as "Getting right with the God inside and outside of me." The Christian concept of Communion, called the Eucharist originates at the Last Supper that Jesus shared with his disciples on the first night of Passover, mere hours before he is arrested and subsequently crucified. During this meal, Jesus took a cup of wine and a piece of unleavened bread, requesting everyone present to drink and eat it, stating that such are his blood and body. Roman Catholicism terms this change transubstantiation. By doing this, Jesus wisely forges the three-way spiritual link of Holy Communion between himself, his followers, and his heavenly parentage. Tuning into and communing with Chokmah opens Qabalists to the transcendent Wisdom encoded therein. *Matthew: 18-20* underscores this: "When two or more are gathered in my name, I am there among them."

When upset due to one sort or another of our old habits, life's stresses and distresses, problems with others, a lack of knowledge, blurred perception, uncertainty regarding what, if anything, to now say and do prevails, the Soul Food of Communion is always available to turn to for the nourishment of Wisdom. When entering this receptive state all thoughts and feelings are fully welcomed and explored. Achieving the impersonal state of Communion then necessitates our full-on willingness to acknowledge and then bypass any personal attachments and aversions regarding how we ourselves, others, and the world *should* or *should not* be. Taking this route we become increasingly open to drawing in the clearest Wisdom we are now capable of receiving in the form of universal and natural laws, truths, and principles. I find this perceptively encapsulated in the *Serenity Prayer* from Alcoholic's Anonymous:

"God, grant me the serenity to accept the things I cannot change,
the courage to change the things I can,
and the *Wisdom* to know the difference."

Through our open-minded and heartfelt contemplation of the teachings of Chokmah we receive cues, such as: Discerning the Wisdom, integrity, or sensibility of an action or decision. Integrating an experience or information that improves our mental clarity and life.

Engaging in this way or via the likes of prayer and meditation or similar practices, dialoguing with an insightful mentor, counselor, teacher, friend, or group assist us in recognizing the true nature or Wisdom of what has, now is, or might arise in the future, Communion is realized. (Getting a good cardio-vascular workout by swimming or biking sometimes brings me needed clarity.) The ongoing enactment of Communion supports us to fulfill the sacred work or contract we agreed to when baptized on the spiritual plane in Kether.

A SEPHIRAH BY ANY OTHER NAME:

CHOKMAH'S ALTERNATIVE TITLES

THE CREATOR-GENITOR: Chokmah is the Creator or Genitor, the projective counterpart and adjunct to the feminine-receptive Creatrix or Genitrix. Together these forces bring the world into being. Wisdom, the Cosmic Father, is dynamic potential, whereas Understanding, the Cosmic Mother, is the elaborator or development of that potential into particularized forms—animal, vegetable, or mineral.

Chokmah sends the invisible, intangible, hidden potency of the Most High received from Kether to Binah and tangibility. He is the movement away from the One towards the many. Functioning in this way, Chokmah is the steward of the universal life force on its way into form. To present a balanced picture, Chokmah is receptive when accepting the energies of Kether, and projective when sending these to Binah.

THE SUPERNAL, CELESTIAL, OR HEAVENLY FATHER: Supernal means "that which emanates from on high or from heaven." Chokmah is the cosmic emanation that enhances and balances out the Supernal Mother, Binah. The Supernal Father is the One Great Spirit in the bifurcated form of Father God, nature's positive polarity that compliments the Supernal Mother, the One Great Spirit in the form of Mother Goddess, and nature's negative polarity. Together they are our heavenly parents from which creation is birthed.

ABBA, AB, FATHER, PAPA, BABA: Both *Abba* and *Ab* translate from Hebrew to mean "Father." Father and God the Father are traditional names given to the male aspect of divinity. It is also an honorable designation given to someone of spiritual eminence in the Judeo-Christian tradition such as a rabbi, priest, or pope. Linguistically, pope stems from the Latin *Papa* and Greek *Papas*, meaning father.

Of course, words and concepts do travel! Baba, the name I was taught to call my Russian great-grandmother, turned out to be an honorific Persian term used for elders of either sex. In India and several West Asian and South Asian cultures, Baba refers to a wise old man, male spiritual teacher, grandfather, father, and in some instances, an endearing name for male children.

THE GREAT STIMULATOR AND INITIATOR: This title speaks of the cosmic vitality that arouses and accelerates all creative cycles. It is the drive of the Universal Life Force toward the manifestation of myriad forms. Chokmah projects this dynamic current of cosmic energy received from Kether into Binah, the womb of the world, to co-create physicality.

THE INNER ROBE OF GLORY: Although possibly blasphemous to some, I liken the Inner Robe of Glory to underwear! Cosmically speaking, it is the undergarment that supports the outer garment of the world. This basic inner fabric of creation is the radiant holy light or Illuminating Intelligence that ignites everything that comes into the physical world with life. Simply, the impersonal Divine Spirit of Kether flows into Chokmah—to comprise the internal support to every external.

THE HIGHWAY OF LIFE: A highway is both a direct and main road between one place and another. Chokmah is such a passageway as it is the first dynamic acceleration, the all-mighty thrust of high voltage cosmic electricity that routes Kether's otherworldly potential outwards into Chokmah. Chokmah then dynamically propels it into Binah, and in this way, the remaining sephiroth and physical form.

TETRAGRAMMATON: The four-lettered Tetragrammaton is the Hebrew's unspeakable, personal name for Father God *Yod, Heh, Vav, Heh*. Judaism's ban against speaking or writing the true name of God was aimed at preventing it from being used as a curse and as a form of humility resulting in it being abbreviated as YHVH, JHVH, or IHVH. Originally used as a sacred medium for ensuring the continuation of life, only the head rabbi could speak this word in the Holy of Holies at the start of the New Year. This concept further suggests the ability to pronounce the Tetragrammaton bestows humans with superhuman powers that Qabalah teaches we are born with, yet are required to cultivate.

Theoretically, each of the four letters represents a step in the descending ladder of existence also known as "the Word." The Tetragrammaton is conjoined with the four Qabalistic Worlds, elements of nature, and a recipe for creation, as follows: Y/*Atziluth*, Fire: emanation-inspiration-ideation. H/*Briah* Water: creative imagination. V/*Yetzirah*, Air: mental formulation. H/*Assiah*, Earth: physical manifestation.

Aligned with Chokmah, the Tetragrammaton is the cosmic power that jump-starts the creation process. Qabalists regard it to be the Western equivalent of the Eastern *AUM*, the sacred, primal vibration of creation through which Spirit conducts the symphony of manifestation into form.

The Tetragrammaton is referred to in the Old Testament by way of the Most High's first words appearing in *Chapter One of Genesis* "And God said..." *The Gospel according to John (1:1-3)* elaborates upon this with the lines—"In the beginning was the Word, and the Word was with God, and the Word was God. All things were made by him, and without him was not anything made that was made."

In ancient Vedantic and Koranic philosophy, "the Word" is synonymous with the command,"Be!" Interestingly, various Christian doctrinal works equate "the Word" with the second person of the

Holy Trinity—Jesus, the son or, as Qabalists interpret it, the "children" of the Most High, the entire physical world.

The Logos: The pre-Socratic Greek philosopher Heraclitus defined Logos as "the rational constituting and controlling principle in the universe." This ancient Greek term meaning "reason," indicating the manifestation of reason, the underlying principle on which everything is founded, is usually translated as "the Word."

Corresponding to Chokmah's positioning between Kether and the remainder of the Tree of Life makes the Logos the intermediary between the ultimate reality and the perceptible world or "the Word," made flesh. Hellenistic Stoics theorized it to be the forceful cosmic generating principle pervading that, which is innate and active in the entire manifest world. A Hindu student aligned it with AUM, the fundamental cosmic vibration that exists and endures to hold physicality together. Paralleling these, Qabalists regard the Logos to be the energetically expressed thought and will of the Most High, the invisible rational principle that activates and permeates the visible world by setting creation into motion in the sphere of Chokmah.

YOD **OF THE TETRAGRAMMATON:** The Hebrew alphabet is called the Flame Alphabet. All letters are derivations of the flame-shaped letter *Yod*, the initial letter in the Tetragrammaton's formula for creation. Attributed to the first Qabalistic world of Divine emanation, inspiration, and ideation, *Assiah*, Yod is likened to a lightning bolt. Paired with the fire element, Yod vigorously jolts the omnipotent force that spurs the life cycle into motion through the sphere of Chokmah.

THE PRINCIPAL THING: Chokmah is the primary activating and enlivening force in the Universe. Qabalists related to it as the primal or original power whereby the earth was founded, designating Chokmah to be the first *tangible* essence of divinity.

THE LIGHT FORCE: This title reiterates and underscores that Chokmah is the Illuminating Intelligence, or light of the Great Spirit of the Universe, radiating throughout the manifest world. The *Book of Genesis* addresses this phenomenon in the phrase, "And God said, 'Let there be light' and there was light."

YANG: Yang is the Chinese term for the projective power linked with nature's positive polarity. Yang is the fast-moving and actively expansive, contrasting, with and complementary to Yin, the actively contractive and receptive still energy coupled with the negative polarity. Archetypical Yang energy, paired with maleness, is responsible for initiating and vitalizing the evolutionary process. Of course, as creation is a blending of positive and negative forces, without coupling with yin energy, creation will not occur. Yang provides stimulation to Yin so that conception and birth will transpire.

IN THE NAME OF HEAVEN:
DIVINE AND ARCHANGELIC PRESENCES

THE DIVINE PRESENCE OF CHOKMAH IS, *YAHWEH*

The Divine Presence coupled with Chokmah is *Yahweh*, which Qabalists translate as "Father of all Livingness." It is the most commonly known and spoken alternative for the unutterable Tetragrammaton, the four Hebrew letters Yod, Heh, Vav, Heh, or YHVH, discussed under Alternative Titles. Yahweh is also referred to as *Jah* and Jehovah. Whenever I see the word Jah I think of the monotheistic Rastafarians who call the Most High Jah, meaning "One Love." Rasta takes its term for "god," Jah, from the King James Version of *Psalm 68:4*, which reads, "Extol him that rideth upon the heavens by his name Jah, and rejoice before him." This group uses the term "I and I" reinforcing their belief that Jah exists in all and that all are one, unified by Jah's love.

The similar Sanskrit word *Jana* means knowledge and Jana Yoga is the yoga of Self-knowledge or Wisdom a prerequisite to achieving the goal of *Raja* or Royal yoga. Yod, the first letter of the Tetragrammaton, translates from Hebrew as "hand," both the hand of God and the human hand. It suggests the hand of Spirit reaching outwards and downwards to initiate creation, the remaining three letters of the Tetragrammaton, and humankind reaching up to Spirit.

Doing Kether's Bidding

The Tetragrammaton is also interpreted as "The One who calls into being," underscoring the fact that Chokmah does Kether's will. Chokmah represents the impetus to establish order from Kether's chaos, exemplified by the Latin phrase *Ex Nihilo Aliquid*, "Something from nothing." It is the primary jolt of cosmic voltage or *chiah*, which sets off the cycle of manifestation by imparting it with the vibrant Life Force. This power also expresses itself mentally as the flash that brings new ideas to light or the recollection of the Wisdom encoded in a universally aligned natural law, truth, or principle—and physically, as the creative impetus to bring an idea into existence.

Bondage, Power, and Impersonality

During the time of Abraham, the biological Father of Judaism, the Hebrew tribe believed in numerous gods. These deities were granted names only after first being worshipped as natural phenomena or objects such as the sun, moon, wind, rain and so on. Simply put, the polytheistic Hebrews, like so many peoples, worshipped the powers that ensured their existence and well-being. It was under Abraham's leadership that the Hebrews began shifting from polytheism to monotheism. (I find it ironic that Abraham's father Terach earned his living selling idols of numerous gods!)

Because survival and protection from harm were foremost, the Hebrews were receptive to Abraham's sales pitch to adopt "Yahweh the Strong." The "sell" was based on Abraham's abiding belief that Yahweh's powers were greater than the combined strengths of all the other gods. After the Hebrews consented to embrace Yahweh, Abraham and Yahweh made their sacred covenant wherein Yahweh agreed to accept the Hebrews, now Jews, as his "chosen people." He vowed to take a special interest in their safety so long as they *only* worshipped him and led their lives according to his dictates. In a world where strength meant survival, Yahweh's protection was more than welcomed. *Romans 4:17* speaks of Yahweh's promise to Abraham and his offspring: "I have made you the father of many nations." Abraham's belief in the God who promised "to protect and create new things out of nothing" further underscores Yahweh's connection with Chokmah.

Historically Speaking

From a historical perspective, the advent of Yahweh was a situation in which oppression and persecution gave birth to freedom. In years to come, Yahweh was believed to have called and inspired Moses to lead the Hebrews out of Egyptian bondage and then to have guided them for forty years in the desert. During this time, Yahweh became more powerful than any other Hebrew god to date. Yet, as Yahweh became increasingly potent, he also became more remote, stern, and invisible. He went from the God who lived among his people to the impersonal God who lived on the highest, most inaccessible mountaintop. Resultantly, many Hebrews secretly clung to their older and lesser deities who provided them with the intimacy and warmth that Yahweh no longer extended.

I find it worth mentioning that some biblical scholars state that events such as the Babylonian Exile and *Diaspora*, the scattering of the Jews beyond Israel, and even the Holocaust resulted from the Jews failing to live by the Ten Commandments, thereby failing to keep to their contract with Yahweh. Although repentance has brought renewal, the cycle continues. An example of this may be seen in Israel's long-term inhumane, apartheid-like treatment of the Palestinians.

THE ARCHANGELIC PRESENCE OF CHOKMAH IS, *RATZIEL*

Ratziel, sometimes Ratziel, meaning both "Bearer of the Word of the Most High" and "Secrets of the Most High," is conjoined with Chokmah. Angelologists state that Ratziel is charged with communicating the *Sepher Ratziel* or *Book of Ratziel*, wherein all celestial and earthly Wisdom is inscribed. Writings claim that these truths were given to Adam to assist the survival of humankind when he and Eve were banished from Eden. It was later passed to Noah as he entered the ark, and then to King Solomon the Wise, Moses, and Jesus, among others. Because this book contains protection for one's home from fire, and one's body from injury, some recommend using it as a protective talisman and sleeping with a miniature version under the bed.

Chokmah is the Illuminating Intelligence, and Ratziel has been experienced and portrayed as pure light with sky-blue wings. This archangel is said to visit when our Wisdom is ready to be amped up, intimating the willingness to put aside our personal preferences for those of a universal nature. Easily called upon through prayer, Ratziel is beheld when doing such as praying, meditating, and sleeping in a conscious dream state. Essentially, Ratziel may be understood as the epiphanies that awaken us to greater awareness—making him an excellent choice to help us persevere in circumstances requiring Wisdom.

The All-Seeing Ones

Ratziel heads the Angelic Order of *Auphanim*, meaning "heavenly wheels" and "Lord of the Stars," the influences that flow through the starry skies to earth—implying the wheel of the zodiac, planets, and luminaries ascribed to Chokmah. Auphanim are also known as "the many-eyed, all-seeing ones," confirming how Wisdom brings the ability to see multiple aspects of life situations. In Christianity, the Auphanim are called the Cherubim or "ones who know," yet another reference to Wisdom. Considered heralds of the Most High, these angels are entrusted with protecting and transmitting sacred secrets to humankind.

Described as composite beings with large wings, a human head with four faces, and an animal body, they are holy guardians. The Auphanim are the first angels mentioned in the Old Testament (*Genesis 3:24*), wherein they safeguard the Garden of Eden and the Tree of Life. *Exodus 25:18* speaks of two Cherubim "of gold," one on either side of the Ark of the Covenant. These fearsome-looking creatures are installed to watch over hallowed objects and places. This angelic order is similar to other holy protectors such as the gargoyle, elephant, chimera, and sphinx.

MYTHOLOGY AND CHOKMAH:

THE GREAT FATHER AND TRIPLE GOD

Chokmah or Wisdom is aligned with all Great Father and male fertility deities, triune gods—a three-in-one Youth-Father, and Elder. He is the co-regent of the three worlds of heaven, earth, and the underworld and potential for fruitfulness. Amongst other qualities, those deities are linked with transformation, intelligence, insight, revelation, or Wisdom.

SUMERIAN

ENLIL: Sumer's Enlil was king of the gods, the universal sovereign who maintained order in the world. Like the Hebrew Yahweh, and others, Enlil lived and ruled from the highest mountaintop.

EGYPTIAN

ATUM RA: At a later era in Egyptian history, Kether's Tum or Atum transformed into the Chokmah's Atum Ra, who birthed from himself all gods, goddesses, humans *and* living things. This gave him rulership over both the Egyptian pantheon and the manifest world.

HEKA: One of the oldest and most important gods in ancient Egypt and the personification of some of Atum Ra's attributes, Heka was considered the primordial source of power in the universe.

PTAH: Although mentioned under Kether, the multi-faceted, Ptah the great god of Memphis is also dually coupled with Chokmah, as he willed the universe into existence through the power of his thoughts and words. In this extended role of Builder of the Universe, Ptah was responsible for forming the totality of creation on earth and in the heavens. He used "speech" to give life to his creations. The Egyptian term for speech means "word," connecting Ptah to Chokmah's other titles, the Word and Logos. Ptah is referred to as "the creator in heaven and earth, who made all things that are," "father of the fathers of the gods," and "the god of light which shows everything," further connecting him with Chokmah, especially the Illuminating Intelligence.

Identified as the Master Builder or Craftsman, Ptah was a patron of Egyptian artisans. Relatedly, Qabalists, Masons, and Rosicrucians refer to God as the Grand Architect of the Universe, a probable throwback to the influence of Egyptology on these traditions.

MAAT: Because Wisdom is conjoined with receptivity, Maat the Egyptian goddess of truth, law, and justice is also paired with Chokmah. While doing some obscure study, I discovered that one of Maat's forgotten names, *Heg-Maat*, is thought to originate from the same Hebrew root as Chokmah.

THOTH: While visiting Egypt, I learned about Thoth and exactly how to pronounce his usually mispronounced name. "Thoth" rhyming with both, is actually the Greek interpretation of the pre-Islamic or Coptic Egyptian name *Tehuti* or *Djehuti* as in Tuh-who-tee. Now that that's taken care of, the supposed author of the *Book of Thoth*, Thoth is believed to have possessed the secret of directing matter by way of his verbal communication—the Word.

Often considered the wisest god in the Egyptian pantheon, myths tell of Thoth, who, much like the biblical Creator, formed the world by speaking and transmitting the formula for creation from on high. This potent god of Wisdom and all forms of communication, Patron of the Arts, Sciences, and Magic is, according to notable Egyptologists, the divine messenger who imparted the totality of heavenly and earthly knowledge to the ancient Egyptians.

ASSYRIO-BABYLONIAN

LAKHMU, LAKHAMU: Parallel to the positive and negative currents of life emanating from Kether, the earliest Assyrio-Babylonian myths tell of Lakhmu and Lakhamu, a pair of enormous serpentine deities, the first progeny to be born from the abyss or Apsu. Together these gods then birthed **Anshar** and **Kishar**, the male and female principles, the celestial and terrestrial worlds, respectively. It was a mating aligned with the relationship between Chokmah, Wisdom and Binah, Understanding, as symbolized on the Tree of Life.

ANU: Anu translates from Acadian to mean "sky." Ruler of the highest of heavens, Anu, like Chokmah, was the supreme god honored by all of the other deities as their father and chief. Anu rarely left the heavenly realm to visit Earth. It is believed that when he did leave, it was only to reside in that part of the sky reserved for him alone called "Anu's Way." He commanded an army of stars known as "the soldiers of Anu." This further suggests Anu's kinship with Chokmah as the "father of all," including the planets and luminaries.

MARDUK THE WISE: At a later period in Assyrio-Babylonian history, Marduk, God of Wisdom, (whose legend is thought to have strongly influenced the Hebrew ideas of Yahweh), with the help of Anshar, destroyed the powerful Great Mother Tiamet to reign supreme. Marduk then divided Tiamet's body into two parts. From one half he created the vault of the heavens, while from the other the solid earth. Next, he organized the world, constructing a place for the gods in the sky and installing the stars; he fixed the length of the year and regulated the course of the heavenly bodies. Although he had accomplished so much, lacking the female principle—nature's negative polarity, Marduk could not make living things and beings.

ARURU: Over time, Marduk the Wise grew wise enough to reintroduce the co-creative feminine principle, as without it there was no life. He accomplished this by calling-up the goddess Aruru meaning "from the seed of humankind." Aruru was less powerful and thereby less threatening than the once all-powerful sovereign Tiamet, making her energy essential to Marduk's rulership and creation of human beings. Although not identical, there is enough commonality to liken the pairing of Marduk and Aruru with that of Chokmah with Binah.

EAST INDIAN

BRAHMA: Brahma signifies the creative aspect of the Hindu trinity, which is dual-aspected. As mentioned under Kether, Brahma's first aspect is Para Brahma, the spirit behind all, while his second is the creative principle in action, Chokmah. Creation may be imagined as Para Brahma exhaling, activating its other aspect, Brahma.

In contrast to the attributeless Para Brahma, Brahma has specific attributes and characteristics. Early Hindu lore identifies Brahma as the father of gods and humans and the Lord of Wisdom. Brahma is said to have given life to the Seven *Prajapati* or spirits. This lines up with how the Godhead, comprised of the Supernal Triad of Kether, Chokmah, and Binah, births the Tree of Life's seven lower sephiroth.

VISHNU: Later Hinduism purports Vishnu to be the supreme god, conjoining him with the fertility of man and nature. Chokmah is linked with the past and Vishnu, the preserver, is responsible for preserving, protecting, and restoring all that has been created. It is believed that from time to time Vishnu materializes as an Avatar, a special physical manifestation of the Most High. Avatars are devoted to enlightening humankind by teaching and maintaining the divine order of the universe. Krishna and Buddha are regarded to be avatars whose activities resulted in the Wisdom Teachings of the *Bhagavad-Gita* and Buddhism.

PERSIAN

AHURA MAZDA: Like Chokmah, Ahura Mazda, as the Zoroastrians of Persia knew him, created the world by the power of thought. Ahura Mazda reigned as a minor deity until about 500 B.C. when he became combined with other gods to become the god of light and Wisdom, Mithra. His following expanded from the Middle East and India into Europe to become the worldwide pagan religion, Mithraism. Even though its rituals were restricted to men, Mithraism was more widespread than Christianity during the 2nd century CE.

MITHRA: Further links between the cult of Ahura Mazda to Chokmah may be found in the story of Mithra. After subduing a sacred bull, from its dying body Mithra brought all of the earth's creatures and vegetation as well as the sacred, hallucinogenic beverage *Haoma*. Haoma juice was ingested to expand consciousness and usher in Wisdom during the Mithraic rites.

GREEK

PROMETHEUS: The titan, son of Lapetus and Themis, is thought to have been the creator of humankind. After fashioning the first human from clay, Prometheus stole fire from the gods in order to help sustain the life he created.

ZEUS: In his dialogue *Cratylus*, Plato speaks of Zeus as "the cause of life always to all things." This King of the Olympians deposed his Titian father Chronos, to become the Great Father of both the Greek pantheon and people. The root meaning of Zeus is "Bright Sky Father," further underscoring his link with Chokmah.

ATHENA: Much as Chokmah springs from Kether, this motherless Virgin Goddess of Wisdom was birthed into the world in full battle regalia from the head of her father, Zeus. In this way, she is similar to the Egyptian Isis. Athena is said to symbolize the concept, "I have come from myself."

Athena is regarded as the guiding and driving force behind acts of bravery and Wisdom. It was her Wisdom, rather than physical might, which saved the Athenians from conquest by the Persians.

Often depicted wearing an owl-shaped helmet and carrying an owl on her shoulder, this universal symbol of Wisdom underscores Athena's connection with Chokmah. A Native American student proposed that the owl is Athena's "totem animal," making it a sacred symbol of her unique life purpose.

ROMAN

JUPITER: Known as the "Lord of Heaven" and "Heavenly Father who rains," Jupiter is the supreme deity of the Roman pantheon. Often depicted bearing a phallic-like thunderbolt, this fertility god impregnated mother earth with his seminal fluid.

MINERVA: As Zeus gave birth to Athena, Jupiter gave birth to Minerva, the goddess of Wisdom. Fittingly, the name Minerva comes from the Latin word *mens* meaning "mind." Minerva goddess of intelligence, knowledge, and philosophy, stimulated all thought, inspiration, and the wisdom that life experience brings. She presided over schools, trade, the arts, medicine, and healing. Unlike her Greek counterpart Athena, the Goddess of War, Minerva was non-violent. She reigned over such hostilities only when the weak and oppressed were being seriously threatened or attacked.

NORSE

ODIN OR WODEN: Odin, meaning "Master of Inspiration," was the chief of the gods at Asgard, the Norse counterpart to Mt. Olympus. Serving in his role as the supreme god of learning and Wisdom, Odin established the laws governing the universe and controlling the destiny of humankind.

In order to drink from the Well of Wisdom at the base of the *Yggdrasil*, the great World Tree or Tree of Life, Odin sacrificed his right eye in the wise giant Ymir's well and threw himself on his spear, in a ritual suicide or ego death. As if this were not enough, he then hung himself from the holy tree for nine days and nights in order to gain knowledge of the sacred runic alphabet of creation. Odin and his brothers later killed Ymir and from his dead body gleaned all of the materials needed to shape the world.

CELTIC

DAGDA: Within Celtic mythology Dagda, identified with magic, fertility, service to the land, and knowledge conjoined with just action, was recognized to be the "Father of All" and "Lord of Perfect Wisdom." Dagda called the seasons of the year into being by playing his enchanted harp. This creative act made him both the guardian of the earth's fertility and responsible for the well-being of all its inhabitants.

TOLTEC, AZTEC, AND MESOAMERICAN

QUETZALCOATL: The Toltec Quetzalcoatl is considered the most important offspring of the primordial androgynous god Ometeotl, linked with Kether. Quetzalcoatl is sometimes depicted as a white-haired old man with a long beard dressed in a feathered robe, conjoining him with Chokmah. He is also known and represented by a "Plumed Serpent," a mix of a bird and rattlesnake.

The Benevolent God of the wind and rain and creator of the world, Quetzalcoatl brought life to the earth in the form of all its inhabitants, deeming him the supreme god of the Toltec and Aztecan peoples. Functioning as the god of civilization, he presided over all learning, culture, the measurement of time, and the preservation of ancient lore and Wisdom.

Some accounts state that Quetzalcoatl required the sacrifice of butterflies and hummingbirds, rather than that of humans. He is often pictured holding a thorn to let blood, a reminder of self-sacrifice—a forerunner to human sacrifice, which he forbade.

OMETECUHTLI: As mentioned under Kether, the self-created Aztecan Ometeotl is sometimes portrayed as containing the husband and wife Ometecuhtli and Omecihuatl, respectively. The male Ometecuhtli corresponds to Chokmah. He is the God of Fire whose name means "Two-Lord" and "Lord of Duality." He resides along with his female counterpart, who we will explore under Binah—Omecihuatl, which fittingly means "Two Lady" and "Lady of Duality." Both live in the thirteenth-highest Aztec heaven. This latitude is parallel to the Tree of Life's plane of causality, whereon Chokmah and Binah are stationed and together are responsible for the creation of the universe and all life within it. Both are further linked with nature's positive and negative polarities, light and dark, motion and stillness, and chaos and order.

OF VIRTUES AND VICES:

Devotion

Devotion rhymes with emotion, underscoring the parts that passion and dispassion play in the development of Wisdom. Rooted in the word vote, as I understand it, Devotion is choosing to wholeheartedly dedicate oneself—with full-on intention, attention, enthusiasm, and a good dose of humor—to engaging with and solving life's endless mysteries.

Qabalistically speaking, Devotion is making a sacred commitment to personal, and in doing so, planetary transformation and upliftment via enactment of the Wisdom teachings or Eternal Verities of the Tree of Life. It is also having the deep and abiding knowledge that all words and actions, no matter how small or seemingly insignificant, may be approached and performed with Devotion, deeming them acts of mystical observance. Of course, Devotion is a profound dedication to one's beloved, what Sufis refer to as their Sacred Beloved. Along this line, Qabalists ask, "After having experienced your Source, what else could you be devoted to?"

Devotion is getting our priorities straight. It is the willingness and ability to pay attention to the Great Spirit that exists within whatever is presently before us—be it a person, creature, plant, or situation. This may be likened to parents being fully attentive to their crying newborn. It is entering into the moment and consciously directing all of our energy, as Chokmah directs all of Kether's energy. As mentioned earlier, Buddhist practitioners liken this to being "mindful" of whatever is immediately before them. Hindus equate this state with perceiving everything one says and does as acts as of Seva, or selfless spiritual service or practice. True mystical-spiritual traditions teach their devotees to regard each mundane act as a chance for conscious worship. Doing this provides the opportunity to focus on the divinity inherent in the totality of life to the exclusion of all else.

Oceans of Devotion

Devotion may be seen in the following: Julia Butterfly lived 378 days in the branches of a1500-year-old California Redwood named "Luna," to prevent loggers from the Pacific Lumber Company from cutting it down. Julia's devotion helped Luna escape the saw and made the tree part of the non-profit Sanctuary Forest. Karen Silkwood was the labor union activist and chemical technician at the Keer-McGee nuclear plant in Oklahoma that was putting the exceedingly dangerous plutonium pellets instead of uranium pellets inside nuclear reactor fuel rods. Silkwood died in 1974 under mysterious circumstances after devotedly investigating and reporting claims of the aforementioned. Certainly, her reporting was instrumental in closing the plant not very long afterward.

There are also everyday folks such as Kyra and Murphy. Kyra gives warm clothing and blankets to the homeless, who due to their various disabilities and preferences, are unable to sleep indoors, and Murphy's upscale restaurant transforms into a soup kitchen on Mondays.

Vice of Disloyalty

Because Chokmah is a direct reflection on Kether, Qabalistic tradition does not ascribe any vice to this sephirah. However, for the purpose of personalizing the impersonal and/or comprehending the elusive, the vice or weakness of Chokmah may be regarded as disloyalty.

From the Qabalistic viewpoint, Disloyalty may stem from the likes of basic ignorance, a wide range of beliefs and emotions, as well as an unwillingness to do what is necessary to live wisely. Sometimes we may know better, yet our humanness stops us from doing better. (Welcome to humankind and the evolution of consciousness!) This shortcoming might be expressed in the misuse of the power of Wisdom (or better said, knowledge), to exert our influence over others to achieve status, control, and financial gain—aka maximizing "ego-building." In this state, we give in to our immature personal preferences rather than to what we recognize to be a wiser choice. When living solely from the personality level without considering the full-bodied consequences of our actions, we renounce and even denounce the presence of anything greater than our self, even the scientifically proven law of cause and effect. In such instances, the relationship between two phenomena in which one phenomenon is the reason behind the other—e.g. thoughtless daily use of Chokmah's medicine-drug cocaine leads to addiction, health, financial, and possible legal problems—is denied.

Awareness of Something Greater

The Spiritual Experience of Chokmah is the Vision of the Most High Face-to-Face. Our immaturities, weaknesses, harmful habit patterns, or vices eventually bring us face-to-face with the knowledge of something greater and more powerful than ourselves. This is the founding Wisdom principle of all Recovery programs aimed at wisely managing and overcoming vices—disease(s) and their symptoms and making choices that support physical, mental, emotional, and spiritual well-being. Again, this change also occurs because we experience the reality of the cosmic order operating within all earthly life. Although being disloyal to this fact may bring short-term gain, it eventually will bring pain.

I have heard it said and have experienced the truth of the statement, "Humor is the source of great Wisdom." Becoming skillful at perceiving and owning the dark or black humor embedded in our immature attitudes and actions, aka personality deficiencies and vices, cracks open the door for Wisdom to enter. Essentially, my willingness to turn on the light of Chokmah's Illuminating Intelligence to see some comedy in my downright asinine, laughable, immature behaviors helps me to more readily accept my own and others' humanness. Taking this path leads me to more mature, wiser ways of thinking and living. I sometimes find it useful to remember that the word Devil is the word "lived" spelled backward!

POWERING-UP: MAGICAL-MYSTICAL SYMBOLS, TOOLS, TALISMANS, AMULETS, AND SIGILS

CIRCLE WITH A DOT: Kether's omniscient, omnipresent, omnipotent life force comes into the world of existence, in the circle of Chokmah. This symbol reminds me of the saying attributed to antiquity's Hermes Trismegistus: "God is an infinite sphere, the center of which is everywhere, the circumference nowhere."

THE SPERM: Sperm is a flawless symbol of divine maleness, as all of its energy is compacted into one tiny seed. Like the workings of Chokmah, the sperm, of the male Creator principle, is potent, yet must be joined with the egg of the female Creatrix principle of Binah, to be fully realized. Because this sephirah initiates the actual beginning of all creative cycles, it may be likened to the cosmic radiation or light force that streams like sperm through the womb of the entire universe, lighting up and consequently impregnating it with life. This symbol offers insight as to why Chokmah is termed the Illuminating Intelligence.

THE *PHALLUS*: This ancient cross-cultural symbol of male generative power is paired with the maker of all life, Chokmah. Although phallus is the Latin word for the image of an erect penis, the organ the sperm uses to eject itself, it is also the embryonic structure from which *either* the penis or vagina develops. In this way, the phallus may be seen as the launching pad for the entirety of creation.

THE *LINGAM*: The term lingam comes from the Sanskrit root word *linga*, meaning, "instrument used for sexual union." Fittingly, the lingam is an ancient Hindu representation of male potency and the production of offspring and Chokmah is the positive polarity or power of the universe, which by way of its union with its negative counterpart, the *yoni*, makes the creation of the world and the perpetuation of life possible. When the lingam is intertwined with a serpent, the Kundalini, or Hindu Life Force, it symbolizes the evolution of consciousness or Wisdom that knowledge of divinity brings.

STRAIGHT LINE: In geometry, all lines are infinite and Chokmah or Wisdom signifies infinite potential. As the shortest distance between two points, the straight line maximizes the energetic potential of this sephirah. Euclid taught, "A point has position but no dimensions. If, however, a point may be conceived of as extending through space, it becomes a line." This illustrates what occurs when the Life Force extends from "the point" of Kether reaches outwards and downwards to Chokmah, and from Chokmah reaches across to Binah, and in this way, enlivens the entire Tree of Life. Kether is the point, and Chokmah is the line, confirming the direction of that point.

The straight line is an ancient way of designating Wisdom. Here is why. If I draw a line two feet long and hide one foot of it, then ask someone how long the line is, they will probably reply, one foot. This is an error illustrating the human tendency to see only what we are presently capable of seeing. Consequently, when feeling lost or disoriented while traveling our life path, our personal "Highway of Life," it is valuable to recall that more of the path, although unseen, lies ahead. With time, and the Wisdom time brings, our way will become evident.

Chokmah is the sphere of the stars and planets. In this sense, the straight line symbolizes the heavenly power that runs through and shapes the entire universe. It is the torrents of radiant cosmic Wisdom continuously descending from above into all celestial bodies. This suggests that it is only a matter of time until we receive the Wisdom already heading our way.

THE MONOLITH OR STANDING STONE: Coming across this term, the image of the monolith vividly depicted in Stanley Kubrick's landmark film, "2001," immediately came to mind. This mysterious massive single block or column of stone was a replica of those displayed and carried in ancient rites and processionals revering the generative power of nature and the universe from which it originates. While I am not certain what director Kubrick was thinking, the film suggested the evolution of humankind from apes and along with it, the advancement of technological Wisdom.

FIGURE EIGHT: The geometrical figure eight, infinity sign, or Mobius strip symbolizes the endless relationship between the One and the urge of the One to continuously manifest itself, the spheres of Kether and Chokmah, respectively.

UPLIFTED ROD OF POWER OR LIGHTNING BOLT: These talismans are tangible representations of Spirit's will, power, and intention as well as the Wisdom that suddenly descends to illuminate us from on high. Such signify the forceful forward-flowing current of positive ions of electricity into the atmosphere, which like Chokmah, is seeking to discharge itself. Here lightning symbolizes the unbalanced, polarized energy of Chokmah, searching for the energy of Binah, to release itself into, thereby grounding and balancing itself out.

MAZLOTH, "THE HEAVENLY HIGHWAY OF LIFE:" This celestial freeway is composed of the entire zodiac—all planets and luminaries. Symbolized by a wheel with either eight or twelve spokes, Mazloth represents both infinite possibilities and the zodiacal cycle of life, respectively. This Wheel is placed on the Tree of Life in the sphere of Chokmah, as a reminder that Kether's limitlessness sets Chokmah's limitedness, in the form of creation, moving.

The zodiac is an imaginary belt of the heavens encompassing the paths of all the heavenly bodies and is divided into twelve constellations, divisions, or signs, within which are the paths of the planets and luminaries. Stemming from the Greek *zodiakos,* meaning "wheel of life," the zodiac is the primordial energy that passes from potentiality to actuality and back again. In other words, the zodiacal wheel's continuous movement is reflected in the physical world's ongoing cyclicity from involution to evolution and back again. The wheel of life's descent and ascent mirrors the Platonic, Gnostic, and Jungian concepts wherein the soul descends into physical existence and then seeks liberation by consciously ascending the wheel of life back to its spiritual origin.

ASTROLOGICAL CORRESPONDENCE TO CHOKMAH:

URANUS, INFLUENCES FROM THE GREAT BEYOND

Qabalistic astrologers couple Chokmah with the planet Uranus, or *Oron* meaning "little light" in Hebrew, with the ancient Greek Sky God, Uranus. This god of the heavens and symbol of masculine potency he and his wife Gaea had many children, including the twelve original Titans. As the first outer or transpersonal planet (those after Saturn), Uranus draws influences from the "great beyond" into our lives. Considered the "higher-octave," or more refined or subtle version of the planet Mercury, Uranus signifies the expansive, uninhibited, transpersonal human intelligence that flowers from intuition in contrast to Mercury's purely personal orientation.

Also known as the "bulls-eye planet", Uranus is linked with electrical energy, the flashes of a greater consciousness that raise our awareness to upgrade or revolutionize and evolutionize our thinking and doing when open to doing such as ceasing to mindlessly follow the crowd. Bearing out this planet's uniqueness is the fact that when compared with the Earth's tilt of 23 degrees on its axis, Uranus tilts almost 98 degrees, making the planet appear as if it is rotating on its side.

Uranus represents the intelligence that compels us past our ordinary thinking and behaving to the extraordinary. It signifies the expansion of our mental capacity for learning, reasoning, and understanding that is validated by intuition—our wise inner teacher. This contrasts Mercury's purely personality-oriented and inherently restrictive thought patterns. Uranus denotes the galvanizing jolts of awareness originating from the great unknown—the superconscious insights and inspirations pushing us out of our comfort zone, urging us to step outside of the conventionality box to experiment with more innovative and spontaneous approaches to life. Uranus represents the irrepressible out-of-the-blue urge to experiment, which raises and expands personal awareness and has the potential to lead to personal and collective transformation.

Concept-Shattering

Spiritual evolution is synonymous with gaining access to the Wisdom of the Wise. Because we humans are the caretakers or "keepers" of the Garden of Eden the earth, and its creatures, we each play a unique and essential role in the cosmic order. Both the cause and effect of doing our part in the scheme of things originate from becoming increasingly open to Chokmah's Universal Wisdom. Uranus connotes the qualities of ingenuity, originality, inventiveness, and behavioral inclinations, which, when genuinely Self-centered, lead to honoring our wiser concept-shattering promptings. One student quipped that the activities of Uranus are "mind-blowing."

Certainly, it is essential to remain open to new input and information. Yet it is wise to utilize discernment before acting, proceed with a healthy amount of detachment from what results, and remain open to learning from the outcome. It came as no surprise when an astrologer friend referred to Uranus as the "Trickster Planet." The Uranian spirit is that of the inspired, freethinking visionary prompting us to shed whatever may be hindering us from integrating heavenly ways of handling earthly situations. The workings of this planet may be seen in this quote from Charles Darwin: "It is not the strongest of the species that survives, nor the most intelligent, but the one most responsive to change."

THE QABALISTIC GRADE OF CHOKMAH:

THE *MAGUS*

The word Magus originates from the ancient Latin root *magh,* meaning "wise one," "one who has power and is able," and "Magician." Magus, the singular for *Magi,* is associated with the Zoroastrian priestly caste, the three wise men or Magi who traveled from Persia to Bethlehem to pay homage to the Christ child, forging a link with the Tree of Life's second sephirah, Wisdom or Chokmah. Achieving the Grade of Magus, we have integrated Chokmah's Wisdom by being intimately acquainted with its Illuminating Intelligence, Spiritual Experience of the Vision of the Most High Face-to-Face, Sacrament of Communion, Virtue of Devotion, and so on. Magi embody the second declaration from Paul Case's *Pattern on the Trestleboard:* "Through me, its unfailing Wisdom takes form in thought and word."

Noted along with Chokmah's Divine Presence Yahweh or Jahweh, the Sanskrit word Jana means Wisdom. In the yogic system, a Magus is a master of Jana yoga or Wisdom. The Jana yogi is adept at using the mind and power of the Illuminating Intelligence through mental disciplines the likes of discernment, dispassion, and endurance, to transcend its identification with self-limiting thoughts and perceptions to unite their inner Self with the oneness of all life and through it achieve complete liberation or *moksha.*

Like the Ipsissimus, Magi have gained control over the five senses—sight, smell, taste, touch, and five functions of the body—speaking, eating, reproducing, eliminating, and moving, and five elements—earth, air, fire, water, and ether. While dominion is the consequence of their spiritual practice, they lack omniscience—the all-knowing state of having infinite awareness, wisdom, understanding, and insight, which only avatars are born with.

The Grade of Magus is the state wherein we are usually born fully conscious mediums, through which Chokmah's Wisdom steadily flows. We live out the statement, "Thy will, not my will." We base our thoughts, words, and actions upon universal and natural laws, truths, and principles, the Eternal Verities or Perennial Philosophy, i.e.: Every part of creation is interdependent with every other part.

Perfecting mental and emotional discernment, Magi think, speak and live wisely. In the simplest of terms, we live fully, "on purpose," doing what is aligned with what we are certain is the wisest action, and if it turns out to be otherwise, we welcome correction and further instruction.

Being dedicated to our connection to the heavens translates into our intention and attention to living a Spirit-centered life. With this inadvertently arises the potential to uplift and inspire others by way of our words and actions. Undoubtedly, negative reactions to a Magus also hold true—with others growing upset, angered, and repelled. In such instances, the Magus refrains from pushing their agenda, unless it is dangerous to do otherwise. As the old saying goes, Magi possess the Wisdom to know the difference.

Magi have the ability to go beyond the yogic state of Samadhi wherein they may come and go between the physical and non-physical worlds in a state of perfect equanimity, free from life's dualities, untouched by all feelings, and connected only to Spirit. Noted under Kether's Ipsissimus, Samadhi is the prerequisite for Nirvikalpa Samadhi, God Realization (I am God), and the ultimate Mahasamadi, wherein we are ready to not only drop our physical body *and* all personal identification and return to the great source of life at the center of the cosmos.

Magicians, Magic, and Alchemy

The term Magus conjures up ideations of magic, magicians and mediums of all sorts. Wisdom, like true magic, is a supernatural power. Magi serve as mediums or Wisdom channels through which the "magic" of Spirit flows through us and out to the world around us by way of our thoughts, words and actions. When we, like the Buddha or Wiseone, apply what we know to more fully develop ourselves, superpowers are activated, and in this way, acknowledge and demonstrate the credibility of their Source. This concept is summed up by the sage words of Rabbi Moses Maimonides, the 11th-century Jewish philosopher and scholar: "Man must become superman to inherit eternity." This statement refers to the miracle-working and prophetic abilities attributed to the Qabalistic Grade of Magus.

The supernatural skillfulness to transform something from nothing or our thoughts into things without an apparent source or physical activity comes with achieving the supernatural Grade of Magus. An example of this remarkable power was seen when Jesus turned water into wine and raised Lazarus from the dead. This ability shows that the Magus has earned dominion over creation in real-time, the instantaneous sequencing of words or thought forms into the materialization of tangible objects. In my experience, witnessing a Magus immediately converting energy into matter versus the relatively slow-motion sequencing of the average human is astounding. This is observed in instances such as the paranormal manifestation of the mystic's apport and powers or *siddhis* of certain yogis.

Devotion is Chokmah's virtue. Through our devoted exploration of the mysteries of the universe, Presto-Chango-Alakazam! we discover the previously unrecognized magical-mystical secrets of life continually happening before our eyes! Miraculous powers are released and realized. However, when selflessness is lacking, the Magus' actions turn questionable, edging toward the realm of Black Magic. While the voice of conscience may be dismissed, the fully evolved Magus experiences it so clearly that it is impossible to mistake it for anything else. In the end, Magi are completely dedicated to integrating what we have discovered to serving the planet and all upon it. We know magic to be living in concert with the spiritual order of the universe as well as protecting and upholding this order in whatever we think, say, and do.

Alchemy and Soul Purpose

Often used as a synonym for magic, Qabalists defined alchemy as "a miraculous change for the better." It is the transformational art and science of viewing ourselves and life situations from an extraordinary or fearlessly reality-oriented point of view. This change results from gaining the Wisdom to consistently apply the teachings encoded within the Qabalistic Tree of Life. While the state of a Magus' life is proof that thoughts create energy and that energy creates matter, it must be noted that there are times when Magi are inundated with extreme hardships. Of course, such are aimed at further testing and trying our abilities and demonstrating that superhuman activities are humanly possible. Magi are living laboratories aware of the multitude of alchemical processes involved in living in concert with the spiritual order of the universe. Doing this subtly broadcasts messages which are deposited in the bank of the collective unconscious, furthering human and planetary development. Because Magi have the cellular certainty that we and all of creation are Divinity embodied in form, our experiences also aim at the soul purpose of assisting our eventual graduation to Kether's Ipsissimus, Unified Existence, union or re-union with the immortal spirit of life at the center of the universe.

CHOKMAH, THE BROW STAR OR THIRD EYE

Chokmah is linked with the Brow Star, the third eye or *Ajna* in the Hindu chakra system, which translates from Sanskrit as "to command and perceive." The term is further conjoined with the functions of intuition, inspiration, imagination and self-realization. The Brow Star corresponds to the left side of the brain, which directs the right eye, ear, and side of the body.

To review the Tree of Life has three pillars: Mercy, Severity, and Equilibrium. These correspond to our spine and the nerves through which the life force moves as follows: the positive solar current, or Pingala in the Yogic system, that heats the body is paired with Chokmah and the sympathetic nervous system's dilation. The negative lunar current, or Ida, paired with Binah, Understanding, is conjoined with bodily cooling and the parasympathetic nervous system's contraction. The neutral central channel of the *Shushuma* is the spinal cord itself. It is from the Brow Star that the solar and lunar currents meet and start spiraling around and radiating out from the neutral central channel initiating the polarity existing in all of the lower stars or chakras. This physiological arrangement shows how the co-mingling of Chokmah and Binah fills the world with creatures containing varying combinations of positive and negative polarities.

Opening to Wisdom

Slipping into and becoming the Tree of Life, Chokmah, topping the pillar of Mercy, becomes the left side of the brain and controls the right side of the body. Conversely, Binah, topping the Pillar of Severity, turns into the right side of the brain and controls the left side of the body. Traditional Wisdom teaches that "Left-brained" individuals are inclined to be more logical, analytical, and objective-skilled in speech, language, reasoning, math, science and writing skills. In contrast, "Right-brained" people are prone to be adept with generalized or holistic perceptions. This group is disposed to being more emotional, unsystematic, subjective, intuitive, and creative—skilled in spatial abilities, art, and music.

Familiarity with neuro-anatomy led me to attribute Chokmah to the area of the left-brain, which contains Broca's region (the third convolution of the left frontal lobe), the center for articulate speech. I liken this to "the Word," the actively expressed creative, revelatory thought and will of the Most High aligned both with the first line of the Old Testament, "And God Said..." and the potency of Chokmah that works through us. This further aligns the Brow Star with the power of speech and Chokmah's authoritativeness.

Of course, when open to acquiring Wisdom, we become Wiser. The burgeoning science of neuroplasticity has been proving that the entire brain is involved in the functions previously categorized into left and right brain abilities. More about the wonders of neuroplasticity appears at the end of this segment.

Induction, Depression, Elation, and Full-On Knowingness

Brow Star is conjoined with the pineal gland, the inner eye or eye of the soul, located between our two outer eyes at eye level within the brain. Hypothesized to be a vestigial third eye comprised of optic nerve cells, it is thought to affect both the endocrine and central nervous systems. The Sanskrit word Ajna is further translated as "to know," much as Wisdom suggests, to have "knowledge of" or intimacy with divinity. While the Crown Star is the door to oneness and union with Spirit, the Brow Star, just below it, is the transcendental portal to Self-realization, the full on knowing that one is Spirit. This underscores the intimate coupling between this Star and intuition or Self-knowledge. The pineal gland, or body, secretes a substance called melatonin, which, among other things, prompts mood changes and regulates sleep patterns and sexual development. Melatonin production occurs when the eyes are exposed to light. Scientific studies show that individuals who have low levels of melatonin, due to less exposure to light, are more likely to experience sleep disorders and periodic depression, or Seasonal Affective Disorder, aptly termed SAD. Additionally, melatonin deficiencies are also found to result in lower calcium levels, leading to bone and tooth loss.

Wellspring of Light and Life

Kether is the wellspring of light and life and when, for whatever reason, we are cut off from this source, depression and a marked loss of inspiration and creativity, the energies of Chokmah often ensue. The pineal gland also contains high concentrations of serotonin, one of the primary ingredients in anti-depressant medications. Dimethyltryptamine better known as DMT, commonly known Dimitri, Rogan and Fantasia, is a naturally occurring tryptamine excreted by the pineal gland, and is a normal part of ordinary neuro-metabolism. Chokmah is linked with time past and the Illuminating Intelligence. It is especially noteworthy, that the pineal gland naturally produces DMT at the moment of death when the lessons of a lifetime are illuminated and reviewed. Because Chokmah is responsible for generating the world, the activities of the pineal body help to generate our drive to create and mindset the overall collection of beliefs that shape how we make sense of the world and ourselves and influences how we think, feel, and behave in any given situation. Because Chokmah is responsible for generating the world, the activities of the pineal body help to generate our drive to create and mindset—the overall collection of beliefs that shape how we make sense of the world and ourselves and influences how we think, feel, and behave in any given situation.

This Star is further linked with the force of inductive reasoning. Inductive reasoning is thinking logically from a specific to the general, i.e.: I create; Spirit creates me and all of creation. It is what Qabalists speak of as "reasoning from the One to the many." The force of induction builds energy to the point wherefrom the speeded-up molecules act as a force upon something else. From another view, stimulated with energy from Kether, the One, Chokmah delivers it to Binah, to become the countless manifestations of Kether's Oneness.

Enwisening Stars

When we are receptive to acquiring Wisdom, we become wiser. There presently are an increasing number of Brain Fitness programs promising to retard aging, renew alertness, memory, and mental flexibility, and rehabilitate neurological injuries. Enwisening stars in this area are proving that our brains, in addition to receiving softwear updates, also receive hardware updates. This means that when because of our physical health and life experiences, neural pathways are injured, fall dormant, and are otherwise discarded, others may be created. This underscores the part Wisdom, in the form of our conscious intention and attention, plays in this re-enlivening process.

A term first used by Polish neuroscientist Jerzy Konorski in 1948, neuroplasticity is one of the most promising state-of-the-art systems in the growing field of neuroscience. Neuroplasticity has been proven to create new neural pathways and alters existing ones by forming, modifying, and reorganizing synaptic connections—essentially rewiring itself in response to reeducation following brain injuries, nerve damage, and other changes. This continually emerging science asserts and has been demonstrating that no matter what one's age or malady, except brain death, the brain can adapt and change. Briefly, the ability of neural networks in the brain may be changed through cortical remapping. Neuroplasticity is validating that carefully designed forms of brain training tap into the brain's innate Wisdom to bypass and reroute neurological and psychological trauma and impairment.

The outcome of wisely directed structural and functional neuroplasticity learning and rehabilitation is the strengthening and permanent change of the synapses or transmission sites between two nerve cells or neurons. Research is showing that neuroplasticity training results in previously unthought-of transformations in response to the harmful impact of a remarkably wide range of physical, mental, and emotional injuries and illnesses. Because it is a relatively young field with new findings and methodologies continually appearing, there is not (as of this writing) one unifying theory.

In closing, about a dozen years ago, Doidge's forward-thinking book "The Brain That Changes Itself" put me on track to rethinking, rerouting, and thereby normalizing a painful, long-standing injury doctors insisted was impossible to treat non-surgically. Chokmah or Wisdom is a state of open-mindedness. I attribute my progress to being receptive to updating my outdated medical prognosis with cutting-edge knowledge and techniques. By doing this, I am not only becoming healthier, but wiser.

THE PALATE REFRESHER:
HOMEPLAY SUGGESTIONS FOR THE PRACTICAL APPLICATION AND INTEGRATION OF WISDOM, CHOKMAH

1.   Apply the scent of musk and wear grey as I experience the Grade of Magus linked with Chokmah.   Ponder the following before, during, or after taking action:

*Using the power of "the Word," or speech, to reshape or transform a situation for the better. *Translating a creative intention into a goal by directing my full intention and attention toward its attainment. *Being mindful of the power of my words—internal and external—on myself and/ or others. *Consciously putting a habitual personality trait aside, so that my One Wise Self may better act through me. *Seeking to thrive-through rather than barely survive-through-a challenging/stressful situation. *Aligning myself with and enacting the principles of Ageless Wisdom although others might not understand, like, or agree. *Considering the potential impact of failing to stand up and speak out against something such as malicious mischief. *Noticing how I vacillate between positive and negative states of mind and emotions.

2.   What comes next holds the promise to expand and deepen my relationship with the presence of Wisdom, Chokmah, by experimenting with the following:

Feel the Tree of Life's Middle Pillar against my back as I take several long, deeply relaxing and centering breaths. Next, send a grounding cord or root down from the base of my spine into the earth and up from the crown of my head to root in the heavens. Continue by sensing my breath spiraling up and down these roots as I breathe. Slowly bring myself into the sphere of Chokmah by doing such as: Imagine showering or surrounding my body in a translucent grey veil, the hue of the sphere, and inhaling the scent of musk. Invoking Chokmah's divine and archangelic presences by sincerely calling out or chanting their names Invoking Kether's divine and archangelic presences by calling out or chanting their names, following under number 19. Summoning the support of the sphere's mythological deities—gods and goddesses—or bringing the coupled flowers, plants, and animals into my mind and imagination. Enacting the aforementioned or whatever else I think is relevant and will help me to kinesthetically, mentally, emotionally and spiritually experience myself in the sphere of Chokmah. I might also focus on my Brow Star, as this is where Chokmah touches my astral body. Now experiment with the following:

A. If and when I am feeling off-center, disappointed, frustrated, or down about who I am and what I am doing or not doing, go to a mirror, and looking into it loudly repeat: "STOP! STOP! STOP!" Continue with something like, "I am looking at the face and body of Divinity, Great Spirit, God/dess, Most High, etc. in human form. I am physical reflection of the One Self."

   Reflect on a challenging or problematic set of circumstances, which in reality mirrors my Wisdom or lack thereof. Could being mindful of the fact that from Chokmah's view, I am looking into the face of the Most High embedded in this situation move me into a different or more thorough mode of problem-solving? Every aspect of physical life is an opportunity to perceive Spirit by accessing the Wisdom that is always available to me. Comment on what insights and/or changes result from this exercise:

B. Wisdom is about the ideas that have the potential to lead to physical activity and ultimately manifestation. Bring to mind a personality trait or ability that I am being spiritually inspired "to call into being." Next, begin ideating or fleshing-out this inspiration. Detail how my life and I could look and be as the result of embodying and living out the result of my inspiration. Follow this by choosing an image that represents this state—a photo, drawing a sketch, making a collage, using a physical object, creating a sigil and so on.

   Remember: Wisdom is the intelligent application of learning. While doing this exercise, notice where in the imaging process I gain and/or lose momentum and energy. What openings and blocks do I become aware of? Generally, openings come from my skillfulness,

Self-confidence, and willingness to learn new things. Blocks stem from my lack of skill, or Self-confidence which produces inertia, fear, pain, anxiety, shame, frustration and the like.

Identify and start planning how I can make the realization of my goal an integral part of my spiritual development and practice. Doing this suggests the likes of praying and asking for wise support, human or otherwise, to help me reason through and then map out my path forward. These aim at opening my mind and heart to discovering ways of achieving my goal while enhancing and remaining attuned to, rather than sacrificing, my true Self and spiritual ideals in the process. It is seeking out and welcoming the light of Wisdom, including other people and resources with more Wisdom than I, for the support, feedback, assistance, and so on to help me reach and manifest my goal.

C.   Experiment with walking in a beautiful place while repeating Chokmah's Divine Name: Yahweh, Yod-Hay-Vav-Hey, Father of All Creation. Doing this affirms my oneness with the Wisdom of the universe, Chokmah. This practice also goes for calling-in Chokmah's archangelic presence, Ratziel Ra-tz-aye-el, Bearer of the Word of the Most High.

3.   Chokmah is known as the Illuminating Intelligence that turns on the light of life and Wisdom within all creation. Consider answering the following:

*Is there one reason why it would be wise for me to regularly reach out to the Wisdom encoded within a consciousness-expanding tool or teachings? *When was I able to hold out the light of Wisdom for another without being attached to whether they perceived or followed it or not? *How have I benefited by inviting the light of higher consciousness to help clarify my clouded thinking and feeling? *When and where did the principles of Wisdom assist me to speak and behave more wisely? *Has my willingness to open myself to the Illuminating Intelligence resulted in a concept-shattering epiphany? *Am I becoming increasingly able to reach for the light of Wisdom when lost in the darkness of ignorance or despair? *In what situation did I/ might I wisely remain quiet rather than speak unwisely?

4.   The Spiritual Experience of Chokmah is the Vision of the Most High Face-to-Face. While many groups believe that no human may directly behold the face of the Most High and live, Qabalists experience this holiness reflected in the countless faces and myriad scenes of daily life. Mull over the following:

*In what commonplace situation have I unexpectedly perceived the Most High Face-to-Face in another and the world around me? *Although it could result in a certain amount of cognitive dissonance, contemplate what I might gain from rising above my habituated mindset to perceive a pressing or distressing set of circumstances—family, friends, community, or socio-political situation—from the extra-ordinary perspective by experiencing the presence or Face of the Most High within it? *Could it be time to enlist help reviewing an unresolved traumatic situation with my father or male caretakers from my childhood, as such has the potential to expand my awareness, bring me Face-to-Face with Spirit and enwisen me, and in doing so, possible others?

5.   Reflect on the presence of the Great Father living within myself, others, and/or in the world around me. Be aware of what happens when I do this:

Ask myself: *In what life situation would I like to receive the nurturance, guidance and support of an wise father-like mentor? *Who has these abilities, and how might I go about asking for their assistance? *Notice what might be stopping me from making this request and how I could I go about overcoming my reluctance, fear of rejection, pride, and the like?

Alternatively: *What insight or Wisdom did I gain from extending encouragement and support in the form of the Wisdom of my experiences to another? *What, if anything, would I now do differently? *Might I benefit from apologizing for how I fathered or did not father a child? *In what ways, I could go about being a better father-like nurturing guide and enwisening presence to myself?

6.   Chokmah's Sacrament is Communion. When my lack of Wisdom, old habits, past mistakes, uncertainty, or blurred perception regarding what has been and how to proceed prevails, Communion is always there for me to turn to for Wisdom. Entering this state, all of my thoughts and feelings are welcomed and explored. Attaining the impersonal state of true Communion—opening to the clearest Wisdom I am presently capable of receiving—then necessitates stepping away from any personal attachments and aversions as to how I, others, and the world *should* or *should not be*. Doing this opens me to the truest Wisdom I am presently capable of receiving. Through my open-minded contemplation of the teachings of Chokmah, I may receive insights into such as: Revealing the Wisdom of a past, present, or possible future actions and decisions, or the integration of an experience and knowledge that improve my mental clarity, Wisdom, and life. In this way, Communion is realized.

In addition to reflecting on Chokmah's teachings, there are other ways of achieving Communion. Here are a few tried and true: *Prayer and Meditation. *Repeating Chokmah's divine and archangelic names. *Dialoguing with a Wise mentor, counselor, teacher, friend, or Wisdom-oriented group. *Mulling over the teachings of Binah. *Consulting a guide such as the I Ching, runes, laying out a tarot spread, bibliomancy—spontaneously opening to a page in a sacred book—and so on. *Taking a "time-out" and walking in nature and/or getting some cardio-vascular exercise. *Oh yes, contemplating the words of the *Serenity Prayer* from Alcoholics Anonymous:

"God, grant me the serenity to accept the things I cannot change,
the courage to change the things I can,
and the *Wisdom* to know the difference."

Remember: When thrown off-track by life's endless changes and challenges, I always have the option to consider the tried and true remedy of Communion. Being receptive to the Wisdom that Communion offers has the potential to help me fulfill the sacred contract I agreed to enact when baptized in Kether above. Note any shift of my Wisdom-perception that results from engaging in the practice of Communion:

How might I become more welcoming to the energies of the Great Father? *Name one way that my pursuit of Wisdom is changing my life and possibly the lives of my loved ones or those around me for the better? *What situation is calling-out to be impregnated with Wisdom? *Where and how am I learning to more wisely use the assertive attitude and powers of Chokmah? *What am I seeding with the dynamic life force of Chokmah to set off a new cycle of creativity?

7. How might I become more open and welcoming to the energies of the Great Father? *Name one way that my pursuit of Wisdom is changing my life and possibly the lives of my loved ones or those around me for the better? *What situation is calling-out to be impregnated with Wisdom? *Where and how am I learning to more wisely use the assertive attitude and powers of Chokmah? *What am I seeding with the dynamic life force of Chokmah to set off a new cycle of creativity?

8. Contemplate the following in relationship to Chokmah, Wisdom:

"The doorstep to the temple of wisdom is a knowledge of our own ignorance." Spurgeon, *Gleanings among the Sheaves*.

"Turn your wounds into wisdom." Oprah Winfrey

"As I work and exercise my powers of creativity I will remember that it is Thou who art working and creating through me." Paramahansa Yogananda

"Our knowledge is the amassed thought and experience of innumerable minds." Ralph Waldo Emerson, *Letters and Social Aims*.

"Wisdom is the principal thing; therefore get wisdom, and with all thy getting get understanding." *Proverbs 8:11*.

"The price of wisdom is above rubies." *Job 28:18*

"Yesterday I was clever, so I wanted to change the world. Today I am wise, so I am changing myself." Rumi

9. Create a personal statement that affirms my ability to access the powers of Wisdom at this time, such as: "My Wisdom is perfect for who I now am, and continues improving with time and experience." My personal statement is:

10. Acknowledge, explain, or list a way in which I embody, or would like to better embody, this line from the *Pattern on the Trestleboard*: "Through me, Its unfailing Wisdom takes form in thought and word."

11. Might I inject a bit of humor to wisely transform an upsetting, unmanageable, mind-boggling situation into one that has the potential to become more manageable?

12. Chokmah heads the Pillar of Wisdom in time that has passed. Ask myself the following:
    *Is a formerly unwise decision inspiring me to now take better and wiser action? *In what area of my personal or professional life am I being given the opportunity to move up the evolutionary scale by using the Wisdom received from a previous experience to perform a new task? *Have I forgotten or discounted the Wisdom I received from a past interaction by repeating it today? *How have I stepped out of my own way and applied Wisdom to an adverse situation to restart a stalled-out project?
    Seated in the past, Chokmah's Wise presence suggests reflecting back on, engaging with, and, if fitting and possible, healing my perfectly-imperfect, possibly wounded, father-caretaker-child relationship with this influential person. Such has the potential to develop and improve my ability to parent, nurture, or mentor others, as well as my physical, mental, emotional, and spiritual health.

13. Chokmah is conjoined with the Virtue of Devotion. Ask myself: Is there one way that my Devotion to Wisdom's teachings has bettered my life, and in doing so, the lives of those around me? To what or who might I be wise to increase or decrease my Devotion?

14. Uranus or *Oron*, the "higher-octave," or more refined, transpersonal qualities of Mercury, is Chokmah's planetary partner. Known as "the bull's-eye planet," this heavenly body is linked with the often sudden dawning of awareness that jettisons us past our ordinary thinking and doing to the extraordinary. It is the expansion of our mental capacity for learning, reasoning, and understanding that is validated by intuition, our wise inner teacher. Among other things, Uranus is linked with electrical energy that elevates and expands awareness, the "zaps" that raise our consciousness to upgrade, revolutionize, and evolutionize our thinking when receptive.

Coming from "out of the blue," Uranus signifies the superconscious insights and inspirations that thrust us out of our comfort zone to step outside of the box of conventionality to experiment with more innovative and spontaneous approaches to daily living.

Explore how the planetary influences of Uranus are being activated in my life by asking myseslf the following: *When and where was my attention being drawn beyond my personal identity to the transpersonal for insights and inspiration? *What insight has suddenly hit me? *Am I perceiving my unhealthy attachment to expanding and, in my opinion, improving another's thinking? *How am I becoming increasingly innovative or revolutionary in my approach to daily living? *Has a concept-shattering idea jolted me out of my comfort zone? *In what ways am I becoming more tuned into and trusting of my intuition? *Where and when did I step away from the crowd, to speak and act from a place of Wisdom, without being attached to anyone agreeing with me? *Has thinking outside of the box brought me unexpected success or failure? *Have I been inspired to reexamine a long-held belief regarding what gives me security?

15.   Wisdom is the evolutionary process that encourages my openness to conceptualize, update, and co-create new and improved neurological pathways in my brain and body. Such are the ways and means of wisely identifying, imagining, and implementing attitudes and behaviors that are conjoined with my prudent insights of what I may do to be healthier. In addition to mental and emotional activities, Wisdom requires actually enacting kinesthetic, tactile learning, or physical actions to facilitate change and etch new neural pathways.

Now zero in on an area in my life in which I am wisely rethinking the value of re-strategizing an unwise behavior or attribute regarding my physical, mental, emotional, and spiritual health and related attitudes and activities. Consistently following a wiser multileveled plan of action results in the encoding of enwisened neurological circuitry into my brain and body. With time, attention, and repetition, this process has been proven to re-wire the brain and nervous system, replacing worn-out and damaged neurological circuitry with updated routes, which will better my health and life.

16.   Reflect on ways the plants, gems, creatures, mythological figures, or other symbols conjoined with Chokmah have the power to serve as helpful daily reminders to improve my life by applying and integrating the teachings of Wisdom.

17.   Be actively receptive to another's Wisdom. Despite previously being closed-minded, experiment with being open; yet not necessarily agreeing with, someone whose values and points of view are different from my own. Notice what change occurs between us when I do this:

Alternatively, open myself to the Wisdom of the Great Father, coming through an inspiring teacher, friend, tool, DVD, CD, book, Zoom call, workshop or other in-person experience—in order to grow and live more wisely. Notice what results when I do this:

18.   In what area(s) of my personal or professional life am I being asked to use the Wisdom I have to seek out and receive the Wisdom I need?

19.   Passionately call out and in Chokmah's Divine and Archangelic Presences. Chokmah's Divine Presence is: Yahweh   F# C C# C Yod-Hey-Va-Hay), Father of All Creation. Chokmah's Archangelic Presence is Ratziel (D A# E F# Ra-tz-aye-el), Bearer of the Word of the Most High, to help me become more attuned with, and to live out the teachings of Chokmah, the sephirah of Wisdom.

20.   Gift myself with the opportunity of deepening my Wisdom of the Qabalistic Tarot's minor arcane and court cards by laying out and contemplating the Four Twos and Four Kings as follows: Notice how *each* card is encoded with Wisdom's/Chokmah's attributes:

- The Illuminating Intelligence.
- Spiritual Experience of the Vision of the Most High Face-to-Face.
- Sacrament of Communion.
- Virtue of Devotion.
- Astrological Counterpart of Uranus.
- And Qabalistic Grade of the Magus, Magician.

THE DESSERT:
AFFIRMING, CONFIRMING,
AND INSPIRING STUDENT EXPERIENCES

The following are the results of class members taking the principles of Chokmah to heart, by applying and thereby digesting and integrating these into their daily lives. When returning to class, they shared what occurred. Each student's Homeplay comments are followed by a few of my own.

■ "Though I call myself Sara, I'm named after the Hindu goddess of Wisdom, *Saraswati*. I was born in early February or *Magha*, the month that she presides over, so my parents gave me her name. Naturally, learning has been especially important. So, here I am with a Ph.D., what I sometimes refer to as 'my expensive, piled higher and deeper education' yet it's not been easy for me to think of myself as wise. While I do have a professional seal of approval, in the form of a full-time teaching position and a good salary at a prestigious university, Wisdom is something else. I think my mindset is mostly due to having been a student for so many years. While I'm known and recognized for being wise about my professional field, my personal life is something else. Chokmah is reminding me how much I could benefit from rethinking my behavior. Usually, when someone tells me something, instead of trusting my inner knowledge and perhaps questioning what they're saying, I automatically think that they know more than I do—that they are wiser than I am.

Coming to understand Chokmah, I've been contemplating a word in Urdu, Hindi and Persian, *Hukhm*, that's very close to the meaning of Chokmah. It translates: 'to be in charge, direct, order, or command.' I see it as being one's own wise parent and authority figure, something I've struggled with forever. For most of my life, it's either been my parents, particularly my father, ex-husband, mother-in-law, teachers, or advisors ordering and commanding me, rather than listening to the orders and commands coming from my inner Self. Directives like these have run my life: 'You can't possibly do that,' when I decided to get my Ph.D.! 'You really don't deserve these,' when I made good grades. 'You must marry who *we* want you to marry, not who you want to marry,' my parents commanded, or better yet dictated! 'You have to take care of the house, before taking care of yourself,' coming from my husband and mother-in-law.

After getting deathly sick last year, I had to wise up, pay attention and listen to what my body is commanding, or else. Guess what? I'm becoming healthier because of it. Chokmah is now underscoring this with the Wisdom that if I'm really going to succeed in life, I need to *keep* listening. This means listening even deeper by tuning into the Wisdom that's within me. You suggested we use personal statements to back up and reinforce the teachings of each sephirah. Here's what I've come up with for Chokmah: 'The Wisdom within me commands and directs me.'"

You are correct, book knowledge is not Wisdom. We may have book learning, but having Wisdom means using spiritual knowledge to handle our life situations. It sounds as if you are sincerely committed to taking genuine inner knowing and applying it to your life. The Spiritual Experience of Chokmah is the Vision of the Most High Face-to-Face. Consider saying your personal statement and recognizing yourself as an aspect of God/dess, while looking in the mirror. You mentioned reminding yourself to rethink your behaviors. When you find yourself automatically thinking negatively about yourself, experiment with taking your desired change a step further by commanding yourself to STOP! *Follow this by consciously acknowledging what you were thinking—a negative pattern or loop—followed by switching to your personal statement. This might be followed by a prayer asking Spirit to help you realize this change.*

While you surely have an image of your namesake, Saraswati, think about adding images of other Wisdom deities—even some males. Putting them in various places has the potential to keep subtly reinforcing your growing ability to honor your one-wise Self. Such can help lessen the hold others and society's directives, orders, and commands have on you. Perhaps this quote from the Gospel of Thomas *will help reinforce the new path you are now following:* 'Blessings on the wise person who has sought truth and, when it's been found, has rested upon it forever, and has not been afraid of those who wish to trouble them.'

■ Joseph, a self-proclaimed Renaissance Man, shared the following: "With the skyrocketing cost of living here in California, I began toying with the idea of either moving out of state or somehow making more money. I did have a successful show at a gallery in L.A. PP (pre-pandemic). My work seems to be getting more in demand, yet I need the income now. Rich people always have money. About a month ago, I sent out some art-related resumes and pictures. So far, nothing has come of it. Despite this, I've been thinking that while my art isn't as profitable as something else might be, it's what I love doing, where my God-given abilities lie and I intend to continue developing some ideas I have.

Being really wise about my situation, I've recognized that getting a job to help support my art isn't only about paying my bills. Opening my mind, it will be reinforcing the takeaway Wisdom I got while in a men's group I was in a few years ago. I learned the value of honoring myself whatever I'm doing, whether it's painting, house cleaning, gardening, or computer graphics. I definitely have other skills. The idea of supplementing my income makes me feel easier about continuing to contribute to the art of painting.

You know what's so great about sharing this with our class? I'm suddenly feeling less stressed than I was when I started a few minutes ago. I'm feeling sparked by Chokmah's energy and enthusiasm to continue painting. I'm sure more work will eventually come *through* for me. (*ED: Joseph finished by looking up as he pointed to the heavens.*) To insure it happens, I've applied to do gardening for a local company and run the information booth at our Farmer's Market."

It certainly sounds as if you're experiencing this line from the Pattern on the Trestleboard *that corresponds to Chokmah: 'Through me, its unfailing Wisdom takes form in thought and word.' Creative self-expression is the process of being inspired internally and externally: internally by the Life Force that compels and inspires us towards manifestation, and externally when we receive the feedback that our creative efforts are being recognized and rewarded.*

Chokmah, the Creator, is sometimes called 'The Great Stimulator.' You're a person blessed with many talents who's been stimulated to co-create caring for yourself plus value your creativity as an artist. Situated in the past on the Tree of Life, your work with Chokmah has further functioned to call up and validate the concept of living on-purpose, *living a life that's fully aligned with your abilities, values and belief—which after listening to you, seems to be everything you do.*

■ "My husband and I spent this past weekend visiting my son at college," offered Roe, a sales rep and family person. "This also meant we got the chance to meet his girlfriend. At twenty-one, this is his first serious relationship and they are madly in love. Initially, my husband and felt pretty uncomfortable because they were all over each other, hugging, kissing, whispering, and giggling. It seemed as if we weren't even in the same room—they were off in their own little world. What amazed me the most was how comfortable they were doing this in front of us, and the whole world! Ah, love!

I awoke on the second morning of our visit, and feeling very confused, I meditated and asked for guidance. I used the suggestions from our assignment of Chokmah to focus on my desire to become wiser. While my husband was sleeping, I quietly ran a bath and meditated, while floating in the deliciously comfortable tub. After calling for Wisdom from Chokmah's Holy Presence, Yahweh, I surrounded myself with the color grey. (Visualization usually isn't easy for me, but because I actually was inside a cloud of grey steam, it was effortless!) Lying there, I almost found myself thinking about Chokmah's placement on the Tree of Life, in time past. I remembered when I first fell in love and recalled how much I wanted to hug and kiss my boyfriend in front of my parents, but didn't dare. Doing this reminded me that my husband and I actually are quite responsible for his behavior. We've always been very affectionate in front of him. So, why shouldn't he do the same in front of us? I shared my insight with my husband while driving over to meet up with the kids. We had a great laugh and shared a kiss at the first red light.

By the time we all got together for brunch, everything changed. I know my change of attitude made a difference. I was even able to joke about what was going on. Stuff like, 'Hey, you two, stop kissing. Your pancakes are getting cold!' Chokmah helped me to get in touch with yesterday so that I could apply its Wisdom today!"

We often forget or would like to forget that what we've experienced in the past often turns up again in the present. Your discomfort motivated you to vividly recall this important aspect of Chokmah. We sow the seeds of tomorrow today! Perhaps if we, as a culture, expressed as much of our love in public as we do of our anger and hatred, the world would be a better place. So, good for you, your husband, your son and his new friend!

■ "As you all know, much of this year I served as a juror in the case of People versus Dorothea Montalvo Puente, the Sacramento (California) boarding house operator charged with killing nine of her tenants," began Amanda, a prolific poet, gardener extraordinaire and family person. "It was a terribly sad and difficult case, though, like the poet William Butler Yeats, 'I have a fascination with what's difficult.' Ultimately, we voted her guilty of three counts of murder and deadlocked eleven-to-one on the other six counts. We also voted for life in prison without the possibility of parole.

Our jury actually broke the record for the longest deliberation in California—history, a record that, I assure you, was not something we were trying to achieve! The entire process was so thoroughly engrossing I hardly missed the time. Just last week a friend commented that it must have been terrible putting my life on hold. Really, it was quite to the contrary. What I learned from the trial, and what's been emphasized and reinforced by the study of Chokmah, is that our lives are never on hold. I now understand that the teacher life is, is always calling upon me to act from the Wisdom I have, to seek out the Wisdom I need."

What a wise and empowering insight! Most of us would feel so much better if we remained mindful of the fact that everything we experience has, in some way, the potential to make us wiser. Essentially, life is a course in self-improvement.

■ Leona, a middle school teacher shared, "I am getting better at expressing my inner Wisdom self. This is the result of allowing myself to be more aware of— better yet, to listen to—what's really going on inside me. I'm learning from the Tree of Life that I am developing the ability to respond to situations in wiser ways than I have in the past. Rather than freezing up or reacting—repeating what I've done in the past out of habit, I am getting better at telling others what I'm certain I need. While traveling over the holiday break, tuning in to the Wisdom within helped me to get out of an extremely upsetting situation. It's something that I've been unable to get through successfully before now.

I drove down to L.A. with Jody, one of my co-teachers who had recently separated from his partner. We talked about school, listened to music, and stopped to stretch, for lunch, and gas. The trip was going fine until he started making sexual advances. He unexpectedly reached out and touched my thigh. I was definitely surprised and moved his hand away. While it's extremely embarrassing to admit, I did this instead of doing what I normally do when being sexually pressured, which is giving in and later feeling hopeless and furious at myself. I can't begin to tell you the thoughts that started racing through my mind.

Deciding I had better center myself, I pulled out our list of suggestions for Chokmah's practical application from my daypack. After reading through the list, I closed my eyes and called in Ratziel, the angel of Wisdom, for first aid. Doing this allowed my Wise Self to take charge. Although what I needed to do turned out to be quite simple, it was not easy. I told Jody that I was definitely not on the same page and felt upset by his actions. Instead of answering me, he asked me to pick out some music and remained silent for the hour and a half or so left of the drive.

Arriving in L.A., he dropped me at my aunt's. After getting my bag out of the trunk, I told him that I'd probably be taking the train back home. He looked surprised and quietly drove off. Less than an hour later he texted me to apologize saying he'd gladly drive and would behave himself. I told him I'd let him know.

Well, I did end up driving back with him and he was completely cool. He apologized again and even made a dumb joke about himself, which I'd rather not repeat. He admitted that he'd been attracted to me for a while, but got that it isn't mutual and hoped that we might be friends. It came down to the truth that I didn't want what he did, and becoming able to express my Self, with a capital S, my inner Wisdom, without getting nasty, helped us to move forward. By setting a wise and healthy boundary, things worked out. Thank Chokmah!"

Chokmah is about both cosmic and personal will, which also may be termed assertion of Self. It sounds as if you have developed a newer and wiser model. Following your inner prompting to turn inwards for Wisdom and assistance from Ratziel and your inner Self, you prudently handled this very uncomfortable situation. Being true to and expressing your Sel, has set the stage for doing more of the same in the future. Keep up the Great Work!

■ "I've been inspired by a little piece of Wisdom," volunteered Sylvia, a physician's assistant and distance runner. "Getting older, I've begun realizing that I am doing many of the same things my parents did and that I condemn them for doing when I was younger. Not long after going into, 'Oh God, I'm just like them,' I had the sense to go into my class notes on Chokmah. These really got me looking at the situation and myself differently. Reviewing some key points last Saturday morning, I got a very real jolt of Wisdom—it was an actual physical sensation that assured me that I'm doing what I am doing for my reasons, not theirs. It was as if a light in my mind was turned on, helping me see that I'm not *really* replicating their behavior.

A year or so ago I took a training program that helped me to expand my perspective on life. It underscored the fact that I always have options when I'm wise enough to wake up and consider what these might be! Of course, new patterns take time to digest, but I'm seeing that what I do is my choice. Chokmah inspired me with the Wisdom to get to that truth. While an external activity may appear the same, what's driving that activity, one's internal motivation, can be, and in this instance was, different. Coincidentally, I had planned to spend time with my mom and dad over lunch the next day.

While visiting my parents, I found myself being less critical and more relaxed, actually breathing deeper and easier, and not looking for their faults as I often do. Chokmah's Illuminating Intelligence jolted my perspective by simply reminding me that I'm me! Noticing their grey hair reminded me that they are wise in their ways, some of which I've definitely benefitted from. Being like my parents is definitely far from being all bad!"

> *Thank you, Sylvia. How inspired and inspiring! Yes, Chokmah's Illuminating Intelligence is synonymous with inspiration and revelation, often defined as* divine guidance, *or* influence exerted directly upon one's mind and imagination. *The word inspire is derived from the Latin* inspirare, *meaning 'to breathe and to breathe spirit into,' and as you shared, you found yourself breathing easier when with your parents once your spiritual perspective was forcefully expanded. You certainly experienced Chokmah's symbol, the lightning bolt that brought you a dynamic flash of illumination or Wisdom.*

■ Barbie, an accountant, enthusiastically began, "I'm getting that when exploring Kether, we are acknowledging the existence of the One Self, and when exploring Chokmah we are being aware of the One Wise Self living through us and all on planet Earth. There's so much going on in my life right now, especially so with the start of tax season. Although the world is whirling and twirling about me with people and circumstances almost pulling me off course, I've been managing to keep calm by remembering the Homeplay suggestion to use the power of 'the Word' to reshape or transform a situation. I'm doing this by putting reminder notes in my car, on my computer screen, refrigerator door, on the kitchen window and bathroom mirror saying, 'I'm living from the center of my Wise Self.' For added reinforcement, I'm reading these aloud almost every time I glance at my reminders! Setting up my 'support system,' it's becoming easier to resist being pulled off course.

I also invite the Illuminating Intelligence and luminous silver-grey light of Chokmah into me when I wake up in the morning. I few times I imagined the early summer fog surrounding me with Chokmah's energy. Oh yes, I've been wearing my comfy grey walking shoes and telling myself that I'm walking in heaven's creation while walking on earth. I considered putting on my housemate's extra grey sweatshirt hanging by the front door, but passed with my yellowish skin tone.

Summing it all up, despite having lots of people and things vying for my time and attention, I'm managing to stay focused on what I really want and need to accomplish. I guess you could say that I had a very uplifting week *living* with Chokmah. I'm looking forward to continuing these practices and feeling more and more Self-centered, Self-directed, and Self-satisfied!"

Congratulations Barbie! It sounds like your plan to integrate ways of living more wisely into your busy daily life is bearing some sweet fruit. You set your goal, and created ways of accomplishing it, through what you're calling your 'support system.' Wisdom is certainly doing what you did. It's also the willingness to stop and shift into neutral and be open to direction, when unsure of how to best proceed. Mentioning this brings the receptive aspect of Wisdom and its many deities to mind. Chokmah addresses the importance of sleuthing out and then remaining attuned to direction. When we, consistently invite the light of greater impersonal consciousness into our minds, our thoughts and feelings become clarified and we are able to act with increasing amounts of Wisdom.

■ "I love Halloween," began Ricky, a dietitian. So, when my partner Paul and I were invited to a costume party, I was ecstatic. That was, until Paul had to fly to Hong Kong on business. I was terribly disappointed because I wanted to share the event with him, and actually considered not going. You know the old stay-at-home-and-mope routine. Yet, when I looked at the Tree of Life diagram hanging on our living room wall, I started thinking about Chokmah and the Wisdom of my decision. Chokmah's creative potential and grade of Magus really stood out in my mind. It was at exactly that moment that I got creative and changed my hocus-pocus focus, from thinking of myself as an 'abandoned child' to thinking of myself as a 'magical child.' I then did some wise, creative thinking that got me one hundred and one percent involved in making myself a hilarious costume complete with some wild makeup. Words can't really express how awesome it was to transform myself. And in the process of transforming myself physically, I also transformed my mindset!

The party was completely magical. Of course, there was even a magician. I loved, loved, loved it! It was a cosmic affirmation of what I myself had done by letting go of my disappointment and welcoming in my creativity. After an awesome performance, I asked the magician how he'd gotten started in his unique career. He shared that nearly thirty years ago a wonderful magician came to entertain at a neighborhood event, and that was that. His interest was sparked! I immediately thought about the sparking energy of Chokmah. He told me how he'd managed to follow the Magician's shows over the state and eventually became his apprentice. When the Magician died, he left him all of his tricks.

Walking home, I realized that I had a great time and didn't even miss my partner. Sure, I wished Paul had been there for the fun, but I gained a lot of Wisdom by him not being there, perhaps even more than had he been present."

Brilliant! You wisely harnessed the initiating and activating energies of Chokmah to initiate having a good time for yourself, rather than allowing yourself to continue initiating misery. Doing this also gave you a taste of the Grade of Magus. At the advanced levels of this grade, the aspirant is no longer distracted by the possibility and glamour of manifesting external forms, but by the magical-transformational qualities of the Life force itself. (Of course, if this service is needed, the Magus can step-up.)

It seems that you've received a taste of the Grade of Magus. Over time, we, like the Magus, change from ordinary to extraordinary humans. Of course, if we think of the Magus only as an ideal of what we may someday become, we miss a crucial and fundamental fact. The Magus already lives at the core of every one of us.

■ Sam, a self-described "household engineer," enthusiastically related the following: "I've been meeting with a writer's group over the last few years. I usually bring pieces of work that are complete and ask for feedback. It's strange, but I've never asked for help when I'm stuck. Well, suddenly there I was with a short story that I'd been unable to complete. I was experiencing 'writer's block,' to the max. At first, I resisted bringing it to the group, thinking 'There's nothing anyone can tell me about my story that I don't already know myself. It doesn't work! It won't work! It will never work! ' Yet during our class on Wisdom, I began thinking, 'Why not be open?' I can take what's useful and leave the rest.

I walked into the next meeting ready to surrender to the group's collective Wisdom. I actually imagined myself carrying a grey flag, that of surrendering to Wisdom, into the room. Well, of course, the comments were more than helpful! I went home energized and with some ideas that will help bring my story to its perfect end.

This great resource has been available to me all this time. While I keep offering others ideas, I haven't asked for them for myself. I'm finally more than ready to put my ego aside and be open to the Wisdom that's there for me. Hey, asking for input doesn't mean that I *must* take what's offered. It's time for me to wake up, wise up, and be more open-minded!"

Sounds like you made a wise decision. Opening your mind to your group's collective Wisdom, you were duly rewarded. In my own experience, being closed has been a defense mechanism—a way of avoiding vulnerability and destructive criticism. I've been amazed to discover that when I let my guard down how much Wisdom is available to me. Doing this has canceled a great deal of the destructive vs. constructive criticism I've been dealt at earlier times in my life. Your growing ability to be discerning will exert a positive influence on your decision to experiment with it again in the future.

■ "The virtue of Devotion and vice of Disloyalty connected with Chokmah really set me thinking," offered Toria, a massage therapist. "First, I've realized that within this last year, I've become increasingly devoted to living authentically, which to me means living according to what I know in every cell of my being to be true. I also know that not doing this is a form of disloyalty.

With the onset of the COVID-19 pandemic, the spa shutting down and school closing, my biggest commitment became helping my eleven-year-old son Milo with his school assignments. He's 'educationally challenged,' meaning he has some significant trouble paying attention. Because recent studies show general online schooling to be rated 5-out-of 10 for effectiveness, I knew I had to get on it. Milo also needs lots of physical activity. He and I play Ping-Pong and shoot baskets. His dad takes him out for runs—he's one fast kid. Of course, being isolated from his friends is a whole other topic.

Although I don't feel fully confident in my abilities, I do know I can learn. My devotion to helping Milo get the best start possible in life is moving me forward. I'm seeing this as a once-in-a-lifetime opportunity that's completely aligned with my decision to live wisely, and in doing so, model how my beautiful son can learn to do likewise.

We go into the *school tent* we've set up in our family room at 8:30 am and get going. It's definitely a full-time job. A good teacher has to be devoted to their students; otherwise, it's a disservice all around. It's so energizing knowing that I am being loyal to my child and Higher Power by doing this. It's inspiring me to do the best I can, and then some.

Milo has always been curious about the tarot, and when I asked him if he'd like to learn more, he got really excited. I decided to give him my tarot card-coloring book and box of pens—some of which are metallic. I was stunned by the almost 3D-illuminated look he gave the Fool! While he isn't the greatest reader, he does have a great eye for color.

I'm contemplating the Wisdom of taking Manly Palmer Hall's brilliantly illustrated *The Secret Teachings of All Ages* and showing it to Milo, for the art and to help him focus as it's so detailed. Now that's something that wouldn't happen in his public school classroom! Through Chokmah, I'm recognizing that much of this situation is about trusting the inspirations, revelations, or Wisdom that comes knocking on the door to my mind."

Chokmah brings knowledge, and through it, the inspiration and Wisdom to sensitively and sensibly do whatever we are being called to do. It sounds as if the situation with your son is an excellent catalyst not only for deepening your knowledge of yourself and your son but for expanding your body of knowledge and Wisdom by being a tuned-in teacher-learning facilitator, as well as an experience of Chokmah's virtue, Devotion. Solving problems is a way of testing and developing our spiritual muscles, aka Wisdom. That said, your virtuous devotion is filling this room with Chokmah's Illuminating Intelligence and thoughts of Milo's 3D-illuminated coloring of The Fool card. Toria, short for Victoria, means victory. It sounds like you're right on track doing you all to help Milo, and in the process of doing it, thoroughly committed to co-creating victories all around.

■ Zara, a young, high-powered saleswoman, began, "Last year I met a man through mutual friends and it was 'dislike at first sight.' Initially, I thought he was insufferably egotistical and overbearing. He personified all the negative male qualities that I could think of. Because we were hanging out with the same group of friends, he and I eventually started talking. What a surprising and enwisening experience that turned into!

I found that while he's propelled by boundless energy, it's with a certain self-confidence that's far from overbearing. He's not afraid to step up and take charge without the need for applause. It's honestly refreshing meeting someone else, besides me, who does this well.

Now I'll finally tell you how my experience ties in with Chokmah. I could see that we were getting increasingly attracted to each other. While I didn't want to put myself out and say, 'I really like you,' he did. It was utterly cool! Here was Greyson, or Grey for short—which so happens to be Chokmah's color—who for the longest time I didn't like and categorized as just another typical misogynistic male waving his you-know-what around. Yet, when push came to shove, he turned out to be the stronger person emotionally. He was the one who came out and said, 'I think you're awesome, but I'm terrified to get more involved because I don't know how you feel about me.' Then he said, 'but I want to take a chance anyhow.' I really admire his courage and honesty.

Out of all of this, I've gained a lot of respect for him. Expressing my feelings isn't easy. I think this a big part of why Greyson came into my life. I sense it's not all about having a relationship with him—it's about feeling propelled and inspired to open to the Wisdom I'm needing for my own growth and development."

Much like the interaction between you and Greyson, Chokmah is the boundless projective Life Force, while Binah receives that energy and is herself activated or inspired by it. Chokmah is associated with the Word or cosmic force, which initiated creation, and you used the word propel, which means to move or to sustain in motion. Your interactions with Grey have propelled you to move your attitude about him.

Although this is getting a bit ahead of ourselves, the energies of Chokmah and Binah are often thought of to be purely projective and receptive, it's helpful to recall that Chokmah is receptive to Kether, whereas Binah projects her energies into the spheres below. Whether we're male, female, or someone in-between, we operate like these sephiroth, projective in some areas and receptive in others. The dance of Chokmah and Binah demonstrates how we humans have the potential to empower and enhance one another.

■ "We've *really* been wanting to move to a different home outside of the city," announced Benny, an Operating Room nurse and parent of three grown children. Although Kim and I have been trying to make our present home livable, the neighborhood has gotten much noisier and more polluted with car exhaust (we're close to the freeway) since we moved in years ago. It's very unhealthy—especially for Kim, who has asthma. BC, Before Chokmah, I was making a big negative monster out of the situation, suffering to the max, instead of asking the Universe for help.

Prompted by Chokmah, I started thinking and repeating the words, 'There absolutely must be a wise way to do this, please, please Great God, show me the way.' Well, out-of-the-blue comes the bright idea that it didn't have to happen in the usual way of calling up the real estate agent, showing the house, waiting for someone to buy it, et cetera, et cetera. So I kept repeating my prayer: 'There absolutely must be a wise way to do this, please, please Great God show me the way.' And Presto-Chango I get this amazing insight from which we were able to formulate a wise and wonderful plan!

Kim is a faculty member at the local college. Because there's no staff housing on campus, they helped us find our house. Well, of course, we simply had to find a faculty member who needed a home! We can then refinance it, since the lending rates have dropped so low, and then have the college transfer the title to the new owner. This can happen without the house ever having to go on the market! This means not having to go through the ugly real estate dance *and* we don't have to do everything involved in showing and perhaps staging it.

So guess what? Kim put the word out and just about instantly found a faculty member with small children and almost exact same job title, but in another department, so I'm sure he qualifies. Of course, he and his family were delighted 'to find the perfect house.' Thank you, Great Wise Chokmah!"

And thank you, Benny, for Letting go and Letting the magic of Chokmah in. Problems hold the potential to open us to Wisdom. Your use of the words 'bright idea' and 'out-of-the-blue' points to Chokmah's connection with Uranus, the planet of cosmic flashes—innovative, outside-of-the-box thinking and doing. Your problem opened you to the Wisdom of going beyond your little self and ideas. Doing this, you opened yourself to receiving the gift of Chokmah's Illuminating Intelligence.

As you know, Chokmah is coupled with the Word, the cosmic power of creation. You put the word out in every way, and look what you co-created. I say co-create because our creative powers are interdependent, not independent. Whether we recognize it or not, we work with what the Universe deems appropriate for manifestation. As I experience it, Spirit always has the last word!

BINAH, UNDERSTANDING

MOTHER OF ALL LIVINGNESS, QUEEN OF QUEENS, CREATRIX, "FROM ME ALL COMES AND TO ME ALL AT LAST RETURNS."

THE APPETIZER: PERSONALLY SPEAKING

After many days of cleaning up our front garden after the stormy winter weather, I discovered numerous piles of dog poop scattered throughout. Although dog excreta is theoretically organic matter, it cannot be left to deteriorate because, unlike cow manure, dog droppings have a high protein-based diet that creates very acidic excrement which is toxic to plants. I love animals and am aware of how difficult the life of a dog, especially a large one, can be in the city. Despite a leash law, some of our neighbors rather than taking the time to walk their dogs let their pets loose to roam the streets in bad weather and late at night. Because the particular street we live on only has very few lights, these stealthy creatures manage to go unseen—and according to some folks, "What's a little doggy poop, anyhow?"

Late one afternoon I was standing by the kitchen window, overlooking our newly restored front garden, when out of the corner of my eye, I caught sight of a huge dog about to squat. Directly behind him, stood a young man who was casually witnessing the proceedings. As instantaneously as Diana Prince turns into Wonder Woman, I turned into a unique combo of the Hindu Kali, the ultimate protectress against evil-doing and Roman goddess Pomona, the guardian of gardens.

Flinging open the front door, I yelled as loud as I could, "Get that dog out of here, NOW!" Both the dog and its owner froze in their tracks. (A dog roaming alone under cover of darkness is one thing, but an enormous canine squatting in my garden in the early evening accompanied by its owner was positively outrageous!) In one emotionally laden sentence, I further spouted that I was done having the garden shat-in, dug up, and destroyed by neighborhood dogs, made easy by their owners breaking the leash law. The man responded by making an ugly face and muttering under his breath. Undaunted, I asked for his address, with the intention of reporting him and his dog to the pound. Nearly spitting out his street name and number, he leashed his pet, pivoted sharply away, and headed down the street.

Thinking that I'd "done my job," I strode confidently back into the house. Watching the events through the window, my son, who was visiting from another part of the state, asked whether I thought I'd communicated effectively. I replied, "Definitely." He, however, had a different point of view, commenting that my threatening attitude, although protective, might encourage this now angry man to allow his dog to visit the garden more frequently, only under the cover of darkness. Still inflamed, I heatedly disagreed.

Following an early Sunday dinner, I slipped into the twilight for a walk. Nearing the ocean, I deeply inhaled the delicious salt air. Feeling calmed, I rested on a bench overlooking the surf. While sitting and enjoying the ebbing and flowing sea my thoughts turned to the week ahead, when I would be sharing the second half of the third sephirah Understanding—or *Binah*, in Hebrew (pronounced Bee-nah in English), the Cosmic Mother. I began recalling how much I delight in sharing the Tree of Life's creation story. It relates the Great Mother principle's impregnation by the Great Father principle, Chokmah, instigated by Kether's Oneness that contains both the positive and negative polarities. These cosmic interactions result in the fluid-like arrangement of atomic molecules and particles comprising the entire physical world, or the Great Sea of Life flowing out from her.

Yes, yesssssss, Understanding! Suddenly the afternoon's events began flooding my mind. I realized that my enactment of the fierce garden protectress was definitely aligned with the dark aspect of the Divine Mother, who brings transformation through fear, destruction, and death. Images of ferocious goddesses began marching through my mind's eye. I then became ready to ask myself if I might have been able to protect the garden without terrorizing, and perhaps permanently alienating, my neighbor.

Going back and forth in my mind, I acknowledged that the young man was first entitled to a civil warning, rather than a wild woman demanding obedience. Shame slowly began seeping through me. Along with it, I began wondering in how many different ways and how many different times I needed to be reminded that such ways of dealing with conflict don't work—either for me personally or for solving world problems. The work I was doing on Non-Violent Conflict Resolution immediately came to mind. Recalling Binah translates from Hebrew as Understanding, I then *understood* that the man and his dog had inadvertently become the recipients of the storehouse of rage I'd been feeling toward all of the loose dogs and their irresponsible owners in the neighborhood and probably in the world! Unexpectedly a verse attributed to none other than Wonder Woman began playing itself through my mind:

Don't kill if you can wound,
Don't wound if you can subdue,
Don't subdue if you can restore peace,
And don't raise your hand at all until you've first extended it!

The sacrament conjoined with Binah is Communion, which asks a practitioner's willingness to acknowledge and then bypass their personal attachments and aversions regarding how they, others, and the world must or must not be. Watching the undulating ocean, I communed with Binah. I felt soothed when one of her alternative names, *Mater Bon Consili*, meaning "Mother of Good Counsel and Understanding," came to mind. It reminded me that Binah bestows compassion and tolerance on anyone who wishes to learn from their shortcomings. She offers comfort when facing pain and sadness—the difficulties inherent in changing one's behavior due to increased Understanding, which results from shifting from the purely personal to a more interpersonal state of mind and heart. I immediately got that I needed to be more Understanding toward my neighbor, his, pet, and myself. Suddenly ready and willing to bring about a better relationship between my neighbor and me—the transforming and resurrecting aspects of the dark and foreboding Great Mother,

Binah—I chose to walk home directly past the young man's home. While walking, I prayed for guidance and gathered my thoughts for whatever might lie ahead.

Seeing a light on, I took a long, deep breath. A dog began barking as I headed up to the door. My heart pounded in my ears as I rang the bell and listened to both man and dog scrambling to answer. As the door opened I blurted out, "Hi, I'm Amber, your neighbor. I'm here to apologize for yelling at you two today. I want to ask that you *please* keep him, (*gesturing to the dog*) out of our garden. Also, what, if anything, might I do to help this happen?"

Looking confused, the man nearly smiled as he readily agreed. After chatting (or communing) further with Byron about the neighborhood, and speaking softly to Elvis, I headed home ready for a relaxing bath. When I told my son what had occurred he said "Good job, Momz." I smiled to myself as he was echoing the basic phrase of encouragement I had sent his way for as long as I could remember.

Understanding is what results when we learn from our experiences. As a consequence of all that had occurred, I fell asleep feeling peaceful due to my upgraded Understanding. While it's true that in certain instances fiercely protective behavior is appropriate, I had not taken the time to find out if, in fact, this was one of them. Although I had misunderstood what the situation genuinely called for, a combination of my son's input and sitting beside Mama Ocean brought me into Communion (Binah's Sacrament) with Binah and a viable plan. Doing this helped clarify my Understanding, bringing me to recognize what I really wanted, a better relationship with Byron and Elvis, a poop-free garden, and a better way of birthing these into being.

THE ENTREE:
GENERAL INFORMATION AND SYMBOLISM

BINAH IS THE HEBREW WORD FOR UNDERSTANDING

The Hebrew name Binah, again pronounced Bee-nah, translated into English as Understanding. Qabalistically, the idea of Understanding underscores the fact that the Universal Life Force stands under or supports all of creation. The Tree of Life illustrates the spheres of Chokmah and Binah to be interdependent, or two halves of the whole of creation—as are the concepts of Wisdom and Understanding. It makes sense that Binah has been likened to a place of mirrors that reflects the pure light of Chokmah, increasing and multiplying it in an infinite variety of ways. By gaining mental cognition and knowledge of a concept—Wisdom—we eventually arrive at a more personal experience of what that concept may actually be. Because doing this involves some sort of sensory and emotional arousal, it is termed Understanding.

Of course, when progressing up rather than down the Tree of Life Understanding leads to Wisdom, the ability to know or discern inner qualities and relationships. Simply, when indicating an action, Understanding means comprehending the true nature of some person, thing, or situation we have come to know or understand. As mentioned when exploring the sphere of Chokmah, the terms "to know" and "to have knowledge of" are used, in the Biblical sense, as euphemisms or indirect references for sexual intimacy. This terminology is fitting when learning about Binah as a cosmic container for the co-mingling of energies originating from Kether and Chokmah.

Understanding evolves from our ability to distinguish one thing from another. It is also the ability to make an idea comprehensible by likening it to an object or idea that is already understood, or paired with some type of tangible experience. For example, we may say," She was behaving like a trapped animal." Understanding is having a personal conception, familiarity, skillfulness, or expert handling of a particular object or set of circumstances. It also refers to having a kind, sensitive, and responsive, sympathetic, or empathic attitude and is used as a synonym for compassion and rapport. In this sense, Understanding is synonymous with tolerance, the ability to reconcile differences. Understanding indicates mutually cooperative and considerate relationships between people, philosophies, and ideologies. Renowned science fiction writer Robert Heinlein's brainchild, "grok," pretty much fits this definition. Along a similar line, Understanding is aligned with the French concept of *détentes*, the relaxation of tension that comes after successful formal meetings and negotiations between nations.

In contrast to the inductive reasoning of Wisdom, Understanding is linked with deductive reasoning. Consequently, Understanding is having the ability to use deduction to formulate and apply concepts and categories to a draw a logical conclusion. For example: From the sum total of information at hand, scientists deduce that despite natural ebbs and flows in climate patterns, the present drought in California is predominantly a byproduct of global warming. Understanding is synonymous with mental clarity—one receives or conceives wisely, as does Binah in her relationship with Chokmah. Qabalists believe that the world as we understand it is conceived, birthed, sustained, and changed by our Understanding. Consequently, when our personal Understanding grows wiser, for example through familiarity with the Qabalistic Tree of Life, our view of the world also grows wiser, or as a friend's Hip Hop DJ daughter calls it, "fresher."

Greater and Lesser Understanding

Greater or universal Understanding is omniscient in that it has complete knowledge of all of existence. As mentioned, yet worth reiterating, such is interchangeably termed Wisdom of the Ages, Perennial Wisdom, Eternal Verities, or what Qabalists like myself refer to as universal and natural laws, truths, and principles. Greater

Understanding may be perceived as a transpersonal agreement between divinity and humanity. Such is the perfectly clear insight and knowledge that supports the well-being of all creation and in doing so, the evolution of consciousness. While at times challenging for the ego and its attending personality, implementing this type of Understanding is what we humans are presently growing into embodying and enacting. Because this brand of Understanding is based upon the development of Wisdom, we are continually being challenged to face tasks with as much awareness as we have in our databank, even when data is lacking or poor. Of course, like a vitamin deficiency, Wisdom deficiency presents us with the opportunity to supplement and upgrade our learning.

Lesser, faulty, or incomplete Understanding, on the other hand, is steeped in the unintentional and intentional misunderstanding of the call we are being asked to answer. In this state, our words and actions are based upon the likes of commonly understood biases, irrational feelings, rigid or outworn ideas, ignorance, and downright stupidity. For example, a student's mother wanted to move to California to live closer to her family, yet put it off for years "because it's earthquake country." This could have been offset by her considering that every part of the world is subject to the forces of nature and that relocation does offer some priceless perks—such as proximity to her daughter, son and grandchildren. Another example of lesser or misunderstanding is witnessing parents with nothing but "good intentions," mapping out their five-year-old child's future, without genuinely considering, or better yet, investigating and Understanding her aptitudes and interests. I recall this whenever I see my friend Warren, whose life as an unhappy lawyer is largely the result of being endlessly pressured by his father to take over his legal practice. (Born under the cardinal water sign of Cancer, he had yearned to become an oceanographer.)

In the state of lesser Understanding, greater Understanding has little or no space to enter. When lost in the land of lesser Understanding, excessive ego, over-emotionality and the like prevent us from being open to viewing a situation from different perspectives. This state also evokes beliefs wherein we are oblivious to, or deny, the part we might have played in what has occurred. The aforementioned is sometimes called "victim consciousness." This is in stark contrast to my student Chris, humorously acknowledging her part in a significant mix-up at work, stating and demonstrating, "When I am busy pointing my finger at someone else's mistakes, three of my fingers are simultaneously pointing back at me!"

Engendering greater Understanding suggests being ready, willing, and able to put aside our lesser Understanding and our attachment to having life be completely on our terms. Doing this clears the path to greater Understanding, supported by Wisdom, to emerge. Eventually, we "get" that our real attachment is to be aligned with increasingly expansive perception, aka greater Understanding. Calling up this form of Understanding is a potent means of directing ourselves, handling interpersonal relationships, and coping with the endless demands of daily living. Embracing this attitude results in views such as "I honestly wish to understand your point of view and trust you wish to understand mine."

Consistently enacting the principles of greater Understanding, we develop mastery over ourselves and our surroundings, and possibly inspire others to behave similarly. One of the most potent ways I have come to this way of communicating is through adopting Non-Violent Communication, or NVC.

NVC may be understood as a style of communication designed to increase empathy and improve the quality of life of those who utilize the method as well as the people around them. This methodology helps us to see our common humanity, using such insights in a way that honors everyone's needs. It offers a solid skill set that helps us create life-serving relationships, families, and communities. Through its emphasis on "deep listening" or the application of greater Understanding to ourselves and others, we become increasingly able to listen to both our own deepest needs and those of others. NVC helps us discover the depth of our own Understanding. Solution-Oriented Non-Violent Communication or NVC emphasizes:

- Observes without judging.
- Communicates feelings without blame, shame, anger, and so on.
- Helps participants to hear one another in a safe, supportive and compassionate environment so that understanding may more easily occur.
- Clarifies and communicates feelings and needs.
- Makes specific requests based on clarified feelings and needs.

Coming full circle—as with everything else we experience, lesser Understanding or lack of Understanding is an essential part of the workings of Spirit. Life is slowly teaching me that my ignorance, unconsciousness, laziness, narrow-mindedness, fearfulness, stubbornness, and the like have the potential to humiliate me to the point wherefrom I start begging for more Understanding.

BINAH IN PICTURES

The Hebrew word for Understanding, Binah, comprised of the letters *Beth, Yod, Nun* and *Heh*, appears on most Qabalistically-oriented tarot decks. Some of the most revealing Understanding of Binah may be received by contemplating the Hebrew letters and tarot cards paired with them: Beth, meaning house—the Magician card. Yod, indicating an open hand—the Hermit card. Nun, translating as, to sprout, grow, and proliferate—the Death card. Heh, signifying a window—the Emperor card. Before reading on, consider mulling over the imagery and symbolism of the aforementioned cards regarding Understanding. My meditation revealed what follows:

The Magician Card and Hebrew Letter, Beth

The Magician card, occasionally named "The Changer," emerged out of the Hebrew letter Beth, meaning house. The magic of Understanding begins entering my consciousness when I start coming to terms with that fact as a consequence of building the house of my life on closed-minded and-hearted, purely egocentric constructs, the garden of my life is not flourishing. Eventually, the misery resulting from my rigidity brings me to understand what I have unwittingly done. Accepting this ego-shattering awareness, I start opening up to examining and changing my intolerant attitudes and behaviors.

The Hermit Card and Hebrew Letter, Yod

The Hermit emanated from the Hebrew letter Yod, meaning an open, helping, and serving hand. When the misery and suffering inherent to living open my tight grasp on rigid attitudes and behaviors, I give new and improved Understandings the chance of entering. Doing this, I become receptive to adopting transpersonal principles that serve me with the chance to review and change the misconceptions seeded in my mind and heart. This leads me to Understanding the value of renovating the house of my personality by being more aware of the facts and information I unconsciously have taken-in and how I communicate.

Death and Hebrew Letter, Nun

Birthed from the Hebrew letter Nun, meaning to sprout and grow, the Death card reminds me that as a result of my growing Understanding, the dead parts of my personality must pass away. Of course, from death comes renewal. Understanding that relinquishing the expired and expiring parts of my personality provides nourishing compost, I open myself to start imagining (the card is also coupled with the Imaginative Intelligence) and thereby creating more realistic, spiritualized reference points on which to base my Understanding of everyday living.

The Emperor and Hebrew Letter, Heh

The Emperor, an extension of the Hebrew letter Heh, meaning window, is fittingly coupled with our eyes, sense of sight, and the super sense of clairvoyance, or clear-seeing. Like all humans, I sometimes live with my eyes wide shut. The Emperor suggests that by opening the window of my mind to see, I have the potential to view the Wisdom of the sages. Understanding this gives me the chance to perceive myself and life situations more realistically. The Emperor sits on a multi-faceted cube holding an observatory. These objects remind me that as my Understanding expands, my ability to observe life's innumerable facets also expands. In the midst of my ego struggling to remain in complete control, remembering this opens my Understanding and betters my life and me.

LOCATION, LOCATION, LOCATION:

BINAH'S PLACEMENT ON THE TREE OF LIFE

The Tree of Life's third sephirah, Binah, located on the causal plane, receives the energies of Kether through Chokmah and tops the Pillar of Severity, completing the Supernal, Divine, or Super-conscious Triad. An elaboration of Kether's One Divine Presence, Binah is the Queen of Heaven. Also called the Upper Shekinah, or feminine divine presence, she is Spirit about to be embodied in the world of form that will again appear in Kingdom or Malkuth as the lower Shekinah, the Queen of Earth.

Future Time

Time-wise, Binah is situated in the future, and for our purposes, biological time. All of the life sciences report that living organisms incorporate biological clocks governing the rhythms of their behavior and in most instances, their life span. Animals and plants also exhibit a circadian cycle of temperature and metabolic rate that have a genetic basis.

Genetic Encoding

Binah, Mother of Matter, is the sephirah most linked with: 1) Physical conception. 2) Genetic encoding. And 3) any limitations natural to the creation of physical form. Simply put, the biological clock of what has been conceived from Binah's interactions with Kether via Chokmah begins running. This is substantiated by the cutting-edge ideas of Gottfried Leibniz. This 17th-century German philosopher and mathematician proposed that the time we experience embodied on earth is simply the length of the program given to us by Spirit. This implies that biological time is nature's way of keeping things from occurring simultaneously!

Causality

Like Chokmah, Binah is situated on the causal plane. Whether we are male or female, every act of creative manifestation takes place through the Cosmic Mother principle. Qabalists believe that everything that lives, lives inside the womb of the Great Mother and draws its life and sustenance from Her. Once the potency of Chokmah reaches the conceptual level of Binah, it proceeds into the physical world. This cosmic ordering process flows all the way down the Tree of Life into Malkuth, the World of Spirit embodied in form. Binah gives birth to the Seven Spirits of the Most High, or the remaining seven sephiroth. From another view, the Binah's activities are like the roots of a tree watered by Chokmah, which then branch out to become the body of the Tree of Life and the entire manifest world.

Insight, Foresight and Natural Selection

In contrast to the Pillar of Mercy, topped by Wisdom and conjoined with time past, the Pillar of Severity topped by Understanding designates the future. Qabalists link acts of *insight, logic,* and *reason* to the Cosmic Father principle, whereas the Cosmic Mother principle is linked to *foresight, intuition* and *creative imagination.* In her role of Mother Nature, Binah continually does this in her work of "natural selection." A shortage of bamboo in a region of China resulted in Pandas from that area ceasing to reproduce and starving to death. However, due to activities on the part of conservationists, their status has changed from "endangered" to "vulnerable." Certainly, it is essential to acknowledge that numerous natural selection processes are askew due to environmental damage, insufficiencies, and catastrophes that stem from the much-discussed, debated, and proven Anthropocene, or human intrusion, upon nature. Nevertheless, from the big or cosmic perspective, everything is in order for the evolution of consciousness.

Generally, Mother Nature plans for the future through the process of natural selection. To date, this means that creatures possessing characteristics advantageous for survival in a specific environment constitute an increasing proportion of their species in that environment with each succeeding generation. Being a fair-skinned redhead who grew up pre-sunscreen and in an era when being tanned was fashionable, I am very prone to skin cancer. That said, I am heartened that the upside to this change is that the seven human races are slowly mixing to become more sun tolerant, less subject to some racially inherited diseases such as Sickle Cell Anemia, and less racist.

The phenomenon of selective increase-expansion and decrease-contraction is also known to result in the development of new species. This change is evident in Senegal where as a result of the extremely hot weather chimpanzees are now growing much less hair and nursing mothers and babies are spending many hours in underground caves that are at least twenty degrees cooler than the surrounding jungle. Nature chooses what works best, and with maturity, we humans learn, through trial and error, to do likewise.

As we grow increasingly aware of the workings of Binah, we increase our Understanding of the how-tos of planning for a better future. Much as the Pillars of Mercy and Severity represent times past and future, the interactions between Chokmah and Binah, the force of Wisdom's insightfulness reaches out to the force of Understanding's forethoughtfulness to evolutionize our species individually and collectively.

In closing, Carl Jung taught that one of the major errors in Christian theology was excluding the divinity of nature within us. We are presently living with the results of this misunderstanding, as evidenced by the environmental catastrophes currently befalling this beautiful planet and all upon it.

Cosmic Conception

Binah is the first form-making sephirah. In the same way that the sperm and egg interact in order to create life, the dynamic cosmic spark of Kether received by Chokmah is then ejected outwards. Yet, without Binah to receive, individualize, particularize, and finitize it into innumerable manifestations, this force is incapable of further development. It is Binah's task to crystallize consciousness into the entire spectrum of physicality. Similar to human conception, Binah is the place wherein the unrestricted life force of Chokmah is shaped into specific life forms, which then function as the animal, vegetable, and mineral realms. Binah provides the cosmic container or womb for the further development, elaboration, and manifestation of the powers of Chokmah and Kether.

Binah, the form-giver to all life, balances Chokmah, the form-instigator. The interaction between these polarities is essential in order for our world to come into being. Birth is a highly specialized and interdependent process. Motherhood or creation cannot occur unless there is activation and impregnation from the Father Principle—turkey basters and in vitro fertilization included. Conversely, Fatherhood cannot occur unless there is a mother or womb (surrogate uteri included), willing to receive and nurture his seed. Whether it is the Great Spirit of Life intending to create the manifest world, or humans intending to birth a child or any physical structure into being, the process is identical: conception, followed by gestation and birth.

Planning for Future Generations

Probably the most mysterious and miraculous of events is the birth of living bodies—what Qabalists envision as the rhythmic dance of life occurring within the Supernal Triad. All of us are like Binah, in that we depend, consciously and unconsciously, upon inspiration as the impetus to create. It is easy to forget that the momentum to bring each creature, object, and so on into existence comes from the infinite.

Chokmah enlivens the entire Tree of Life by instigating conception in Binah—the Understanding or parameters of the progeny to be gestated and birthed. Qabalists relate to Binah as the face of the Most High that we can best relate to and understand. As the Great Mother, Binah bestows each soul with the physical characteristics needed to fulfill its baptismal contract. To complete the picture, when each biological clock runs out, Binah welcomes its accompanying soul back into her comforting presence.

Naturalist D'Arcy Wentworth Thompson, in his masterwork *On Growth and Form*, regards the forces that shape life thus: "Life is always in motion, responding to the deep-seated rhythms of growth," which create physical bodies.

According to James Gleick, one of the great science writers of all time: "Scientists studying the formulation of the patterns of physical reality conclude that behind the particular, visible shapes of matter must lie ghostly forms (patterns or matrices) serving as invisible templates. Forms in motion." Binah is about form being conceived, gestated, and born in the midst of Chokmah's formlessness. Scientifically, the interaction occurring between Binah and Chokmah is that of life extracting order from a sea of disorder

Gleick also quotes quantum physics pioneer Erwin Schrodinger: "A living organism has the astonishing gift of concentrating a stream of order on itself and thus escaping the decay into atomic chaos." Qabalistically speaking, the aforementioned refers back to the Source, Kether. From another view, physics professor Joseph Ford succinctly states, "Evolution is chaos with feedback."

Lastly, a biology student likened Binah's function as the great womb of life to that of a morphic field that defines the entire biology of every living being. It provides a force field that guides the development and behavior of an organism as it grows. Morphogenic fields are the organizing blueprints of things, especially living things, right down to their atomic structures.

Upgrading, Embracing and Spiraling

Binah's mothering creates, preserves, restricts, and transforms. She elaborates, fleshes out, and cares for the potential of Kether and the potency of Chokmah for future generations. Binah maintains, nourishes, and expresses the storehouse of Wisdom inherited from Chokmah, the side of the Tree representing time past. Ideally, moving into the future is the result of carefully examining and Understanding our past actions and distilling our future plans from these. Doing this gives us the chance to upgrade our actions and attitudes, thereby giving birth to better, increasingly sustainable outcomes. Finally, when ready for another go-round, the basic process is repeated to further refine and perfect the next generation of results, and in doing so, we ourselves.

Again, Understanding is related to our growing capacity for forethought and foresight. Essentially, it is our intention and increasing ability to map out and follow a reasonable plan of action with tender loving care. Although redundant, thoughtful planning is the outgrowth of hindsight and our desire to either change or repeat what has occurred. Understanding is synonymous with being willing to compost our previous experiences to fertilize a better future. Essentially, growing increasingly Understanding, we cannot help but upgrade our evolutionary software.

In addition to reviewing our past successes and failures, examining our passions and aptitudes can prove invaluable when contemplating a career change. After retiring comfortably, JR, a software engineer with time on her hands and a decades-long passion for astrology, decided to create softwear programs for beginning, intermediate, and advanced astrology students. After several learning experiences in which she misunderstood her student's learning curves, she re-birthed a series of excellent and well-received programs. Nature selects what works best, and with time and Understanding, we do too.

Spiraling through our developmental cycles, the Wisdom of Chokmah slowly but surely inspires us to put aside our angst about the future and conceive that when we live in accord with universal and natural laws, truths, and principles, everything works out over time or in the and in the Big Picture—demonstrating the farsighted Understanding of Binah. This is suggested by the statement Paul Foster Case ascribed to this sephirah: "Filled with Understanding of Its perfect law, I am guided moment by moment, along the path of liberation." Spiritual evolution is the fruit of growing increasingly aligned with the perfect way in which the laws and cycles of nature and the greater universe operate—and living by these, to whatever extent I am presently ready, willing and able.

QABALISTIC IMAGE OF BINAH: A MATURE WOMAN

Maturity is synonymous with physical ripeness and the gleaning of Understanding. Along this line, the *Sepher Ha Bahir*, or *Book of Brightness* from the twelfth-century states: "For you shall call Understanding, Mother." The archetype of a mature woman, also implying her other stages of development of virgin and crone or elder, is fitting when considering Binah as the "Mother of All." It is essential to note, that although Understanding is usually regarded as the by-product of time and experience, tending to make it synonymous with aging, spiritual maturation may occur in any gender or non-gender, at any age and time.

Such Understanding is seen in the lives of these Indian Saints. At age twenty, it was revealed to Sri Anandamayi Ma: "You are everything. I realized that the whole Universe is my own manifestation when I met directly with the One, manifested as the many." Sri Ramakrishna began experiencing his spiritual ecstasies at age 6 while worshipping the suddenly enlivened Divine Mother, Kali.

THE SEPHER YETZIRAH, NAMES BINAH

THE SANCTIFYING AND SEPARATING INTELLIGENCE

To sanctify means to consecrate, regard as holy, blessed, and free from sin—as well as to possess miraculous or supernatural power, reserve for sacred use, and make productive of spiritual strength. The Sepher Yetzirah pairs the Sanctifying Intelligence, the mental attitude of the sacredness of all life one adopts when Understanding or assimilating Binah's teachings. For many ancient groups, sanctification meant "to bless with blood," suggesting ritual sacrifice as well as the sanctity of menstruation and birth. Because all that lives comes from the womb of the Great Mother, it is hallowed and untainted by the sin, which some religions use to shame and entrap practitioners. The concept of wholeness was first evident in the early agrarian societies wherein worshippers of the Great Mother Goddess held that fertility, which enlivened everything surrounding them, was holy.

Of course, there is the sacred ritual of becoming blood brothers—joining participants' families. On a somewhat different note, Mesoamerican and African societies, among others, are known to have cut a body part to release blood in order to communicate with their deities. In ancient Mesoamerican groups, rulers performed bloodletting rituals on themselves when asking their people to make a sacrifice such as going to war. If our world leaders were required to do such as shed their own blood or disfigure their genitals in public prior to declaring war, I would guess that many conflicts could be resolved nonviolently.

Tragically, there are also individuals who, needing Understanding, deliberately hurt their bodies with some form of external or internal bleeding as a way of dealing with their mental and emotional pain, rage, anger, frustration and so on. Although not one of sanctification, this activity fits with some of Binah's alternative titles and Spiritual Experiences such as The Vision of Sorrow, covered shortly.

Binah blesses all that she gives birth to with divinity in the form of a sacred soul and the body that best accompanies it. Again, Qabalists term this divine nature the *neshama*, which translates from Hebrew to mean "breath of the Most High." Binah bestows the neshama, the specific soul, on the non-specific *élan vital* or vital Spirit of life sent to her from Kether via Chokmah.

Mother, Binah, gives the holiness of a flesh-and-blood form and features to Father, Chokmah's, Illuminating Intelligence. This is how she makes further evident and tangible the Hidden Intelligence of the Most High described in Kether. According to both spiritual and scientific systems, every part of creation is designed to perform some specific task in the greater scheme of things. Simply, all that comes through Binah's primordial womb into form are purposefully planned to fulfill some part of Divinity's special and sacred use. Each one of us is a consecrated vessel endowed with a particular purpose to accomplish on earth. Because all of creation is divine in essence and origin, the power of the Sanctifying Intelligence reminds us to respect ourselves, others, and the world around us.

Lastly, Understanding springs from the ability to distinguish, or separate one thing from another. The Binah brings about the miraculous transformation of indistinguishable, infinite energy into distinguishable and finite physical forms. This is also why Binah is known as the Separating Intelligence.

THE SPIRITUAL EXPERIENCE OF BINAH:

THE VISION OF SORROW

Movement from the timeless, limitless, infinite universe emanating from Kether to Chokmah, and then into Binah's time-constrained, limited, finite world of creation is what forges Binah's link with the Vision of Sorrow. Creation is the process of objectification—the flow of ever-existing invisible forces becoming temporarily visible beings and objects. Sorrowing arises from the fact that what is fixed only endures briefly. The conversion of spirit into matter causes its entry into the life cycle that in time gives way to the 3 D's: Decay, Death, and Dematerialization of physical forms.

Decay and death result in dematerialization, or the release of tangibility into intangibility—the metamorphosis we have learned to call and relate to as death. Yet from a scientific view, physical life is not really the beginning of anything, but part of a natural cycle in which eternally existing forces take on temporary forms, aka materialize. As mentioned under Chokmah, because energy is the movement of mass, and the movement of mass cannot be created or destroyed, energy simply changes from one form into another. Materializations remain for a certain time— their life cycle—and then dematerialize back into invisibility that at another time will again manifest to repeat these changes. While the disappearance of tangible beings and forms opens us to loss and sorrow, it simultaneously opens us the potential to increase our Understanding.

Motherhood and Mothering

From another older view and as mentioned earlier, biologist Rupert Sheldrake's theory of morphic resonance may also apply. Similar to Jung's theory of the collective unconscious, morphic resonance has shown that the influence of previous structures on similar succeeding structures occurs by way of morphogenic fields. Simply, morphic fields enable the building of physical structures (a cardiac field will become heart tissue or be directed to replace damaged or missing cells), as well as memories to cross both space and time from the past—the likes of living in a warzone, imprisonment, bigotry, slavery, political oppression, religious persecution, environmental toxicity, starvation, alcohol or drug use, being sex trafficked, in this or other lifetimes—must also be mentioned.

Whether through biology, intentional or unintentional actions or inactions, mental, emotional, or physical abuse, neglect, or abandonment, many of us were significantly traumatized. In any event, the sorrow resulting from this impacts the person we grow into, how we live, relate to ourselves, others, and the world-at-large. In psychological circles, this is called the "Mother Wound." Note: although we are exploring Binah, the Great Mother, I am going to use the term Parent Wound to refer to who helped shape us into the person we are today whether that was a biological parent, or a parent figure such as an older sibling, relative, step-parent or grandparent, or teacher.

The fact us that no matter who you call "parent," this person held power over your development throughout your life, and they may not have been the parent you needed, yet were the parent Spirit bestowed. Whether through intentional malice, physical or emotional abuse, or unintentionally through absence or other life circumstances, we may find ourselves wounded by the "parent figure in our life, due to their actions of inaction. Aside from your mother and father, it may be a parent figure such as an older sibling, aunt-uncle, or step-parent, whose actions or lack thereof cause harm. This wound influences who we become and how we live—and any harmful impacts can ripple through our relationships with ourselves and everyone in our lives.

Engaging with Sorrow

As I have known and engaged with it, the Spiritual Experience of The Vision of Sorrow suggests we humans:

1. Become as aware as possible of what occurred-—some instances are not fully traceable.

2. Acknowledge, what is now occurring as a result.

3. Feel our feelings.

4.   Give ourselves time to mourn our losses.

5.   Put aside our ego to reach out for help as needed.

6.   Achieve the Understanding that what has occurred or is occurring, is part of being born into a physical body.

The Vision of Sorrow's linkage with Binah suggests committing ourselves to the repair work needed to heal. While undoubtedly damaging and tragic, the sorrowful mother-child relationship has the potential to function as a powerful incentive for physical, mental, emotional, and spiritual growth and development for oneself and others. I vividly recall my mother crying while apologizing, "I am so sorry. I only did to you what was done to me."

Sorrow is a state others may help to alleviate; yet, in most if not all instances, no one can take it away, as in the case of grieving the death of a loved one. These events must run their course. Some of life's most important lessons are learned through the sorrow of separation. Whether the parting is from those we love, a long-standing belief system, a cherished object, or something else, sadness is sadness. As the words of the poet and mystic Kahlil Gibran express, "The deeper the sorrow carves into your being, the more joy you can contain."

Going from Sorrow to Sorrow

While sorrow is disruptive, it is also instructive. When misery results from the breaking down and dissolving of misunderstanding, it is valuable recalling that this process is the prelude to creating a womb-like space into which Understanding may be conceived, gestated, and born. This is why the wise say it is by going from sorrow to sorrow that much of our evolutionary progress occurs. Binah is synonymous with time, cueing us to recall that with the passing of time, our Understanding expands to the point wherein our automatic responses to sorrow and its sibling, pain, have the potential to grow increasingly less debilitating.

In the closed-minded, ego-centered state of misunderstanding, sorrow manifests as the grieving one—the tormented, despair-ridden victim. However, an alternative to the state may come to the fore. The result of opening to the spirit-centered state of Understanding appears the hopeful, uplifted one and victor. (At one of the lowest points in my life, my yoga teacher gave me the name Jayanti, meaning "Victorious," for my birthday.) At such junctures, we empathetically come to recognize that sorrow goes along with having a physical body and the feelings accompanying it. Along with this, we have the opportunity to begin using our circumstances to focus on the bigger picture such as the Eternal Verities—the universal and natural laws, truths, and principles—and thereby gain perspective and increase our Understanding. Proceeding in this way, we also get to put a deposit in the bank of the collective unconscious, which has the potential to subtly encourage others to respond similarly. This scenario more than suggests why Binah is perceived as the creative, protective, destructive, and transformative facets of life, united in one Mother Goddess.

Witnessing, Intervening, and Letting Go

The Spiritual Experience of Binah may be likened to Mary, the mother of Jesus, or any parent—such as my friend Karla whose daughter was killed in a drive-by shooting, Understanding their child's path in life and at times enacting a sorrowful role of standing by and witnessing its unfoldment. Certainly, in some instances, foresight moves us to intervene. I could not stop thinking about this while viewing Michael Jackson's heartbreakingly impaired last performance in his documentary concert "This Is It." Yet intervention is a question of the individual's

Understanding, plus the ability and determination of the interventionist to act, while simultaneously letting go of their desired outcome.

Separation and Sorrow

Again, Binah is also known as the Separating Intelligence. This title reminds us that when the one and only life force becomes the many life forms, we have the sorrowful experience of feeling temporarily separated from our Source. Qabalists agree that some of the anguish conjoined with Binah points to the fact that in this sephirah the soul is so close, yet so far from a reunion with Spirit.

Psychologically, deep depression and anxiety are sometimes attributed to the unconscious sadness stemming from leaving the complete care and safety of our mother's womb and entering the care-riddled and relatively unsafe world. Partnering with this is post-partum depression, the grief of separation that mothers sometimes experience after childbirth. Despite all of this and so much more, the Spiritual Experience of the Vision of Sorrow innate to being born into our flesh suits, spurs, compels, goads, and inspires us towards increasing our awareness and Understanding. In doing so, we consciously return to Binah's welcoming womb when the dream of separation ends or our body clock times out.

FEATURING: BINAH

NUMBER, THREE: Binah is numbered three. Like Binah, the third point in the Supernal Triad, three is often regarded as the number of wholeness as it contains the beginning, Kether, middle, Chokmah, and an end, Binah. Numerologists equate three with creative power and the joys of living, for which Binah opens the way. Three signifies the forward movement of energy, the overcoming of duality, and synthesis. As the third sephirah, Binah forms the co-equal counterpart to the polarity of Chokmah, which, when combined with the One of Kether, moves beyond dualities to create the third element of new life. As the Maternal Crown of Creation and Mother of Matter, she and number three signify the stabilization of the Life Force via physical structures.

Linguistically, three was the first number to which the meaning "all" was given. Lao Tzu spoke of Binah when he stated, "One engenders two, and two engenders three, while three engenders all things." He further termed the physical diversity of the universe the "ten thousand things." Similarly, the *Piraha* people of the Amazon also use a "one-two-many" system of counting.

COLOR, BLACK: Analogous to how the black pupil of the eye admits light, Binah admits the light and life of Chokmah. Characterized by the absence of light, black absorbs all others back into itself. Unlike white and other hues, pure black can exist in nature without any light at all. Because every creature and thing, animate and inanimate, is born from and returns to the dark womb of the Great Mother, it is understandable that Binah is linked with this hue, deeming black the color of mystery. It is also a symbolic reminder of the Vision of Sorrow, since in many cultures it signifies death and mourning. Black is the densest of colors, and within this sephirah, the molecular structure of what has been seeded is getting increasingly concentrated. It is within Binah, the Mother of Matter, that the basic substance of life is beginning to thicken, or in scientific terms, condense and take form.

Sociologically, black, when compared with its opposite, white, is often attributed to negative and unclean energies. In many cross-cultural systems, women are linked with black and men with white. This is evidenced in many art forms in which the hero and virgin are depicted wearing white, while the villain and whore are clothed in black. Furthermore, women have been, and in some instances still are, considered unclean due to their bodily functions of bleeding, birthing, and their role in changing diapers and bedpans being negatively categorized. Such has also been true of dark-skinned people within Western society, who for centuries have been relegated to performing many of the "dirty" and menial jobs of life. While living in India, I was appalled to learn while reading the newspaper advertising eligible brides that darker-skinned women were less desirable as marriage partners. Sorrowfully, women and men with dark skin are deemed inferior by racists and the ignorant.

GEMSTONE, THE PEARL: Binah is paired with the pearl, particularly black pearls. The lustrous seed-like pearl is the gem linked with Binah. It has been a multi-cultural tradition to give young women pearls at puberty. This gift signifies the recipient's purity and potential fertility—the virgin and mother aspects of Binah. Binah "seeds" each incarnating body with a soul, and in ancient times pearl divers believed each pearl had a distinct personality and soul.

Pearls require numerous layers of effort to be formed, and so does Understanding. Akin to Binah, the host and womb of the world, pearls are hosted in the oyster's womb-like environment. The oyster secretes enzymes which soothe the discomfort the annoyance creates, and in the process form pearls. A like process occurs when I keep perseverating over an irritating situation until I reach some soothing "Understanding," or pearl of wisdom.

A Biblical reference to the pearl occurs in *Revelations 21:21* states, "And the twelve gates (of heaven) were twelve pearls...." Looking at the Tree of Life from the bottom to the top, Binah is the first sephirah above the abyss that separates the physical from the non-physical worlds. This resonates perfectly with Binah's link to the "Pearly Gates," the portal to heaven.

SCENT, MYRRH: Myrrh, or Balm of Gilead spoken of in the Bible, the scent conjoined with Binah, is the most ancient gum resin known to humanity. Yahweh instructed Moses to use it for sanctification: *Exodus 30: 23-25* states: "Take the fines of spices: of liquid myrrh…and you shall make of these a sacred anointing oil, as blended by the perfumer; it shall be a holy anointing oil." Myrrh is a secretion that forms naturally in various small deciduous trees and shrubs of the *Commiphora* species. This substance was sacred to the ancient goddesses who were the givers and takers of life, as is Binah.

Coincidentally, the word itself originates from the Arabic *murr*, meaning bitter. The exudations formed by this resin when secreted from the tree are tear-shaped reminders of Binah's link with the "Vision of Sorrow." No wonder it was chosen by the insightful Magi as a gift for the Christ Child. It has been proven that the impression left upon the Shroud of Turin (reputed to be the cloth that Jesus was wrapped in after the crucifixion) occurred because he was embalmed with myrrh, which, over time, left an imprint or negative image on the shroud that was then photographically processed to reveal his face—definitely worth a "look-see."

Binah is the Sanctifying Intelligence. Highly esteemed in the Near East and Mediterranean regions, myrrh has also been used since antiquity as incense for sanctification: christenings, last rites, funerary and purification rituals. Myrrh served as a fumigant and antibacterial agent in mummification and as an antioxidant and aromatic additive to medicine. This resin is still called upon to help purge stagnant blood due to amenorrhea. Aromatherapists employ myrrh to help patients process personal sorrow and allay fear and anxiety about the future, the time frame in which Binah resides.

PLANT, THE LILY: Like Binah, womb-of-the-world, the lily stores nourishment in its womb-like bulb. This flower has long been acknowledged as a religious symbol of purity, fertility, life, death, and rebirth aligning it with Binah's three faces of Maiden, Mother, and Crone or Elder. The triple goddess aspect is regarded by some sources to be symbolized by the fleur-de-lys, meaning "lily flower."

The bell-shaped lily is sometimes called the trumpet flower: hence its association with Gabriel, the archangel of annunciation. Much like the Word or vibration of creation, Chokmah fertilizes Binah. Gabriel is said to have impregnated Mary through the sound of his trumpet. Qabalists consider this idea to be a metaphor for how the Word or formula for creation passes from Chokmah into Binah to birth the world.

PLANT, THE CYPRESS: The cypress tree bears both male and female cones, signifying Binah's fruitful and all-embracing nature. Greek mythology states that cypress trees mark the entrance to Hades. When available, coffins are traditionally made of cypress wood. The tree's leaves and branches are fashioned into funerary wreaths and decorations, whereas its potent scent is used to cover the stench of death and decay. All underscore the cypress's link with Binah and the Vision of Sorrow.

ANIMAL, THE DOVE: Qabalistically, the dove symbolizes the soul sitting in the upper branches of the Tree of Life, waiting to be born. Pertinent to the caretaking aspect of Binah, the dove feeds its young with "milk," or food regurgitated from the parent's crops. Similarly, in alchemy, the dove signifies the sublimation or diversion of its biological impulse—instead of feeding itself, the parent feeds its chick.

In religious art, the dove is emblematic of the Holy Spirit, peace, and gentleness. Of course, after the flood, a Dove brought Noah an olive branch indicating the peaceful restoration of nature.

However, in India, the call of the dove, particularly that of the mourning dove, is regarded as a harbinger of grief, death, and misfortune. The aforementioned forges another potent link with Binah's Spiritual Experience.

Finally, the Dove, Pelican, and Sparrow are considered psychopomps, creatures responsible for safely conducting newly deceased souls to the afterlife, where their Understanding of the life they have lived will be examined. This explains why some traditions deem it unlucky to harm or kill these birds.

ANIMAL, PELICAN: Another reminder of Binah's nourishing and nurturing aspects is seen in how a pelican feeds its young from its large pouch. This bird is an ancient and often religious icon of self-sacrifice and the Sacred Heart of Jesus. Another related idea stems from the ancient Egyptian belief that a mother pelican fed her young by wounding her own breast and then letting her blood flow into the mouth of her nestlings. (Of course, the father does this, too.) Binah's connection with the process of natural selection appears in the fact that a mother pelican will kill her sick and weaker young so that the stronger nestlings may survive.

Pelican is an ancient term used in chemistry for a vessel with tubes leading from its head to its body, within which distillation and condensation occur. Such offers another explanation why the Pelican, as an important alchemical symbol, is conjoined with Binah, the sphere in which spirit is condensing into matter.

ANIMAL, THE SPARROW: Sparrows are known to survive the harshest of physical conditions and reproduce prolifically. I vividly remember putting breadcrumbs and seeds out for these tiny birds with my mother throughout our long and severe Northeastern winters. This hardy avian is a reminder of the enduring qualities of both the Great Mother and Mother Nature.

MEDICINE AND DRUG, SOMA OR HAOMA: In Indo-Iranian Vedic Religion, Soma or Haoma, now thought to be an East Indian leafless vine, was of immense importance in religious ceremonies. This Sanskrit word, literally translated, means "distill, extract, sprinkle." It was worshipped as a deity and ingested in the form of milk-like juices made from this leafless, now unknown plant. After pressing its stalks between stones, the fluid was then filtered through sheep's wool and mixed with water and milk. This highly intoxicating juice was believed to have caused many of the supernatural powers and visions mentioned in Hindu and Parsee mythology to heighten creative self-expression. Devotees also used the juice both as an offering to the gods and as a drink of immortality. Analogous to the ritual of Holy Communion, eating this sacred food heightened one's ability to commune with the gods and goddesses and become temporarily Divine. Whether Soma or Haoma, this psychedelic plant's mystical powers are mentioned in the earliest scriptural writings of both groups. Soma is also the Greek word for "body," creating a viable link with Binah and the sphere's transformation of spirit to physical bodies.

In some instances, the Priestess or Priest ingested the sacrament and then urinated out a sacred drink that was shared with devotees. This intoxicating liquid is believed to have caused many of the supernatural powers and visions mentioned in Hindu mythology and to have greatly heightened creativity—linking it with Binah. In ancient Vedic symbolism, Soma was akin to ambrosia, the Food of the Gods, and as such bestowed partakers with divine ecstasy. The Ninth Mandala for the *Rig Veda* is entirely devoted to Soma and is called the "Soma Mandala. The following excerpt strongly suggests the interchange of energies between Chokmah and Binah: "The sweet-flavored soma waves go to the wielder of the thunderbolt as a cow with the milk to the calf."

Ancient Persian tradition claims the prophet Zarathustra carried the founder of Zoroastrianism, Zoroaster's spirit to earth on the branches of the Haoma. It is further noted that Zarathustra consulted with an angel called Haoma. Whether Soma or Haoma, the plant's supernatural, powers is mentioned in the earliest scriptural writings of both groups.

Egyptian mythology tells that those who lived by the laws of Maat, the Egyptian Mother goddess of Truth and Justice, akin to Binah, drank something comparable to Soma as a sacrament. The liquid was believed to confer a ritualistic type of purity similar to the Pagan and later Christian "washing in the blood of the lamb." Egyptian scribes wrote: "My inner parts have been washed in the liquor of Maat." Maat's potion is said to have brought life after death to the virtuous, but hellacious death without end to those who violated her laws. Additional research suggests that there may also be a link between the Pharaonic initiation rites and the Soma-like sacrament of ergot.

Finally, Soma is also the drug mentioned in Aldous Huxley's futuristic novel, *Brave New World.* Citizens take this mind-altering drug to produce a mind-altering escape from the stresses and strains of living in a totalitarian world state under the absolute control and surveillance of a central government. The government dispenses it as means of fabricating a sense of serenity, distracting and controlling the population through pleasure. It is prescribed in wide a variety of situations to increase sexual prowess and pleasure, deepen relaxation, improve concentration, boost self-confidence, refrain from future planning and so. From what I learned, Huxley's concoction appears to be a single-chemical combination of many of today's drug effects, offering users a full hedonistic spectrum depending upon the dosage.

THE SACRAMENT OF BINAH, UNDERSTANDING, IS COMMUNION

As mentioned under Chokmah, the paired sephiroth share the same plane, Seven Inner Stars, and sacrament. By receiving the *non-specific* imperceptible universal energy of Chokmah, originating from Kether, Mother Binah conceives, gestates and simultaneously gives birth to the *specific* shapes of perceptible creation and the sephiroth below the abyss. The fleshy forms or bread of life that Mother Binah delivers as the physical universe are the result of her Holy Communion with Kether through Father Chokmah's fertilization with the wine of his life force.

Intimate Exchange

Again, the Latin root of communion is *communionem*, meaning mutual participation, sharing, fellowship, or partnership. Communion is synonymous with intimate exchange, the sharing of thoughts, feelings, and experiences, inter-communication, petitioning, communing, closeness, togetherness, mutual acceptance, and rapport. Practitioners of Judaism, Islam and other religio-spiritual traditions are instructed from childhood, to speak, or communicate with God daily. The Universal Life Force descends from Kether on the spiritual plane, into Chokmah on the causal plane. Nature's negative polarity in the form of Cosmic Mother Binah then draws these energies in to commune with, and have "knowledge of," her soul mate, Cosmic Father Chokmah. This Holy Communion or cosmic intercourse is what brings the world into being.

Soul Food

The practice of habitually interacting with Spirit through prayer and meditation, rituals, teachers, guides, groups, and so on, is ancient. One student described this as "Getting right with the God/dess inside and outside of me." To reiterate, the Christian concept of Communion, known as the Eucharist, originates at the Last Supper of Jesus and his disciples on the first night of Passover, mere hours before he is arrested and subsequently crucified. During this meal, Jesus took a cup of wine and a piece of unleavened bread, instructing everyone present to drink and eat it, stating that such are his blood and body. Roman Catholicism terms this change transubstantiation. By doing this, Jesus compassionately forges the three-way spiritual link of Holy Communion between himself, his followers, and his heavenly parentage. Tuning into and communing with Binah opens Qabalists to the transcendent Understanding encoded therein. *Matthew: 18-20* underscores this: "When two or more are gathered in my name, I am there among them."

When upset due to one sort or another of our old habits, life's stresses and distresses, problems with others, a lack of comprehension, blurred perception, or uncertainty regarding what, if anything, to now say and do prevails, the Soul Food of Communion is always available to turn to for the nourishment of Understanding. When entering this state all thoughts and feelings are fully welcomed and explored.

Achieving the impersonal state of Communion then necessitates our full-on willingness to acknowledge and then bypass any personal attachments and aversions regarding how we ourselves, others, and the world *should* or *should not* be. Taking this route, we become increasingly open to drawing in the clearest Understanding, we are presently capable of receiving in the form of universal and natural laws, truths, and principles. Again, I find this befittingly summarized in the *Serenity Prayer* from Alcoholic's Anonymous:

"God, grant me the serenity to accept the things I cannot change,
the courage to change the things I can,
and the Wisdom to *Understand* the difference."

By way of our open-minded and heartfelt reflection on the teachings of Binah Spirit sends cues, such as: Understanding the soundness, integrity, or sensibility of an action or decision. Integrating an experience or information that improves our mental clarity and life.

Connecting in this way or through the likes of prayer and meditation or similar practices, dialoguing with a perceptive and supportive mentor, counselor, teacher, friend, or group, assists us in Understanding the true nature of what has, now is, or might arise in the future, Communion is realized. (Chanting often opens me to receiving needed Understanding.) The ongoing enactment of Communion supports us to fulfill the sacred work or contract we agreed to when baptized on the spiritual plane in Kether.

A SEPHIRAH BY ANY OTHER NAME:

BINAH'S ALTERNATIVE TITLES

THE CREATRIX-GENITRIX: Binah is the fertile and vital feminine-receptive counterpart and adjunct to the masculine-projective Creator-Genitor. Together these forces bring the world into being. Wisdom, the Cosmic Father, is dynamic-potential, whereas Understanding, the Cosmic Mother, is the elaborator or development of that potential into particularized forms, whether animal, vegetable, or mineral.

Binah makes tangible the invisible and hidden potency of the Most High received by way of Chokmah. She is the movement away from the One towards the Many. Functioning in this way, Binah is the Understanding stewardess of the forces of nature and the physical world. To present a balanced picture, Binah is projective when giving birth, as Chokmah is receptive when accepting the energies of Kether.

THE SUPERNAL, CELESTIAL, OR HEAVENLY MOTHER: Supernal means "that which emanates from on high or from heaven." Binah is the cosmic emanation that enhances and balances out the Supernal Father, Chokmah. The Supernal Mother is the One Great Spirit in the bifurcated form of Mother Goddess—nature's negative polarity that compliments the Supernal Father, the One Great Spirit in the form of

Father God and nature's positive polarity. Together they are our heavenly parents from which creation is birthed.

THE GREAT RECEIVER: Binah draws to her, receives, and admits the Universal Life Force and impetus to create form, emitted by Chokmah.

THE GREAT MULTIPLIER: In her role as the Great Multiplier, Binah is the reproducing and fructifying agent inherent in nature. Just as a single cell proliferates over and again, so does Binah and the life forms she births.

GIVER OF THE SOUL: Binah bestows the soul or holy neshema and its unique characteristics to every living being.

DURA MATER: Fittingly, *Dura Mater* is Latin for the primal, ever-enduring, imperishable Mother of Matter. In order to be continually birthing and sustaining the physical world, Binah must be resilient! It is no coincidence that the outer layer of the brain, called the Dura Mater, functions to cushion it from trauma.

QUEEN BEE: All of the other bees are completely dependent on the Queen Bee. Like the Queen Bee, Binah is the Mother of the ever-buzzing hive of creation. Unlike humans, every bee knows the Queen is their mother as evidenced by them continually feeding, bathing, warming, cooling, protecting, and even caressing her.

TRIPLE GODDESS: Binah is the Triple Goddess of antiquity and counterpart to the Triple God. Essential to fathoming her fully is acknowledging that in addition to being the Mother, she is also the Virgin and Crone or Elder facets of the Great Goddess. Taken a step further, Binah is life's fertile potential, fruitfulness, decay, and death, giving her reign over the three worlds of heaven, earth, and the underworld.

MATRONIT: While a significant amount has been written in Hebrew tradition about the three-fold aspects of Binah, the Virgin *Almah* and Mother, *Aima or Ama,* less has been written regarding Binah as the mature woman, Matronit—the Dark Mother of Bitterness and Sorrows.
  Matronit, in her ancient Talmudic role as the bringer of death and sorrow, patiently awaits the homecoming of all she has sent forth in her potent Virgin and fecund Mother aspects. The *Book of Proverbs* writes of Matronit as follows: "Her feet go down to death; her steps take hold in hell." The *Book of Splendor* goes on to state: "...man at times tastes the other bitter side, and then her face is dark." Binah, in her personification of the Dark Mother, patiently awaits the homecoming of all she has birthed forth in her potent Virgin and Mother aspects.

MARAH: Marah is a name for the Great Cosmic Sea, which gives forth life. The world is made of what Qabalists term "cosmic mind stuff," and Binah is its primal source. Just like water, this cosmic substance remains itself no matter the form such takes. The fluid-like mental arrangement of atomic molecules and particles, which makes up the entire physical world, flows from Binah, the Great Cosmic Sea and Root of Water.

Marah means Bitter Mother, is further paired with Binah's Crone aspect. *Exodus 15:23* addresses this aspect of her nature: "And when they (the Israelites who had been wandering in the wilderness) came to Marah, they could not drink of the waters of Marah, for they were bitter." On a similar note, bitter herbs called *marrah*, are eaten during the Passover ritual, signifying freedom from the bitterness that the Jews experienced as slaves in Egypt.

The ending of her reproductive cycle signifies that the crone is no longer able to become pregnant. Yet this aspect of her continues serving as the comforting womb to which every physical form returns after its biological cycle has ended.

Of course, release from reproduction offers more time and energy for the human female to devote her accumulated Wisdom and Understanding to creative self-expression and to birthing other creative endeavors, such as the words you are reading.

MATER DOLOROSA: Mater Dolorosa is Latin for Mother of Sorrows. This title underscores Binah's availability to ease the grief and the sorrow that accompanies life in a physical body. At those times when we cannot soothe our own or others' suffering, we can turn to her for consolation and Understanding.

MATER BON CONSILI: Also from Latin, and one of Binah's more obscure titles, it translates as "Mother of Good Counsel" or Understanding. When we honestly desire to face up to our weaknesses and the like, this aspect of Binah offers support in the face of what lies ahead.

THE VIRGIN MARY: As Binah's is impregnated by Chokmah, God the Father impregnates the Virgin Mary. As I have come to Understand, males and females are actually surrogates for this cosmic process. Qabalists, like many of the oldest mystical-spiritual traditions, understand the title "Virgin" to indicate purity of spirit, not necessarily the state of *vagina intacta*, or physical virginity.

HEH: This second and fourth letter in the four-lettered Tetragrammaton Yod, Heh, Vav, Heh is the facet of the Most High that receives energy from the Yod of the Tetragrammaton and then passes it on to the remainder of the letters to continue and consummate the creative process. This occurs in much the same way that Binah conceives the life force from Chokmah, to begin birthing the rest of the Tree of Life and thereby the physical world.

More specifically, Yod ignites and launches the drive to create the first Qabalistic world of Atziluth, Emanation. Heh symbolizes the conception of the entire spectrum of physicality in the second Qabalistic world, that of Creative Possibilities and Imagination—Briah. The Tetragrammaton's Yod and Heh are sometimes coupled with the nose and mouth of the Most High through which the Cosmic Breath enters and exits. Here, the Yod represents Chokmah and inhalation, while Heh is Binah and exhalation. (Note: I will continue outlining the Tetragrammaton's remaining letters in later chapters.)

OUTER ROBE OF CONCEALMENT: Binah's Outer Robe of Concealment is the physical body, which covers and obscures Chokmah's Inner Robe of Glory. Binah attracts and binds the free-moving and limitless force of Chokmah into a limited form. It is in this way that Binah bestows the non-specific force of Chokmah with a specific form.

YIN: Yin is the Chinese term for the in-taking power linked with nature's negative polarity. Yin is still, open, and actively receptive in contrast, yet complimentary to Yang, the actively projective, moving energy coupled with the positive polarity. Archetypical Yin energy, paired with femaleness, is open to stimulation and in that way vitalization of the evolutionary process. Of course, as all of creation is a blending of positive and negative forces, without coupling with yang energy, creation will not occur. Yin energy provides a specific structure to the Yang force.

IN THE NAME OF HEAVEN:
DIVINE AND ARCHANGELIC PRESENCES

DIVINE PRESENCE OF BINAH IS, *ELOHIM*

The Divine Presence conjoined with Binah is *Elohim* or *Yahweh Elohim*, which means "God of Creation." Elohim is unusual in that it is a feminine noun with a masculine plural, indicating Binah's power to conceive and birth the entirety of creation. It also serves as a reminder that each sephirah contains the energies of the previous sphere and that the entire manifest world is some combination of Chokmah's and Binah's positive and negative polarities.

With Chokmah we translated Yahweh as "He who calls into being." Coupling Yahweh and Elohim reiterates and celebrates the principle of polarity originating on the Tree of Life's causal plane. Such is the bipolar, co-creative force underlying the manifest world. Bearing this in mind, it fits that the most accurate translation of Elohim appears in *Genesis 1:26* "God says, Let *us* make man in *our* image." The use of *us* and *our* proclaims and emphasizes Binah's potential to birth all sexes.

Elohim also translates as Host or Hostess. Biologically speaking, the word host is an organism in or on which another organism lives. Giving it some thought, Creation is a parasitical organism that draws its sustenance from Binah, the Great Mother. Furthermore, a Host and Hostess provide hospitality and nourishment to others. Binah is "The Divine Assembly," an obscure yet fitting translation of Elohim who delivers the totality of creation. As a student quipped, "She's the emcee to the world, who gives her kids a home away from home." This reminds us of the fact that we originate from both our physical mother and our Cosmic Mother. Binah's multi-faceted nature gives and sustains our lives, and when our biological clocks run down, welcomes us back to her waiting womb.

THE ARCHANGELIC PRESENCE OF BINAH IS, *TZAPHKIEL*

Although angels are physically gender-neutral, Tzaphkiel is said to represent the feminine aspect of Divine creation. She heads the Jewish *Aralim,* or "valiant ones or heroes," the celestial hierarchy equated with the Christian Order of Thrones. Believed to be composed of white fire, these angels reign in the third heaven. Accordingly, Binah is the third sephirah and is assigned to watch over, protect, and nurture the fruits of creation. The Talmud says of the Aralim: "The Aralim prevailed, and the sacred ark was captured." Because an ark is a container, this cryptic phrase more than suggests the workings of Binah in which each sacred soul "captures" a sacred physical body or container. Tzaphkiel's activity of limiting or condensing the life force by assigning it a form is further underscored by Binah's link with the planet most linked with physical boundaries and structures, Saturn.

Contemplation of God

The angelic presence of Binah is Tzaphkiel, meaning "Contemplation of the Most High God," and "Beholder of the Most High." When we think about it, this is what genuine Understanding is about. Tzaphkiel strengthens us by increasing our Understanding—perceiving Spirit present in all—and by doing so, imparting the Wisdom needed to foster spiritual growth. Essentially, Understanding is "getting" that divinity is "standing under," or embodied in, whatever life presents. Tzaphkiel passes on the value of loving unconditionally, resolving conflicts peaceably, developing forgiveness and thoughtfulness, and inspiring humankind with the motivation to help others in need.

Since Tzaphkiel knows and understands all, she is also called the "Knowledge of God." Again, Biblical texts refer to sexual intercourse as "having Knowledge," revealing Tzaphkiel as the angelic power presiding over the Vehicles of Manifestation—flesh-and-blood bodies. Simply, the *Life Force* of the angel Ratziel reaches out from the sphere of Chokmah to the *Life Form* of the angel Tzaphkiel in the sphere of Binah. This interaction gives Tzaphkiel dominion over the archetypical forms, the original matrices or patterns. These are termed by scientists such as Rupert Sheldrake "morphogenetic fields" or forms, from which the manifest world is made. (Because of this, Qabalists refer to Tzaphkiel as "One who Beholds the Most High in Manifest Form.")

MYTHOLOGY AND BINAH:

THE GREAT MOTHER AND TRIPLE GODDESS

Binah is aligned with all of the Great Mother and female fertility deities and triune goddesses—a three-in-one Virgin, Mother, and Crone or Elder. She is the life cycle's potential for fruitfulness, decay, and death, as well as the co-regent of the three worlds of heaven, earth, and the underworld. Amongst other qualities, those deities are linked with sorrowfulness, transformation, insight, and empathy, or Understanding.

EGYPTIAN

HATHOR: Self-manifested Hathor is the oldest of the Egyptian deities from which all others are derived. A fitting symbol of Binah, Hathor, or the "Womb Above," was the Egyptian's Queen of Heaven and mother of the sun god, Ra. In her role as Mother of the Gods and the physical world, she bestows the *Ka* or soul on all of creation. The personification of Divinity, nurturance, and the heavens, Hathor is represented as a star-studded cow or woman with the head of a cow and a solar disc between her horns.

SEKHMET: This sister and dark side of Isis, was the goddess of war, bearer of disease and death. To balance this out, she further functions as the goddess of transformation, conjoined with medicine and healing.

ISIS: In a later era of Egyptian history, Isis grew into fulfilling the role of the Great Mother of Gods, humans, and nature. She presided over love, loyalty, death, resurrection, and transformation.

Isis was also the widow, mourning her murdered husband Osiris. The symbol of the widow is venerated in Masonic tradition, wherein Isis and Mary Magdalene, said to be the widow of Jesus and the mother of his son (or daughter in other circles), are given this venerated position. The phrase Masonic rituals use as an appeal for help for a troubled brother, "Is there no help for the widow's son?" refers to this belief. In some ancient circles, Isis was regarded to be the Ark, the fertile container or womb that gestates and births her son Horus, the reincarnation of his slain father Osiris.

NEPTHYS: This sister of Isis and counterpart of the earlier deity Sekhmet is recognized as the bringer of decay, death, darkness, and metamorphosis. She helps Isis locate her slaughtered and dismembered husband, Osiris. Her healing powers facilitate the resurrection and transformation of Osiris into Horus.

BABYLONIAN

LILITH: According to the Babylonian Talmud, Lilith was "the first Eve," paired with Adam. Yet, due to her non-compliant, self-determining nature, the first woman who stood up for what she believed and pushed for equality despite the consequences. She enjoys her sexuality and is banished and replaced by a compliant consort, "the second Eve." Resultantly, Lilith is linked with the dark side of Binah. Although the Old Testament presents only one somewhat veiled reference to Lilith in *Isaiah 34:13-16* of the Masoretic Text, she has a central position in Jewish demonology. Along this line, Lilith is sometimes said to be the Serpent curled around the Tree of Knowledge planted in the midst of the Garden of Eden.

In old Kabbalistic (Jewish-related) astrology, Lilith was related to the planet Saturn, conjoined with Binah. All who share a dark, depressed, melancholic disposition, or "black humor," are her children. Lilith's two primary roles are as the strangler of children—more commonly known as crib deaths—and the seducer of men, from whose nocturnal emissions she conceives and bears demonic progeny. More recently, Lilith was linked to the dark of the moon, the furthest point of the moon's orbit around the earth, and the shadow side of one's personality. Conjoined with our primitive, deeply buried subconscious impulses, such as repressed sexuality, hurt, and anger, the aforementioned may lead to depression.

ETHIOPIAN

THE BLACK MADONNA: The Black Madonna is portrayed in iconology from the Caucasus, Italy, Egypt, Africa, Haiti, and elsewhere. In the Bible's *Song of Songs*, King Solomon likens the Ethiopian Queen of Sheba to a bundle of myrrh, Binah's scent. Symbol of womanhood and compassion, Sheba is said "to contain the blackness of wisdom," just as Binah contains the energies of Chokmah.

Still actively worshipped in Catholic churches in parts of Europe, the Black Madonna is an updated version of Isis and other ancient mother deities who had dark skin, as did the Semitic Virgin Mary. However, she does have some additional unique contemporary history originating from seventeenth-century Czestochowa, Poland. It was here that her image caused invaders to flee Jasna Gora church and monastery, when it began bleeding while being attacked by invaders.

ASSYRIO-BABYLONIAN

TIAMET: Binah is sometimes called the Great Sea. In Assyrio-Babylonian mythology, Tiamet is the primal personification of the sea or Apsu and the feminine element, which gives birth to the world. She is brutally murdered by Marduk the Wise (ha!) who, when then lacking the feminine principle, becomes unable to create life. Marduk eventually has to wise-up and engage the goddess Aruru to help produce the first human, Enkidu, from clay.

GRECO-ROMAN

RHEA: Binah is conjoined with the Greek goddess Rhea, a Titan. As wife and sister of Chronos and mother of the gods and goddesses, including Zeus, Pluto and Demeter, Rhea is worshipped as Magna Mater, or Great Mother, of ancient Greece.

DEMETER: Binah is also associated with the Greek fertility goddess and Mother of Persephone, Demeter. In Greek the word "De" in De-meter means delta, signifying both fertility and the womb, while "meter" denotes "mother," rendering the goddess Demeter the fertile mother. Binah's Vision of Sorrow may be equated with Demeter pining for her daughter Persephone, who is abducted by Pluto and taken to the Underworld.

PERSEPHONE AND HECATE: The Orphic mystics considered Persephone or Kore to be two aspects of the triune goddess. She was both the virginal Persephone and the crone Hecate, Goddess of the Dead, and Queen of the Underworld. Over time Kore's linkages were lost, leaving Persephone to be both a virgin and a crone.

OPS: This fertility deity and wife to Saturn is the Roman counterpart to Rhea.

EAST INDIAN

MA SHAKTI: Ma, the basic mother-syllable of Indo-European languages, is often used as the primary name of the Great Mother Goddess. Shakti means "Cosmic Energy" or animating power that projects, maintains, and dissolves the universe. Ma Shakti is the title of the Great Goddess or Devi, consort of the Great God or Deva, (interchangeably called Shiva, Brahma, and Vishnu). She is the feminine creative force, the innermost soul of all creation.

KALI: Comparable to the Egyptian Sekhmet is the goddess Kali, whose name translates from Sanskrit as "She who is black." Kali signifies the "other" or dark side of the Mother of Life—the Mother of Death and Transformation in the Hindu pantheon. This potent goddess is "the devourer" who takes back all life and worlds into her primal womb at the end of their life cycles. Complete union or reunion with her occurs at death, when she embraces and absorbs the soul of the dead.

MALAPRAKRITI: The dual-aspected female goddess, Malaprakriti is often considered the counterpart or consort of Brahma. She is the personification of the primordial substance and its innumerable derivations, the most basic element from which all life is derived. This goddess presides over the highest, most primal level of the soul. Fittingly, Binah is the sephirah wherein the specific individual soul, or neshama, is bestowed upon the non-specific Life Force rushing in from Chokmah. Malaprakriti is also the counterpart to Binah's role as Mother Nature.

NORSE

FRIGG: Frigg or Freya was the Great Mother of all the Norse gods and goddesses, who at a later point in history became wife to Odin. Akin to Binah's relationship with Chokmah, Frigg is believed to have shared Odin's Wisdom. Among her numerous roles, she was the goddess of foresight, fertility, motherhood, and matrimony. The contemporary slang term "friggin'" is an obscure reference to her link with fertility and sexuality.

SKADI: Skaki means shadow, making her the Norse sister of Sekhmet, Kali and other dark goddesses.

ROMAN AND FRENCH

STELLA MARA: Although the church does not regard the Virgin Mary as a goddess, worship of the Holy Mother had its origins, long before the advent of Christianity, in the pagan traditions of antiquity. As a means of attracting and keeping heathen followers, the early Roman Catholic Church employed adoration of the Great Mother in the form of "Mary, Mother of God." Similar practices were revived centuries later in Southern France when church membership was waning. Akin to how Binah is impregnated by Chokmah, Father God impregnated the Virgin Mary. This act is said to symbolize the sacred marriage, ritually termed the *heiros gamos* in Greek.

Catholic church doctrine proffers that Mary, or Our Lady, as she is known, helps by way of intercession with the redemption of humanity. This concept is embodied in the Rosary prayer: "Hail Mary, full of grace, the Lord is with you; blessed are you among women, and blessed is the fruit of your womb, Jesus. Holy Mary, Mother of God, pray for us sinners now and at the hour of our death."

Along a somewhat similar line, research studies have shown that even in cases wherein personal relationships had not been the best, in times of great need or death some people will call for their mothers. (I recall doing this while laboring to birth my son.)

MIDDLE EASTERN

FATIMA: Binah has also been conjoined with Fatima, meaning "Creatrix." She is the Islamic counterpart to Mary and the mythological daughter of the Prophet Mohammed. An ancient Shiite text says she appeared "at the creation of the material world." Her symbol as Holy Virgin, the crescent moon, is depicted on Islamic flags.

TOLTEC, AZTEC, AND MESOAMERICAN

QMECIHUATL: Out of the Ketherian line of Ometeotl emerged the positive and negative polarities, or husband and wife, the Aztecan duo of Ometecuhtli and Omecihuatl. Parallel to Binah's pairing with Chokmah, this couple is responsible for the creation of the universe and all life. Aptly adorned by earns of corn, Omecihuatl is known as the "Constant Creatrix of Life," and "Lady of Flesh and Sustenance." This primal goddess functions as the mother of the gods and of the natural world. She lives, along with her male counterpart, Ometecuhtli, in the highest Aztec heaven. Like Binah, she sends the souls of infants from heaven to earth.

OF VIRTUES AND VICES:

The Virtue of Silence

Binah, synonymous with creativity, is aptly conjoined with the virtue of Silence. Learning this immediately prompted me to recall the old Latin saying used by practitioners of magic and others: "To Know, To Dare, To Will, and To be Silent." When starting out or in the midst of the creative process, these words imply the value of discerningly directing our time, attention, and energy into the project at hand, rather than wasting or even losing it by talking about what we are creating. On a different, yet similar note, mystics believe that some Understandings are best kept unspoken unless one is asked or is in a teaching situation. This is done to 1. Refrain from dissipating the power of our often fully inexplicable experiences. 2. Conserve the energy needed to digest and enact what we have come to Understand. And 3. Abstain from boasting, inciting envy, causing harm, and so on. Oh yes, some teachers find it exceedingly beneficial to answer a student's questions with silence or very small hints, leaving them to figure out the rest.

Most Eastern and Western monastic systems require members to take vows of silence as part of their training. Silence is often seen as essential to deepening a relationship with God. It is also considered a virtue in some religions. In the Buddhist tradition, a monk's vow of silence is a way to practice proper speech and avoid saying something detrimental by avoiding revealing anything that comes to mind. For them, speaking with silence is a way to practice nonviolence. After contemplating suicide so that his family could benefit from a life insurance payment, the legendary inventor and visionary Buckminster Fuller took a two-year vow of silence. This courageous leap resulted in the advent of Fuller's humanitarian views and cutting-edge inventions aimed at bettering life for all on planet Earth. Another potent example of the workings of this virtue is seen in how, when the Virgin Mary was impregnated by the "soundless sound" of Gabriel's trumpet, she simultaneously received the Understanding of the life her son, Jesus, would have and the essentiality of remaining silent about what was revealed.

It is often only through silence that we may achieve the calm and centered state needed to receive the Understanding and spiritual guidance required to gather the creative energies necessary to conceive, gestate, and give birth to a new idea or project. Many of us yearn for silence to allow the voice of our muse to whisper into our ears.

To Speak or Not to Speak, That is the Question!

Binah reigns supreme over the great silent secrets of conception, gestation, birth, and death. She is the still womb of life responsible for the existence of all on the physical plane. Mother Binah sends us forth from the Great Silence into life and draws us back into it at death. Silence implies the Understanding that each soul grows in its own way and time and that often the best advice or comments to give—unless solicited, the danger is imminent or essential—is none. It is often better to remain silent, listening, watching, and waiting until one is asked.

There are instances in which my Understanding compels me, whatever the consequences, to break my silence. Of course, I do this when wearing my hat as a Tarot Consultant. When proceeding to communicate with my children, I would tell them that it was my obligation as their mother, who loves them, to communicate so that they would never say to me, "Mom, why didn't you tell me that." (I did give them complete permission to plug up their ears while I was speaking!) I was recently moved to doing this when a long-time friend called to vent about a severe and long-standing health problem. When I had previously asked her if she was "open to a suggestion," she unhesitatingly declined. After refusing any input, she continued crying and complaining. I then found myself with several choices: I could excuse myself from the conversation, continue listening, or take a chance and push forward. Due to the gravity of her situation, I knew that I could not live with myself unless I shared my Understanding and pushed ahead without any further expectations. As it turned out, she called several days later to say "thank you" and reveal that she had made an appointment with a specialist to discuss her severe, life-threatening health crisis.

In these instances such as these I receive the inner peace, knowing that I have not withheld what I am certain is vital information, yet without being attached to anyone doing anything differently or quite honestly, in some instances continuing our relationship—personally or professionally. To my recollection, I have rarely, if ever, said, "I told you so" when the worst happened. I have also experienced people avoiding me, and more, after doing this. This is why, despite its drawbacks, my creed remains "Life is not a popularity contest."

Binah's links with silence and sorrow are reminders of how some parents and caregivers do not speak to their children out of ignorance, among other things. Not knowing what or how to communicate, they propagate what they themselves likely experienced while growing up. (A friend's mother took this route when at about age 8 I innocently asked her the meaning of the word "rape.") Certainly, silence is also used as a form of punishment, such as giving someone "the silent treatment" and in this way withholding love and approval.

Vice of Greed

Babies come into this world crying, "I need love! I need food!" Despite the fact that it is part of each parent's job description provide, many children are not well nurtured and nourished, and as a result, will sometimes grow into greedy adults. Greed, aptly known as "The Mother of all vices," is the pathological state of being insatiably desirous of possessions, wealth, or the love and attention of others. It is the unbalanced desire to produce, own, and in some instances hoard, more than what one needs, can reasonably care for, and consume.

I am not implying that the frills of life are unimportant. However, when "things" are used to replace love, humans may become seriously wounded and greedy. Might the current epidemic of obsessive-compulsive behaviors—excessive spending and shopping, eating, drinking, drugging, sexing, working, and the like—be unconscious attempts at filling the void left by a deficiency of "Vitamin L," Love? Is it possible that a major cause of materialism and greed rampant in the world are byproducts of societies so skewed in their values that insatiable needs for money and "stuff" have become valued above all else? Similarly, has the greed for belongings become an unconscious substitute for belonging to loving families and the deep-seated need to genuinely connect with Spirit?

A close friend, now deceased, friend used to pose the question "What is enough?" when examining his wealth in the face of other needs. Over time, I witnessed him, as anonymously as possible, bailing political demonstrators out of jail, leaving baskets of food on doorsteps, slipping cash-filled envelopes into mail slots, and buying struggling artists the tools they needed yet could not afford. (Not too long after receiving an electric guitar, one tremendously talented, poverty-stricken musician was featured on the cover of *Downbeat Magazine.*)

We are Her Distributing Agents

Binah is conjoined with Mother Nature. Is it likely that the current natural disasters brought on by climate change and diseases such as COVID-19 are giving humankind a wake-up call to allay greed and bring us together with the common Understanding that we are One, when we fail to get the message otherwise? From the Qabalistic view, Mother Nature always creates enough for everyone. Yet like Mother Binah, the more fortunate humans among us are innately charged with the assignment also to create and share. Generally, lack comes from the unequal distribution of wealth by avaricious people, businesses, and governments. These spiritually impoverished, immature souls, and their minions are deficient in Understanding that She is really the Great Provider and Multiplier of form and we are Her distributing agents.

POWERING-UP: MAGICAL-MYSTICAL SYMBOLS, TOOLS, TALISMANS, AMULETS, AND SIGILS

THE *YONI*: This Sanskrit word refers to all female genitalia. The yoni receives the lingam, corollary to the penis and phallus, to create the world. This primary object of worship in Hinduism represents both the Great Mother goddess, as well as the veneration of women considered living expressions of the goddess. Some of its age-old symbols of fertility are the egg or double-pointed oval, fish, cornucopia, triangle, and triangularly-shaped Greek letter Delta.

THE WOMB: Binah is the womb, the organ where life is conceived, gestates, and exits at birth. Mysticism and psychotherapies alike propose that we are driven by a deep-seated desire to return to the womb. The womb is a sacred space, and the Sanskrit word for any temple or sanctuary is *garbha-grah*, meaning womb. Of course, the words tomb and womb are linguistically related and are a throwback to antiquity when tombs were designed as "wombs" in which the dead might be reborn.

THE ARK: The word ark is derived from the Latin *arca,* meaning to contain, enclose, hold, and protect. In Her role as the Supernal or Heavenly Mother, Binah provides the physical vessel in which the soul protectively rides the ebbing and flowing seas of the manifest world.

THE *KETIS:* Ketis is the Greek word for cowrie or scallop shell, a symbol of the vagina. This shell has been used as a sign of fertility and protection cross-culturally. Amazonian Indians decked their fruit trees with cowries in an effort to induce productivity. Ancient Egyptians decorated tombs with these shells as charms to ward off evil and ensure rebirth. Moslem women claimed cowries worn during pregnancy kept both mother and child from harm. Indo-Europeans donned Kauri shell necklaces to shield them from ill will.

THE HOLY GRAIL: Pagans and mystically-oriented Christians alike believe the Holy Grail represents the womb of the Great Mother, the place from which all life comes, and to which all eventually returns. To these peoples, the Grail is one with the Holy Cauldron of Regeneration, the blood-filled vessel symbolizing the Great Mother's womb of birth, death, and regeneration. Alchemists refer to the Grail's contents as the *Prima Materia*, the First Matter or Mother, the substance of life. It is the mixing bowl for the totality of elements from which physical reality flows. The Grail is also referred to as the "wish-fulfilling gem" and the "pearl of great price."

Over time, the Grail became coupled with the cup used by Jesus at the Last Supper, when pouring wine for his disciples to drink, saying, "This is my blood," *Matthew 26:28*. Here Jesus acts with nurturing energy similar to that of Binah-he receives and holds the energies from above, and then pours them out upon the world.

THE FIG AND POMEGRANATE: The orb-shaped fig and pomegranate are ancient symbols of this sephirah, in the form of the Great Mother Goddess and womanhood. These plentifully seeded fruits have signified Binah's fertile and abundant nature since antiquity.

ASTROLOGICAL CORRESPONDENCE TO BINAH:
SATURN, TIME MARCHES ON

Qabalists couple Binah with the planet Saturn, or *Shabbathai*, meaning "Saturday, Sabbath, day of rest," in Hebrew. Saturn is called "The Ringed Planet," a nickname arising from the large, magnificent, and extensive ring system, mostly made from chunks of ice and carbonaceous dust, encircling the planet. It is for this reason that Saturn is often considered the most awesome entity in the solar system.

Apt to Mother Binah, many astrologers associate Saturn with one's biological mother in a birth chart. Binah is the "root of form," and Saturn formulates boundaries, limits, and structures, with Understanding. The underlying force driving such creation also conjoins Saturn with our Spiritual Mother, Binah. Consequently, Saturn's seven rings may be seen both to be enfolding the planet and suggesting

Binah's gestation of the remaining seven sephiroth below. Furthermore, much as Binah functions to turn Chokmah's non-specific cosmic energy into tangible configurations, Saturn is associated with the crystallization, refinement, and concentration of non-specific cosmic energy into specific physical forms. In order to have finite sizes and shapes, there *must* be a boundary or constraints imposed upon infinite possibilities—a reference to the planet's constraining rings.

The mention of constraint is a compelling reminder of the "Mother Wound," the long-term effect of a psychological deficiency in the mother-child or parent-child relationship that is passed down through generations. This wound tends to reflect how children have been parented and affects how they later parent. Children who were raised by alcoholics, drug-addicted parents, or those with mental health conditions, either undiagnosed or untreated, may struggle into their own adulthood. There are also children who are brought up by parents who do not have these challenges, who provide for the physical needs of their children, and even interact with the children in a positive way, yet do not know how to provide the deep love and attention that children need. They may not have been abusive or neglectful, and never engaged in negativity in their relationships with their children yet they were always "cold," distant, and less tuned into the emotional needs of their children. Usually this behavior, and in some instances one's physical health, is a reflection of how we were or were not parented.

Binah places a limited terrestrial construct upon the unlimited, free-flowing, celestial potential of Chokmah that starts creation's biological clock ticking. It makes sense that *Cronos*, the Greek God of Time and seed sowing, is paired with Saturn's inherently restrictive yet also liberating nature. Similarly, Binah signifies the limited duration of earthly embodiment and the constraints inherent in having a flesh-and-blood body. The astrological symbol for Saturn is the ancient scythe of Father Time, or the T cross. This glyph suggests how we, in time, learn to lay aside our ego and do the work physical embodiment presents. The scythe is also a reminder of Mother Nature's unstoppable cycles of birth, growth, decay, and death.

In response to my quest for freedom and Saturn's restrictive influence in my astrological chart, a wise teacher offered me this then astounding, yet potentially liberating perspective: "Freedom is the choice of your disciplines." Saturn is the planet of the work of life and the discipline it takes to get these labors accomplished. It makes sense that Saturn, often called the Taskmaster, is linked with the Qabalstic opposites of Freedom and Slavery. This underscores how much of life is a matter of our attitude towards whatever comes our way. In addition to assisting us in Understanding the value of discipline, Saturn prods us, at times most uncomfortably, to scrutinize, question, critique, contemplate, thoughtfully focus on, and in certain instances re-configure self-made rules and regulations and the internal pressure to conform. Along with this comes those behavioral codes passed along, and in some instances demanded, by external authority figures—parents, teachers, the media, religious training, governing bodies, peers, and so on. Saturn's influences represent the point in time when we start questioning and rebelliously revising the likes of such to align with ourselves making these decisions.

Restriction, Individuation, and Liberation

When engaging with Saturn's limiting influence, it is beneficial to recall that it often limits in order to educate, liberate and, in certain instances, keep us safe. As the story goes, when little Peter Rabbit's prudent and loving mother instructed him not to go into Mr. McGregor's garden, it was for his own health and safety. Here and in similar instances, restrictions are a form of love. Of course, using Saturn's authoritativeness as a means for unnecessarily controlling or power-tripping others is another story. While naturally inhibitive to the ego, Saturn aims at divesting us of the traits hampering Self-awareness and Understanding of our greater purpose. This second-largest planet in the solar system is further associated with patience, maturity, and wealth. Essentially, many personality-level conflicts and discomforts brought forth by the saturnine aspects of life have, with endurance, the potential to bring enrichment beyond dollars and cents.

Saturn is known as the taskmaster and teacher. In the sphere of Binah, the soul takes on a body and along with it, the assignment of Understanding that whatever life presents us with is offering us how to be more responsive to and responsible for our actions towards ourselves, others, and the world at large. These refer to Saturn's sobering, strict, and controlling influence. It is understandable why so many addicts of one sort or another use substances to avoid this unavoidable fact of life.

Saturn is aligned with the individuation and maturation process of Understanding one's true self and place in the world—and the liberation that follows. Astrologers link this with the planet's 29½-year cycle—we can have up to three Saturn Returns in one lifetime. This means Saturn *returns* to the same astrological sign it was situated in at the time of our birth, with each cycle offering another level of tests and trials or opportunities for advancement. Genuine maturity is developing the Understanding that our words and actions are best aimed to "benefit all concerned."

I recently came to the aid of a little girl who, as a result of being improperly seated in a supermarket grocery cart, was doing her all to escape, while her mother was busily shopping several yards away. In the midst of gently reseating the child while explaining that she could fall and get hurt by standing, her distracted mother returned. Seeing me interacting with her daughter, she viciously threatened to hit me for "not minding my own business." Relating this to Saturn, behaving responsibly, we become increasingly willing to assume adult roles in our lives, rather than remain hapless children. While doing this does open us to the entire spectrum of harsh consequences, it simultaneously opens us to the opportunity to maturely re-author our life scripts.

Tester of Souls

Saturn is the "tester of souls," pointing to the principle that all life events come from the One and are intended to expand our Understanding, and in doing so, unify us with the One. On that note, Saturn is also coupled with the Black Bile of medieval science, what is presently known as depression, and its companions—endless sadness, hopelessness, and misery. Of course, in some instances, depression stems from some type of misunderstanding the likes of anger or fear turned inwards wherein communication, external input, and/or an attitude adjustment—such as evaluating an event with the help of another or viewing what has transpired from the bigger, spiritual picture, is curative.

There are also situations when despair is the result of poor nutrition and a lack of cardiovascular exercise. A family member's mood improved after she began receiving vitamin B12 shots and absorbing more Vitamin D by regularly riding her bike in the afternoon sunshine. Last, yet not least, imbalances may be a consequence of our genetic makeup and low levels of neurotransmitters like serotonin, a deep and sometimes unreachable trauma, and exposure to poisons and toxic environments. In circumstances when too much time has elapsed, and one's outlook cannot shift to become more solution-oriented, the great elixir of Understanding is needed. Achieving this state may involve reaching for the potion of scrupulously honest Saturninan self-examination facilitated by masterful professional help. The brother of a student suffering from PTSD due to his participation in Operation Desert Storm was significantly helped by psychedelic therapy administered by the local Veterans Hospital.

Astrologers term Saturn the "Greater Malefic," as it is related to the dark side of life—tragedy, grief, and pain. This planet also represents hard work, determination, and responsibility. Recalling Binah's Sanctifying Intelligence and the holiness at the core of all life can be key to the hard work and determination needed to responsibly accept and work through the Vision of Sorrow that is part of living in a sacrosanct physical body. Over time, our experiences usher in a greater Understanding of the human condition and along with it, the growing ability to nurture ourselves by conscientiously working with and through its gloomier aspects. Saturn's glyph is a T-cross—a reminder that at such crossroads, recalling that seeds germinate best in the dark may shine the light of Understanding onto troubling times and situations.

THE QABALISTIC GRADE BINAH:

MAGISTER TEMPLI, "MASTER OF THE TEMPLE"

Watchwords of the Grade of Master of the Temple, Magister Templi, (plural *Magistri Templi*, Masters of the Temple) are encapsulated in Paul Foster Case's *Pattern on the Trestleboard*: "Filled with Understanding of Its perfect law, I am guided moment by moment along the path of liberation." Coming to grips with and mastering the realities of daily living offers unending challenges and benefits galore. Qabalists assert that unless aspirants are thoroughly committed to handling their mundane responsibilities they are unprepared to successfully engage with the forces and responsibilities above the physical plane.

The title of the grade Master of the Temple, as with all others, indicates an experiential Understanding of the principles of this sephirah through its Sanctifying Intelligence, Spiritual Experience of the Vision of Sorrow, Vice of Greed, Virtue of Silence, and so on. These skills grant aspirants dominion over their "temple" or physical body and surroundings or temple of the world. Fitting to the workings of Binah's placement on the causal plane, Magistri have the potential to develop the miraculous power to gather atoms and molecules together and materialize physical objects and even to raise the dead.

Mystics, adepts, and yogis from previous ages regarded their physical bodies as liabilities to spiritual attainment. They denied, neglected, abused, and even tortured their physical body through the practice of harsh and abusive treatment. Christians aptly term this austere practice "mortification." Mortification includes wearing sackcloth and ashes—symbols of mourning and repentance—fasting, abstaining from all of the pleasures of physical life, taking vows of silence, and engaging in self-flagellation practices such as flogging, lashing, tanning, whipping, and imitating Christ's crucifixion. While these have receded into the background, the evening news recently showed a man in the Philippines playing the role of Jesus Christ during Holy Week by being crucified for the 33rd time on Good Friday.

In contrast, we Magistri understand that our physical bodies and senses are a viable means for experiencing Spirit embodied in form. Instead of propagating the outdated split between our body and our soul by mistreating our living temple, we have a cellular Understanding of the body's place in our soul's evolution and honor it with the care and respect it, and all life forms, deserve. I recently recalled this while driving to recycle some questionable household items, rather than mindlessly tossing them into the garbage.

Mastery Over Decay and Death

In the process of achieving loving dominion over our physical, mental, and emotional bodies, we Magistri in rare instances achieve, in addition to the possibility of raising the dead, earn some degree of mastery over our own death and decay. We are, in truth, our body's keeper. In this r- being to the best of our ability, to more easily and productively live out our karmic purpose. This does not mean that the body will not die; of course, physical death is inevitable. Yet, it does mean that through a combination of living in alignment with Binah's laws of nature, Magistri may prolong our lives beyond the normal time span. History shows instances of rare individuals living well beyond the normal life expectancy. Generally, this occurs so that a Magister may continue and finish their particular work assignment. Although one knows in each and every cell of their being, that they are not their body, they proceed to honor it as the "Temple" medium or means through which to perform and complete the spiritual agreement or Understanding they signed onto when baptized on the spiritual plane in Kether prior to their physical birth. In the yogic tradition this is the first level of Samadhi, the experience of oneness with God/dess, which leads to its subsequent states of Nirvikalpa Samadhi and finally Mahasamadhi.

Miracle Workers

With further regard to the issues of decay and death, it is essential to mention a tiny minority of miracle workers. Since Binah is the Mother of Form, some Magistri Templi may create, maintain, and or dissolve their physical bodies at will. These individuals have achieved a level of mastery over decay and death, resulting in this ability. Furthermore, upon death, these exceptional individuals ascend to the spiritual world along with their physical bodies. Examples of this are seen in the Old and New Testament's accounts of Enoch-Metatron, Elijah-Sandalphon, the mysterious Mechelzidek, and Jesus.

There are documented instances of significantly advanced Magistri who, when needing to enter and exit a physical form, have done so without going through the normal birthing process and passage through, aging, decay, and death. This means a Magister has the ability to create a physical body at will—and may go between the non-physical and physical worlds when duty calls. The renowned yogi mystic Babaji, who always appeared as a young man, was according to some accounts about 500 years old around the late 1800s. Although never looking more than middle-aged, the Count of Saint Germain lived well into his nineties. Christ is believed to have physically appeared on several occasions following his "death" and crucifixion. Although visibly aging, Sathya Sai Baba, dubbed "The Man of Miracles," is known also known to have materialized himself in more than one place at the same time. Examples of other miraculous powers or siddhis as they are known in India, are the ability to increase or decrease one's size, be impervious to heat and cold, or feel hunger and thirst.

Somewhat different, yet relevant, are the Buddhist and Yogic practitioners who inhabit a "Rainbow" or Mind-Created Body. These bodies are free of any interspaces, bones, or substances; they glow like incandescent rainbows. Buddhist Dzogchen practitioners have accomplished this throughout the ages; Khenpo A–Chos achieved this in 1998. Similarly, the Catholic Church exhumes a body after it has been buried 100 years to judge its level of decay before conferring Sainthood. Paramahansa Yogananda's body showed no physical disintegration upon its burial 20 days following the demise of his body. I recently read that although he left his body in 1952, it remains uncorrupted to this day, more than 70 years later.

The Pure Soul Liberated

Because Binah is the first sephirah above the manifest world, this grade suggests the mystical-spiritual experience of the pure soul liberated from its entanglements with the personality and physical matter. Reaching this point in their evolutionary journey, one has achieved a living Understanding of the workings of the universe and their soul spirit Self. Again in the words of Case, the Master of the Temple is "Filled with Understanding of its perfect law," and therefore is "guided moment by moment, along the Path of Liberation."

This grade represents the type of mastery that empowers the spiritual aspirant to "cross the abyss" seen on the Qabalistic Tree of Life as the Higher Mental Plane up to the Causal Plane at will—that is, to have the power to enter into or depart from the physical world and a physical body, as necessitated by their life's work. A particularly stirring example of this is seen in the yogic master Sri Yukteshwar's remarkable post-death appearance to his mourning disciple Yogananda. So fully Understanding Yogananda's sorrowing state, Sri Yukteshwar appeared to him following his death and burial, demonstrating the power of yoga.

BINAH, THE BROW STAR OR THIRD EYE

As explained under Chokmah, the horizontally paired sephiroth share the same star, the Brow Star and the pineal gland. Binah is conjoined with the introverted right side of the brain, which directs the left side of the body, the Brow Star, the third eye, or Ajna, in the Hindu chakra system. In summary, the Ida, and her yin negative lunar current, are coupled with the parasympathetic nervous system's *contraction,* bodily cooling, the right side of the brain's introverted activities, and the left side of the body. The Pingala and his positive, yang solar current are coupled with the sympathetic nervous system's *dilation,* bodily heating, the left side of the brain's extroverted activities, and the right side of the body. The Ida and Pingala emanate from the neutral central channel or Shushuma to the lower energy centers. The liaison of Binah and Chokmah populates the physical world with creatures composed of varying blends of positive and negative traits.

While yogic tradition terms the Brow Star, the Ajna, or the third eye, alchemists among others label it Mt. Abiegnus, meaning pinecone. Mt. Abiegnus is the fir tree-covered mythical mountain located in the center of the earth symbolizing the tests and trials inherent in spiritual evolution. This star is above the physical plane, linking the pinecone with the top of the wand carried in the Bacchic and Dionysian traditions and divine intoxication. "Pine" from the Latin *pinea* is also the root of pineal, the gland star coupled with Binah and Chokmah.

Parsing Out Parts

Understanding is intuitive awareness, foresight, and knowledge that can present itself as a flash of inspiration from one's inner Self—or the "heart of the mind," as one student spontaneously called out in class. Generally, the right side of the brain is associated with the perception of things (objects, situations, etc.) in their entirety rather than in their parts, whereas the left side of the brain is linked with the perception of parts, rather than their entirety. The right brain is frequently conjoined with nonverbal and nonlinear Understanding such as the origination of creative imaginings, dreams, fantasies, and precognitive experiences. This area may also be connected with feeling states, humor, the appreciation of music and art, and deductive reasoning—in contrast to the inductive processes of Chokmah.

Deductive reasoning is reasoning from a general concept to a specific concept—what Qabalists speak of as "from the many to the One"—from the idea of human beings in general to the idea of a *particular* human with their unique physical characteristics and personality traits—a fitting match for Binah. Simply, Binah creates precise life forms from the rush of imprecise energy generated by Chokmah. In contrast to the speeded-up inductive activities of Chokmah, the deductive Binah slows energy to the point wherefrom molecules condense into form. Further illustrating this is the elementary mathematical concept of deduction or subtraction. Binah subtracts small bits of energy from the Prima Materia or infinite substance of Chokmah to create finite life forms.

Knowledge and Perception

Another translation of Ajna is knowledge, implying Understanding that comes from memory or automatic recollection—deeming Understanding to be the result of knowledge put to the test of time and then recalled as needed, or Wisdom. Last, yet certainly not least, Ajna is synonymous with "perception," becoming aware directly through the senses.

Perception calls up the notion of creative imagination, the impact of sensory stimulation—whether sight, sound, taste, touch, or smell—on our minds. The stimulation of a sense causes some type of neural impact. Such results in a mental image, pattern, matrix, or morphogenetic form that has the potential to conjure up (in magic speak), or generate actual physical forms—as in the case of a Master of the Temple manifesting another body. The slightest whiff of lemon causes me to instantly see a glass of lemonade, complete with ice and a straw. The strength of this image may then move me out the side gate to pick lemons to then make this refreshing beverage. It also has the power to have me imagining my grandson and me gleefully juicing lemons for lemonade and singing, "When life gives you lemons, make lemonade!"

By nature, perception indicates the activation of certain neurological processes, what Qabalists term our "inner sensorium" that stimulates the faculty of creative imagination inherent to the Brow Star. Creation takes place through sensory impact or stimulation, and this star is the main receptor site for prompting! On that note, I will close with thoughts of the extraordinarily creative poet and artist William Blake. When referring to humanity's limited perception of the world around us he said, "If the door of perception were cleansed, everything would appear to man as it is, Infinite."

Wisdom and Understanding

When we are open to acquiring Wisdom, we become wiser. When we are open to acquiring Understanding, we become so. As mentioned, there are presently an increasing number of Brain Fitness programs promising to retard aging and renew alertness, memory, and mental flexibility. Techniques in this area are proving that our brains, in addition to receiving softwear updates, also receive hardware updates. When due to our physical health and life experiences neural pathways are injured, fall dormant, or are discarded, others may be imagined and created. The repair of neural networks in the brain occurs through cortical remapping or rewiring. This demonstrates the brain's innate and extraordinary ability to continue creating new neural pathways, and to bypass and alter existing ones by developing, modifying, reorganizing, or rewiring synaptic connections.

Binah's Understanding is conjoined with deductive reasoning based on factual evidence. Scientific evidence is consistently pointing to the part that Understanding, in the form of our conscious intention, attention, and physical application plays in the regenerative process. The permanent alteration of the transmission sites or synapses between two nerve cells or neurons is accomplished through the reeducation of mental, emotional, and physical efforts of those undergoing treatment.

The science of neuroplasticity is proving that no matter what one's age or physical malady, except brain death, the brain is capable of adapting to and ameliorating trauma and impairment. Such is accomplished by those who wisely understand the part they play in their rehabilitation. Yes: Wisdom, Chokmah and Understanding, Binah are two sides of the same brain!

Again, there are different ideas and theories on what biological processes allow neuroplasticity to occur. Perhaps the fact there is no one unifying theory contributes to the fresh Understanding that keeps creating, like Binah, fresh forms of expression.

Final Word

Again, Norman Doidge's cutting-edge book "The Brain That Changes Itself" inspired me to put aside my doubts, pain, and fear to start using neuroplasticity to reroute and normalize a decades-old injury that doctors insisted was impossible to correct non-surgically. The prerequisite was opening to the Wisdom of neuroplasticity, through which I began Understanding that I was not hopelessly stuck.

THE PALATE REFRESHER:
HOMEPLAY SUGGESTIONS FOR THE PRACTICAL APPLICATION
AND INTEGRATION OF UNDERSTANDING, BINAH

1. Apply the scent of myrrh and wear black as I experience the Grade of Magister Templi or Master of the Temple, linked with Binah. Contemplate the following before, while, or after taking action:
    *Calling upon Understanding to help clarify and possibly reconcile seemingly irreconcilable differences. *Conceptualizing more environmentally sustainable ways of living. *Understanding my thoughts and feelings in the midst of a tenuous situation. Despite my resistance, caring for my physical body and surroundings with the Understanding that these are the "Living Temples," and as such, are tools through which I am doing my spiritual work. *Understanding the place death and loss have in my life. *Encountering and coming to terms with the principle of natural selection as it is unfolding in the world of nature. *Doing what I am able to respect the holiness of all life forms. *Engaging with my reluctance to extend Understanding to another.

2. What comes next has the potential to facilitate a deeper comprehension of Understanding, Binah, by experimenting with the following:
    Feel the Tree of Life's Middle Pillar against my back as I take several long, deeply relaxing and centering breaths. Next, send a grounding cord or root down from the base of my spine into the earth and one up from the crown of my head to root in the heavens. Continue by sensing my breath spiraling up and down these roots as I breathe. Slowly bring myself into the sphere

of Binah by doing such as: Imagine showering or surrounding my body in a translucent black veil, the hue of the sphere, and inhaling the scent of myrrh. Invoking Binah's divine and archangelic presences by calling out, or chanting their names, following under number 19. Summoning the support of the sphere's mythological deities—gods and goddesses—or bringing the affiliated flowers, plants, and animals into my mind and imagination. Enacting the aforementioned, or whatever else I understand is fitting, will help me to kinesthetically, mentally, emotionally and spiritually experience myself in Binah. I might also focus on my Brow Star, as this is where Binah touches my astral body. Now experiment with the following:

A.   While mentally or physically touching, and in that way, consciously sanctifying and dedicating each to serving as a living temple, in and through which Spirit, The Universe, Great Mother, A Higher Power, Divinity and so on lives and operates. After becoming comfortable doing this, consider mentally and emotionally extending this sanctification process into my immediate environment, family, friends, and community, and then out into the world around me.

B.   Alternatively, consider who or what, despite my good intentions yet lack of Understanding, I might be s-mothering? On the other hand, who, due to their good intentions, yet lack of Understanding, am I feeling s-mothered by? On the Tree of Life, Binah is positioned in the future. Consider whether or not I am sincerely wishing to improve my relationship and Understanding of the connection between this individual and myself from here on out. If so, proceed to cut the etheric or non-physical umbilical cord that is tying us together in dysfunction by experimenting with the following:

Sketch out and then imagine two ladders with three steps each facing the other. Climbing from the bottom up, the steps represent the physical, mental-emotional plane, and spiritual planes. Imagine myself and the other person approaching and then ascending the opposite sides of the ladder until seated on the top step facing each other. Create a current of infinite spiritual energy in the shape of a Mobius strip or figure eight flowing around and between the both of us.

Proceed to communicate, outline, and explain why I will be severing the umbilicus. For example, start with the statement: "I have come to the Understanding that cutting this tie will benefit my, and our, growth and well-being because:"

Next, tune into any response the other individual might have being certain to fully acknowledge his/her thoughts and feelings.

Then, sever the cord with a tool pre-selected for this purpose—a laser beam, scalpel, knife, scissor, or the like.

Immediately apply a pre-selected healing balm or ointment to the severed areas.

When ready, take whatever might remain of the separated umbilicus and descend the ladder to the physical plane. Dispose of the cord as fitting: burning, burying, composting, and so on.

Please note that this entire meditation is best done before going to sleep for 28 days or one lunar cycle. Remember, it is essential to continue attending to the remaining wounds until healed.

C.   Experiment with walking in a beautiful place while repeating Binah's Divine Name: Yahweh Elohim, Yod-Hay-Vav-Hey Aye-lo-he-ee-mm, Mother of All Creation. Doing this affirms my oneness with the Understanding of the universe, Binah. This practice also goes for calling-in Binah's 's archangelic presence, Tzaphkiel Tza-ph-key-aye-el, Beholder of the Most High.

3.   Binah is known as the Separating and Sanctifying Intelligence. Mull over answering what follows:
*In what ways has a misunderstanding separated or alienated me from someone beloved? If fitting, note a few steps I might take to renew Understanding. *From whom or what might the process of separating myself usher in perspective, and along with it new or renewed Understanding? *How could ceasing to unnecessarily separate myself from others be beneficial?

In her role as the Sanctifying Intelligence, Binah consecrates all she gives birth to with a sacred soul. Reflect on responding to the following:
*In what way(s) might I invite this Understanding to remind me to treat myself, others, and/or my surroundings with increasing amounts of respect? *How may I key into recalling the fact that when I am behaving respectfully, I am sending others the message to do likewise? *What are some ways in which I might become increasingly cognizant of the sanctity of my physical body? *How is Understanding helping me feel blessed to have been born into the physical world at this time? * Might I benefit from being more reverential of the fact that all physical forms are holy vessels endowed with their particular purpose in the scheme of things?

4.   The Spiritual Experience of Binah is the Vision of Sorrow. Contemplate what follows: *In what ways is sorrow expanding my capacity to feel joy? *What great distress did I experience, and how is it nurturing my maturation? *What death, defeat, or failure am I presently mourning/do I need to mourn? *Am I learning to accept that pain, suffering, and the like are inherent to being born in a physical body? *Might I be grieving the loss of a particular physical function, skill, or ability? *Could my reaction to death and loss be altered through a combination of dispassion and a more mature Understanding of Binah's creative, destructive, and transformative cycle?

Am I coming to understand the fact that at times there is nothing I can say or do to relieve others' pain and sorrow? Instead of trying to "fix" another's distress, experiment with making the time to patiently listen to them expressing the full range of their sorrowfulness. Doing this further suggests acknowledging their upset with something like: "I am so very sorry for the loss of your beloved." If fitting, then ask: "Is there anything I might do to ease your sorrow?" Although I could not take away a student's grief due to the unexpected death of her young niece, I could plant a "Tree of Life" in her memory.

5.   Contemplate the presence of the Great Mother living within myself, another, and/or in the world around me. Be aware of what happens when I do this:

      Ask myself: *In what life situation would I like to receive the nurturance, guidance, and support of an Understanding mother-like mentor? *Who has these abilities and how might I go about asking for their assistance? *Note what, if anything, is stopping me from making this request? *How could I overcome my reluctance, fear of rejection, pride, and the like?

      Alternatively: *What insight or Understanding did I gain from extending encouragement and support in the form of the Understanding gleaned from my experiences to someone else? *What, if anything, would I do differently in the future? *Might I benefit from apologizing for how I mothered or did not mother a child? *In what ways, can I go about being a better mother-like, nurturing guide and Understanding presence to myself?

6.   Binah's Sacrament is Communion. When my lack of understanding, old habits, past mistakes, uncertainty, or blurred perception regarding what has been and how to proceed prevails, Communion is always there for me to turn to for Understanding. Entering this state, all of my thoughts and feelings are welcomed and explored. Attaining the impersonal state of true Communion—opening to the clearest Understanding I am now capable of receiving—then requires my deep, heartfelt willingness to step away from any personal attachments and aversions as to how I, others, and the world *should* or *should not be.* Doing this opens me to the truest Understanding I am now capable of receiving. Through my open-minded contemplation of the teachings of Binah, I may receive insights into such as: Understanding the true nature of my past, present, or possible future actions, decisions, or the integration of an experience, and knowledge that improves my mental clarity. Through these, Understanding and, Communion are realized.

      In addition to contemplating Binah's teachings, there are other ways of achieving the state of Communion. Here are a few tried and true possibilities: *Prayer and Meditation, *Repeating Binah's divine and archangelic names. *Dialoguing with an Understanding mentor, counselor, teacher, friend, or Understanding-oriented group. *Studying the teachings of Chokmah. *Consulting a guide such as the I Ching, laying out a tarot spread, bibliomancy-spontaneously opening to a page in a sacred book—and so on. *Taking a "time out" and doing something uplifting such as walking nature and/or getting some cardio-vascular exercise. *Oh yes, reviewing the words of this adapted version of *Serenity Prayer* from Alcoholics Anonymous:

God, grant me the serenity to accept the things I cannot change,
the courage to change the things I can,
and the *Wisdom* to *Understand* the difference."

Remember: When thrown-off track by life's endless changes and challenges, I always have the option to consider the tried and true remedy of Communion. Being receptive to the Understanding that Communion offers has the potential to help me fulfill the sacred contract I agreed to enact when baptized in Kether above. Note any shift of my Understanding-perception that results from Communion:

7. How might I grow more open and welcoming to the energies of the Great Mother? *Is my commitment to better Understanding changing my life, the lives of my loved ones, and those around me for the better? *Am I open to being impregnated by the dynamic life force of Chokmah to set off a new cycle of creativity? *What am I wishing to conceive, or have already become pregnant with and am gestating? *Where and how am I learning to better use the receptive attitude and powers of Binah? *What situation is calling for an influx of Understanding?

8. Contemplate the following in relationship to Binah, Understanding:

"Her children rise up and call her blessed." *Proverbs 31:28*

"The noblest pleasure is the joy of understanding." Leonardo di Vinci

"The mother of all living." *Genesis 3:20*

"Understand is a two-way street." Eleanor Roosevelt

"Peace can't be kept by force; it can only be achieved by understanding. Albert Einstein

"Your pain is the breaking of the shell that encloses your understanding." Kahlil Gibran, *The Prophet*

"Man (Humankind) masters nature not by force but by understanding." Jacob Bronowski, Mathematician

"Everything in nature acts in conformity with law." Immanuel Kant

9. Create a personal statement that affirms my ability to access the powers of Understanding at this time, such as: "My Understanding is perfect for who I now am, and is expanding with time and experience." My personal statement is:

10. Acknowledge, explain, or list the ways in which I embody, or would like to better embody, this line from the *Pattern on the Trestleboard,* "Filled with Understanding of its perfect law, I am guided, moment by moment, along the Path of Liberation."

11. Consider where in my personal or professional life it might be appropriate to enact the principle of natural selection, rather than have the principle of natural selection be enacted on me. For Example: Take the time to weed my garden before the weeds take over to become my garden.

12. Binah heads the Pillar of Mercy situated in the future. Consider asking myself the following:
    *What new Understanding is offering me the potential to plan for a more satisfying future? *How is Understanding myself or another changing because of Binah's teachings? *In what way(s) could my Understanding of Mother Nature's cycles be the first aid needed to help me feel less regretful about my past actions and more hopeful about what I do in the future? *What area of my life is offering me the opportunity to move up the evolutionary scale by applying the salve of Understanding?
    Seated in the future, Binah's Understanding presence suggests the value of better Understanding and healing my perfectly-imperfect, possibly wounded, mother-caretaker-child relationship with this influential person. Such has the potential to develop and improve my ability to parent, nurture, or mentor others, as well as my physical, mental, emotional, and spiritual health.

13. Binah is linked with the Virtue of Silence and the Vice of Greed. Ask myself: How likely is it that my present Silence on an important issue will help or harm myself or others down the line? Briefly, explain my Understanding of the question, "What does it mean to have enough?"

14. Consider Saturn or *Shabbathai,* the planetary link to Binah is known as the "Root of Form" and "Taskmaster." Among other things, Saturn is conjoined with the formation of boundaries, restrictions, limitations, concentration, work, and discipline, as well as the crystallization, refinement, and concentration of non-specific cosmic energy into physical form.
    Discover how the planetary influences of Saturn are being activated in my life by reflecting on the following: *In what way am I growing more appreciative of discipline after applying it to complete an uncomfortable, yet essential task? *Could I be freeing myself from internal conflicts and unhealthy

limitations by being more willing to dispose of obsolete habits, beliefs, rules, and regulations? *What restriction has Understanding moved me to impose upon myself or others? *Am I in the midst of Understanding the value of learning to work more effectively with a family member, boss, neighbor, etc., who has a sour, harsh, or abrasive personality? *What new Understanding is daring me to concentrate on re-writing my life script? *Can I name one way that the passage of time and the experiences it brings is increasing my Understanding and spiritual maturity? *How have I committed myself to facing and healing the childhood wound I sustained from my mother-father-parent? *Might I further materialize a creative project by placing finite limits on its infinite possibilities? *In what situations am I Understanding the need to accept or give constructive, versus destructive, criticism improving? *Am I noticing an area of my life in which the passage of time and the experiences it brings is increasing my Understanding and spiritual maturity? *Have I been recognizing the value of accepting and learning from an initially unacceptable restriction? *In what ways is Understanding supporting me following the death of a loved one? *Could I be celebrating the freedom I found by challenging a powerbroker or my own harsh inner critic?

15.   Understanding is the evolutionary process that encourages my openness to re-conceptualize and birth new neurological pathways in my brain and body. Such are the ways and means of identifying, imagining, and then enacting attitudes and behaviors that are aligned with my increasing Understanding of the routes I can take to healing.

In addition to mental and emotional activities, Understanding requires engaging in kinesthetic, tactile learning, or physical actions to facilitate change and etch new neural pathways.

Identify an area in my life in which I am Understanding the value of improving my creative conceptualizing or image-making and participating in the physical, mental, emotional, and spiritual health, attitudes, and activities to support this change. Consistently following a multilevel plan of action results in etching new neurological pathways into my brain and body. With time, consistent attention, and repetition, this process has been proven to re-wire the brain and nervous system, replacing or updating worn out, flawed, and damaged neurological connections with new routes, which will upgrade my health and life.

16.   Contemplate ways the plants, gems, creatures, mythological figures, or other symbols associated with Binah have the potential to serve as helpful daily reminders to improve my life by applying and integrating the teachings of Understanding. One of the first things I do each morning is to drink pure water and lemon juice from a special cup, which I imagine to be the Holy Grail. While drinking deeply from its sacred waters, I imagine the liquid cleansing, nourishing, and sanctifying my entire being.

17.   Open myself to Understanding another. Despite previously being closed-minded, become open to Understanding, not necessarily agreeing, with someone whose values and points of view are different from my own. Notice what change occurs between us when I do this:
       Alternatively, open myself to the Understanding of the Great Mother coming through; an inspiring teacher, friend, tool, DVD, CD, book, Zoom call, workshop or other in-person experience in order to become more Understanding. Note what results when I do this:

18.   In what area(s) of my personal or professional life am I being asked to use the Understanding I have to seek out and receive the Understanding I need?

19.   Passionately call out and in Binah's Divine and Archangelic Presences.
       Binah's Divine Presence is: Yahweh Elohim (F C C C #C Yod- Hay-Va-Hay, E F# C F G# Aye-lo-he-ee-mm), Mother of All Creation. Binah's Archangelic Presence is: Tzaphkiel (A# C A# E F# Tza-ph-key-aye-el), Beholder of the Most High, to help me become more attuned with, and live out the teachings of Binah, the sephirah of Understanding.

20.   Gift myself with the treasure of expanding my Understanding of the Qabalistic Tarot's minor arcana and court cards by laying out and contemplating the Four Threes and Four Queens as follows: Consider how *each* card symbolizes Understanding's/Binah's attributes:

•   The Sanctifying and Separating Intelligences.
•   Spiritual Experience of the Vision of Sorrow.
•   Sacrament of Communion.
•   The Virtue of Silence and Vice of Greed.
•   Astrological Counterpart of Saturn
•   And Qabalistic Grade of the Magister Templi, Master of the Temple.

THE DESSERT:
AFFIRMING, CONFIRMING,
AND INSPIRING STUDENT EXPERIENCES

■ Eli, a postal worker, shared the following: "Since learning about the Binah's virtue and vice, silence and greed, I've been remembering how, as a child, which wasn't very long ago, I used silence to manipulate others and gain control. In early childhood, I cried a lot and showed all of my feelings—happiness, anger, fear, sadness, and so on. I was often made fun of for doing this, especially when sad, which got me even more upset. So, as I got older, I didn't want to give my parents, or really anyone, the satisfaction of knowing how I was feeling—good, bad, or indifferent—so I stayed silent.

Learning about Binah, I'm Understanding that my childhood and teenage habit of keeping silent turned into greed in my adulthood. This is not greed in the traditional sense, but that I greedily accumulate and hang onto this backlog of feelings. (Sometimes doing this even upsets my stomach.) I remain silent in situations where speaking up would actually improve my life and relationships.

Working with Binah is turning me around enough to see—is giving me the Understanding to know when silence is and isn't the best way to go. I really want to communicate better and learn to use Silence as a positive rather than a negative force. I want to turn it into a tool to help me, rather than using it as a weapon to get back at others and continue hurting myself."

Binah's teachings are empowering you with a better Understanding of your old habit along with the desire to better your communication skills. Silence can start out as a way of gaining some modicum of control in situations where one feels hurt, powerless, or fearful of expressing ourselves when significant others don't or can't listen to our thoughts and feelings. Of course, remaining silent when communication is needed can grow into a detrimental automatic habit. As you've experienced, this behavior creates the illusion of power and physical side effects like stomach aches, yet does not grant real power—the power to be understood as well as to understand others. Binah's astrological partner is Saturn or Taskmaster. You've more than earned Kudos for assigning yourself the 'task' of self-improvement.

■ "My lover, Rosa, and I had a huge discussion this past weekend that transported us to a place of better Understanding," offered Francesca. "She likes being affectionate with me in public. Most of the time, I don't mind, while at other times, I do. Since ours is a new relationship, I'm still a little shy about talking about things. While we were out together last weekend, she put her arm around me in front of some business acquaintances and it didn't feel completely right. Although I did my best to gently edge away, I sensed that her feelings were hurt.

Following lunch the next day we had a very productive talk about what happened the night before. She told me how she doesn't want to hide parts of herself anymore, that the painful time of her 'being in the closet' is over and done. I was able to listen and understand because I feel the same way. We agreed that it sometimes takes courage to be an openly lesbian or gay couple in this still sometimes-homophobic environment.

After listening to her, I got to explain how in some situations, and with certain people, I don't want my private life to be public. For me, it's a loss rather than a gain of power. I become 'Fran the lesbian' rather than 'Fran, the person.' Her response was to ask whether I think I lose power by letting people direct my life. Great point! Yet, I explained that, for me, choosing to be more private about the image I project actually makes me feel more powerful. I was also able to explain that I don't believe in being either all open or all closed about everything. I'm very much an in-between kind of person. I act according to what I sense each situation calls for. Rosa really listened carefully and said she understood my position. I also understood and took responsibility for not being completely clear about this up until now.

We decided that in the future we'd do our best to honor our differences. Rose said she would work on not feeling rejected when I needed to be private. I said I would work on being more communicative to avoid upsetting her with my needs. Our conversation brought out so much Understanding on both sides, it strengthened our partnership."

Understanding can be defined as "reaching an agreement through the reconciliation of differences as well as the ability to differentiate one thing from another." You and Rosa had to separate yourselves from each other in order to better understand each other. Doing this helped you reach a clearer Understanding of who you are personally and inter-personally. Sometimes we hold back talking about our feelings and defining our needs and ourselves because we fear alienating others…losing love. Of course, not doing so is equally detrimental, since it alienates us from ourselves and creates relationships that are based on withholds or untruths, rather than facts. It takes a good deal of Self Understanding and courage to be real about who we are. While doing so has the potential of bringing discord, in the end, it makes real relationships better and the unreal ones either transform or fall away. Taking this position also offers us the chance to experience how differences can expand our perception of the world.

Lasting relationships are based on how much acceptance and Understanding we are willing and able to extend to ourselves and others. Congratulations! It's so empowering when we can listen to another's thoughts and feelings and perceive that what they are saying is true for them. Your efforts have more than validated this statement by Eleanor Roosevelt, "Understand is a two-way street."

■ "My job has had me traveling a lot this last month," began Valerie, a marketing consultant for a large company. "As a result, I've missed class and have had to spend a lot of boring time waiting in airports! Typically, I would get irritated and think along the lines of, 'This person is standing in front of me blocking my way. That person is purposefully taking too much time chatting while checking in. The person sitting next to me on the plane is taking up more than their share of the seat.'

So at one point, while having to wait in the San Francisco airport because of a weather delay, I started thinking, 'Maybe these people are thinking similar things about me!' I then experimented with sitting still and putting myself into the consciousness of some of the people who came by.

First an elderly, overweight woman came trudging by. When I imagined myself inside her body, my feet hurt, my clothes felt way too tight, and I was annoyed by people having their belongings spread out and not leaving me enough room to get a comfortable seat in the departure area. I did the same when a middle-aged man who was busy talking on his cell and wheeling his over-loaded carry-on bag plopped down across from me. It turned out that he was exhausted, longed to take a hot bath, and wished that the loud airport announcements would stop distracting him from his business call.

I kept doing this exercise until it was time to board my flight. I found it very enlightening how my Understanding of others expanded my Understanding. We're all the same kind of being but perceive things through different eyes, bodies, and life experiences. My airport exercise had me feeling less alienated and more connected to everyone around me. It's so easy for me to get caught up in myself and miss the fact that we are One!

Speaking of number one, one of the best parts of what happened to me is that when I arrived home I found the Homeplay for Binah sitting right where I'd left it—on the kitchen table. The suggestions: 'Extend Understanding to yourself or another in an area in which you might have formerly been closed-minded. Strive to Understand another although his/her point of view seems alien to yours,' were perfect for me! I guess I've been here, although my body has been in Dallas!"

As Mother Nature, Binah has dominion over the process of natural selection. From the standpoint of our personal nature or personality, such may be seen as the manner by which, over time and through evolution, we naturally come to select the personality traits to develop and those to let go of. There's the tendency to forget that we're all made of the same basic stuff. Spiritual aspirants spend years, not to mention lifetimes, aiming to experience this sense of Oneness. Your discomfort led you to let go of your harsh judgments of others, and in doing so, you self-selected to experience and understand this potent truth.

■ "Looking sad and exhausted, Thomas, a dedicated Qabalah practitioner and carpenter, presented our class with the following: "I got a close-up and personal look at the sorrowful side of Binah this week! Although I've been nurturing this 'new' vision of family and the ways to create and procreate, it hasn't worked. It's turning out that I'm living the 'old' family tradition instead. My ex-girlfriend is pregnant with my child, we no longer have a relationship, and she absolutely won't have an abortion. I'm feeling completely horrid. Upsetting as it is, my situation is identical to the one my mother and father were in when I was conceived. Although been feeling so much more Understanding for my parents since this happened in my life, I had fooled myself into believing I'd wanted to stop this dysfunctional cycle.

Our break-up, which happened a month or so ago, was a mutual case of 'irreconcilable differences.' Yet now she's saying she loves me and wants to get married. I absolutely know it won't work. I'll definitely be there for her while she's pregnant, and I'll be responsible for my daughter or son, but I don't want to be married to her and subject a child to the many unsolvable problems in our relationship. I honestly believe that if she weren't pregnant, she wouldn't want to be married to me, either. I absolutely don't want to compound the pain and sorrow. I'd get married in a second if we had a workable relationship, but we don't, a fact that a year of counseling more than showed us. The situation is a genuine example of Binah's Vision of Sorrow. I didn't want to continue the hurful pattern from my childhood, yet did it anyhow!

In the middle of all the upset I've continued saying the *Pattern on the Trestleboard* daily and have been led into some deep contemplation of the statement that goes with Binah: 'Filled with Understanding of its perfect law, I am guided, moment by moment, along the Path of Liberation.' Focusing on this truth is helping me shift my attitude from running away to making the situation somehow doable. Looking at it from Binah's perspective is slowly moving me away from 'I'm a failure, our lives are over, and the child will be miserable,' to making the best of it.

I've had to face myself—ugly stuff like having unsafe sex with a woman I had no future with. My lack of consciousness, or better said, Understanding, when overcome with lust. To be even more honest, I'd call my behavior a form of greed. Difficult as it is, I'm coming to terms with my automatic patterns. Through universal Understanding, I'm aiming to make peace with myself. I'm creeping forward with Understanding, and as a result, am not feeling nearly as frightened and regretful as I first was."

Time-wise, Binah's situated in the future. It's often only through our experiences, rather than those of others, that we learn how to plan for what's ahead. Sometimes our unconscious drives are stronger than our conscious motivations. There's an older Hip-Hop song called, "Be a Father to Your Child." It addresses all "absent fathers," the children who suffer the loss of a father's presence in their lives, and the mothers who are shamed and abandoned. It describes the Vision of Sorrow and wounding everyone concerned experiences as a result.

Your sorrow has led you to show love, yet not to the point of being self-destructive—a condition that's sometimes goes along with this kind of situation. Listening to you speak, I'd label what's transpired as being Self-instructive. Binah is paired with natural selection. We select and plant the seeds for tomorrow, today. Your present Understanding is causing you to choose some new patterns that will be helping you to co-create a more fulfilling future and heal your own childhood trauma in the process.

■ "A nurse who needs nursing best not nurse others," emphatically declared Maureen a nurse, mother, and grandmother. "The universe has been trying to send me this message for a long time, now I think I've finally received it. As you know, I broke my arm and wrist a couple of weeks ago and have been trying to wrap my head around why it happened.

Lately, I've been distracted by what's going on in my daughter Jane's life. She and my grandchildren are moving out of state. It's one of those situations where I'm happy and sad. I'm truly happy she has a new job that she's looking forward to going off on her own. I'm also sad to see them all moving so far away. I'm Understanding that I must let go of her and what she does with her life more than ever before. It's more than time for her to make important decisions without me interfering unless asked.

While thinking about her packing and moving, I wasn't looking where I was walking, tripped over a gurney in the hospital, and fractured my left arm and wrist when trying to break my fall. Normally I'd have jumped in and started taking care of things for my daughter, but the break also broke my worn-out 'mom to the rescue routine.' I was stopped in my tracks. Plain and simple, this means not smothering her with mothering! She must learn to work through things herself.

Because Jane's such a procrastinator, watching her get ready to leave has made me extremely anxious. She and the children are flying out next week and there are still some important legal matters that she had to have done a month ago but didn't. When I asked how things were going she started telling me about all that had to do. Hard as it was, I kept my mouth shut and listened. Instead of being after her to take care of things ASAP, offering advice, or doing it for her, I decided to enact Binah's virtue and remained silent. In many ways, it's been harder to zip my lips than to intervene. Nevertheless, the pain in my arm has both reminded and stopped me—I can barely drive, cook, or babysit my grandkids, not to mention go to work. I'm feeling like a bird with one wing!

Binah's connection with Saturn, the planet of time and limitations, has prodded me to recognize my personal limitations. Being honest about my limits, manifesting in the form of my need to be taken care of and tendency to care take others in excess, is bringing a great deal of Understanding. I'm Understanding that I need to cut the umbilical cord of misunderstanding by letting go and asking for help, rather than helping. Of course, similar things came up for me at work. It's amazing what creative solutions my daughter is finding without me. Binah's teachings are turning out to be perfect for me!

While I'm Understanding what's going on, sometimes I sure don't like how it feels to understand. I'm like an addict with a habit, and I'm going through withdrawal. Old habits do die slowly and hard!"

> *Like Binah, you've been receptive to "The Word" powering across the Tree of Life from Chokmah. It's often challenging for those of us in the "helping professions" to know when and when not to help others. It also offers the power to recognize when and where we ourselves need help.*
>
> *Enacting Binah's virtue of Silence regarding your daughter is a big one. I'll be the first to admit how difficult it is to be quiet, especially when one is accustomed to taking charge. As you've been experiencing, sometimes the best thing we can do is to remain silent and allow others to learn for themselves. Certainly, at other times, silence is detrimental, such as when one is ill or genuinely incapable of handling a situation without input. You're Understanding how valuable it is to examine our impulses and the bottom line about the situation at hand before speaking or doing. In the process of facilitating your daughter's maturation, you've planted seeds for some of the same. You've realized she's capable of doing what was needed, in her way and time, as are you. Not only have you broken your arm and wrist, but you've also broken some old patterns along with it.*

■ Lou, an engineer for a large semiconductor company, shared a recurring work issue from the perspective of Understanding. "The homework question, 'What new Understanding have I derived from a past experience that is helping me to plan and prepare for a more satisfying future?' definitely had my name next to it. With the New Year, I started a great new job, and with it has come some new, but not always great, experiences. What else is new?

I continually have people with opposing ideas opposing me. I've tended to get really pissed off and react to them at the time, or take my feelings home and become even more upset. I've frequently done both. Because this situation doesn't occur with just one person all the time but comes at me from many directions at almost any time, my whole body is constantly on alert. I can feel the adrenaline pumping through me.

In an effort to make it better, the other evening I finally began seeking Understanding. I wanted to find out why my reaction is so severe and negative and aim to make things better. So, I picked out someone who was opposing me and thought about the situation from his/her point of view. Doing that was easy. However, what surprised me most was that I came to think of it from a third or overall point of view.

I unexpectedly realized that the work wouldn't be nearly so much fun if people weren't opposing me and got me upset! I wouldn't be nearly so creative! We wouldn't be getting as much done, or done as well if there wasn't this friction! In all honesty, I would be kind of sad and bored if the opposition went away! It made me feel a whole lot better to see it as a kind of game and not take it seriously."

Binah conceives, and many of our intellectual conceptions are strongly influenced by our preconceptions. These originated from your past experiences and as it turned out, they are actually inappropriate for both present and future planning. You've demonstrated the fact that true Understanding may be obstructed by our initial or superficial evaluation of a situation because it leans toward being more reactive than proactive. Your creative evaluation of the situation revealed this to be true. Yes, evaluating our life situations more thoroughly in the present offers us a better opportunity to continue doing likewise in the future.

■ "I'm losing the love of my life, making it an excruciatingly painful week," began Mauri, choking back her tears. "It's been terrible to suddenly be excluded from his life. Changing my picture of how our relationship should be to how it actually is has brought up so many deep feelings. Most prevalent has been feeling like an abandoned child. After our final conversation last Thursday, I cried from the time I left work until the time I fell asleep. I'm not quite sure how I managed to drive home. It's strange, but at another time in my life, I would have gotten very busy. I would have paid all my bills and re-arranged my drawers and closets. I would have gotten so busy I wouldn't have felt what I was feeling. I'd just go numb. Instead, I let myself go into that great sea of tears and sadness.

While this awfulness has been going on, my good friend Marsha had to have an emergency mastectomy. I believe this has definitely contributed to my upset. I was experiencing this profound grief about her all day, compounded by my final encounter with my ex. It was all too much for me to bear. In the midst of all this, I had the need to listen to some *Kiertans*, the Yoga of devotional chanting and singing.

I turned on this magnificent CD called *Jai Ma*, which is dedicated to none else than the Universal Mother. Jai Ma means 'Praises to the glorious Divine Mother full of bliss.' I turned it on as I cried and cried. While listening, I lit a candle in the pottery candleholder that Marcia gave me for Christmas years ago and asked the Great Mother to help us both.

Recently, my therapist began encouraging me to write. As I mentioned, when I get into pain I usually turn outwards. I get busy doing all to block my feelings. However, this time I told myself to stick with my feelings. And what do you know? I started writing a poem to the Universal Mother. It really helped me deal with some of the grief and angst I was feeling. I felt as If I'd buried my head in her compassionate bosom. Unlike my physical mother, I know she's always there to love, comfort, and understand me."

It sounds as if you are receiving a dose of Binah's compassion. Wonderful that you gave yourself permission to be as you were, which moved you into beginning to process your feelings. While doing this can be difficult, it's also liberating! From my own experience, tears have a cleansing and healing quality. We best mourn our losses; otherwise, they stick around to haunt us forever. Doing this, in time, gives way to the Understanding that everything and everyone has a place in the greater scheme of things, whether we like the form events take or not.

Yes, some of your grief seems to go back to your childhood and your relationship, or lack thereof, with your mother. (You might review the class segment on the Mother Wound.) Likely you recall that one of Binah's names Alternative Titles is Mater Bon Consili, Mother of Good Counsel. *It's uplifting to hear that you are doing grief counseling and getting nurturing and support from an Understanding therapist. Especially so since it's directed at encouraging you to better understand, accept, and nurture yourself unconditionally, as well as to activate the creative-mother part of yourself to accomplish this. Learning how to love ourselves unconditionally is one of the most rewarding things in life.*

■ Cecily, a high school counselor in a severely economically deprived area, shared the following. "I have been pondering the Practical Application and Integration Suggestion: 'Open myself to Understanding another. Despite previously being closed-minded, extend Understanding to someone whose values and point of view are different from my own. Note what happens when I do this:'

It hurts my heart working where I do and seeing children come to school in tattered clothing and hungry. While waiting in line at the post office the other afternoon, I got my chance. The universe just happened to put me next to a well-dressed woman who when I admired the baby girl she was holding, told me she has two more girls at home and is praying to get pregnant with a son. (I noticed a small gold cross around her neck while looking at her sweet baby daughter.)

After getting into a conversation about her very talented, beautiful, healthy daughters I asked her what she thought about some politicians wanting to do away with the Affordable Care Act or ACA, which helps the poor afford to get medical treatment when needed. Her immediate response was that she thought it was costing her and other taxpayers too much money it should be defunded.

Okay, here comes Understanding. First, I acknowledged that she wanted that the Affordable Care Act defunded as it was costing the taxpayers money. She immediately answered, 'Definitely!' I then very gently, asked her what Jesus taught about ministering to the sick and poor. The woman immediately turned bright pink straight up from her hands to the roots of her honey-blond hair. Before she could finish blushing and answer me, the clerk called out, 'Next!'"

You definitely get an A plus, plus in your practical application of Binah, Cecily. You were more than able to extend Understanding to this woman whose values and views differed from yours. You followed by asking her a heart-opening question about the teachings of her teacher Jesus. Binah presides over the future, and you surely planted seeds of Understanding that may eventually bear fruit. Excellent!

■ Noel, who is working part-time and applying to graduate schools, brought his experience to class: "Economic necessity has pretty much forced me into living with my parents after being out on my own during college. It's quite a challenge or, more honestly, a pain in the rear, living with my mother, whose tendency is to smother rather than mother me. She is so overbearing that being with her sometimes gets absolutely and completely intolerable. A couple of times, I've actually felt as if I'm suffocating. I want to be treated like an adult, but for whatever reason, she just can't do it, and I can't manage to convince her that I'm an adult.

It's been through our studies of Binah that I started Understanding that the Cosmic Mother is working through her to mother me, to teach me about love and compassion. I was at my wit's end after a go-round with her last Saturday so I decided to try some prayer and meditation to mend myself. You've suggested we invoke the divine and archangelic presences of each sephirah. I've never done it outside of class, but at this point, I thought it might give me some relief. I called out the name of the archangel Tzaphkiel and asked—I should really say begged—for guidance.

I *know* I was heard because in a while I got some real Understanding. I realized that I want her to change, but it's me, my attitude, that needs changing. I clearly understood that my mother needs Understanding. This next revelation is embarrassing, but I also got the Understanding that I allow her to get to me. I allow myself to get locked in verbal combat with her. I realized we would both probably do better if, when she starts her smothering routine, I could simply hear her out. Instead of getting defensive and argumentative, I could thank her for her advice and interest and give her a hug. Well, I've done it twice and it's working! Thank you, Tzaphkiel."

Tzaphkiel is known as both the Contemplation and Knowledge of the Most High, and as Noah demonstrated, how through contemplation or prayer and meditation we receive knowledge. When we genuinely ask for Understanding, we receive. It amazes me how often we must get to the end of our rope before opening to guidance.

It sounds as if there may be more reasons than economic necessity for you to be living at home. The world is filled with people like your mother, and by living with her you are getting, and she—or the Great Mother Binah, operating through her, is giving you—the opportunity to learn how to deal with personalities like hers more effectively. If fitting, you might consider sharing that some of her concerns are your concerns, too. You could add that you are now learning, just as she did at an earlier time in her life, how to take care of yourself, and while you value her input, there are times when you need to arrive at decisions in your own way and time in order to grow. You might consider adding that watching you struggle probably isn't easy for her. I'll offer you something which has taken me a long time to learn: when I act like an adult, my chances of getting treated like one are better than when I don't. In my experience, immature people engage in power struggles. Adults recognize them as such and then, like Binah, are selective in imagining other ways of handling situations.

■ "I co-own my home with my ex-husband," began Alex, a medical assistant, "and last week he got in touch asking me to buy him out. After leaning toward doing this, thanks to Binah, I received a completely different Understanding of his request, and one that made me feel cautious about doing so.

While learning about each sephirah the first thing I do when I awaken is to review our Suggestions for Practical Application and Integration and meditate on it for a while. Well, no surprise, the morning after I spent the night struggling to get some Understanding of how to handle my ex's request, I got into my usual routine. After a minute or so, I got the greater Understanding I'd been seeking, the real purpose behind all of this upset with my husband. I understood that I'm looking for security! Along with it, I realize that buying his share of the house and getting into debt will not give me this.

So I've decided to start some information-gathering techniques such as looking at the comps—shopping houses like mine that are for sale and for how much, the housing trend, including interest rates. Of course, I should talk with a realtor or two about the market value of my home, and the possibility of moving elsewhere (I'm honestly not very attached to the house), before reaching a decision. I need to take care of myself! So, I'm seeking out the information or Wisdom to give me the Understanding to do what's best! I suppose I'm experiencing how in life, just as on the Tree of Life, Wisdom and Understanding are interconnected.

I am clear that I'm not looking to harm my ex only to take care of myself, which in his mind might be misunderstood as not taking care of him. My genuine intention is to make it a no-loser situation. That's my bottom line Understanding and come to think of it, It's how I'll begin my conversation with him."

Understanding means one has a clear perception of something, and it appears that your contemplation of Binah delivered. Qabalists call Binah the Separating Intelligence. Understanding comes from the ability to distinguish or separate one thing from another, and your Understanding helped you to get the importance of distinguishing your needs from those of your ex. As you experienced, genuine Understanding is the clear and conscious insight that contributes to the well-being of ourselves and others. Certainly, due to personality differences and ego struggles, such does not guarantee the satisfaction of everyone concerned, at least in the short run. It signifies one is motivated with the intention to help rather than to harm. The best medicine doesn't always taste the best. Understanding refers to individuals and groups bearing tolerant, humane, or empathetic attitudes, those who base their words and actions on the likes of the universal and natural laws, truths, and principles coupled with our Tree of Life studies.